M000287821

English as an International Language

PEFC

PEFC/16-33-111

CATG-PEFC-052

www.pefc.org

NEW PERSPECTIVES ON LANGUAGE AND EDUCATION
Series Editor: Professor Viv Edwards, *University of Reading, Reading, Great Britain*
Series Advisor: Professor Allan Luke, *Queensland University of Technology, Brisbane, Australia*

Two decades of research and development in language and literacy education have yielded a broad, multidisciplinary focus. Yet education systems face constant economic and technological change, with attendant issues of identity and power, community and culture. This series will feature critical and interpretive, disciplinary and multidisciplinary perspectives on teaching and learning, language and literacy in new times.

Full details of all the books in this series and of all our other publications can be found on http://www.multilingual-matters.com, or by writing to Multilingual Matters, St Nicholas House, 31–34 High Street, Bristol BS1 2AW, UK.

NEW PERSPECTIVES ON LANGUAGE AND EDUCATION
Series Editor: Professor Viv Edwards, University of Reading, UK

English as an International Language
Perspectives and Pedagogical Issues

Edited by
Farzad Sharifian

MULTILINGUAL MATTERS
Bristol • Buffalo • Toronto

Library of Congress Cataloging in Publication Data
A catalog record for this book is available from the Library of Congress.
English as an International Language:
Perspectives and Pedagogical Issues
Edited by Farzad Sharifian.
Includes bibliographical references.
1. English language--Study and teaching--Foreign speakers. 2. English language--
Globalization. I. Sharifian, Farzad.
PE1128.A2E47245 2009
428.2'4--dc22 2008035195

British Library Cataloguing in Publication Data
A catalogue entry for this book is available from the British Library.

ISBN-13: 978-1-84769-121-7 (hbk)
ISBN-13: 978-1-84769-122-4 (pbk)

Multilingual Matters
UK: St Nicholas House, 31–34 High Street, Bristol BS1 2AW, UK.
USA: UTP, 2250 Military Road, Tonawanda, NY 14150, USA.
Canada: UTP, 5201 Dufferin Street, North York, Ontario M3H 5T8, Canada.

Copyright © 2009 Farzad Sharifian and the authors of individual chapters.

Reprinted 2010

All rights reserved. No part of this work may be reproduced in any form or by any
means without permission in writing from the publisher.

The policy of Multilingual Matters/Channel View Publications is to use papers
that are natural, renewable and recyclable products, made from wood grown in
sustainable forests. In the manufacturing process of our books, and to further
support our policy, preference is given to printers that have FSC and PEFC Chain
of Custody certification. The FSC and/or PEFC logos will appear on those books
where full certification has been granted to the printer concerned.

Typeset by Techset Composition Ltd., Salisbury, UK.
Printed and bound in Great Britain by MPG Books Ltd.

Contents

Acknowledgements

I wish to thank the authors of the chapters in this volume not only for their valuable contributions but also for their help in serving as internal reviewers of other contributors' chapters. The external reviewers and Professor Viv Edwards, the series editor, also deserve a special word of thanks for their helpful comments on the earlier versions of the chapters. Finally, I am grateful to Anna Roderick, Tommi Grover and Marjukka Grover at Multilingual Matters for their help and support during the preparation of this volume.

Farzad Sharifian
Melbourne

Contributors

Farzad Sharifian is an Associate Professor at the School of Languages, Cultures and Linguistics, Monash University, Melbourne. He has a wide range of research interests in linguistics and applied linguistics, including intercultural communication, pragmatics, language and politics, and English as an International Language. He has published numerous papers in international journals such as *World Englishes*; *Language and Education*; *Pragmatics & Cognition*; *Journal of Politeness Research*; *Language Sciences*; *Language and Intercultural Communication* and *Language, Culture and Curriculum*. He was the editor (with Gary B. Palmer) of *Applied Cultural Linguistics* (John Benjamins, 2007). He has recently developed innovative courses in English as an International Language at Monash University.

Adrian Holliday is Professor of Applied Linguistics at Canterbury Christ Church University, where he supervises doctoral research in the critical sociology of language education and intercultural communication, and is also the Head of Graduate School. He is author of *Doing and Writing Qualitative Research, 2nd edition*, Sage, 2007; *The Struggle to Teach English as an International Language*, Oxford, 2005, which deals with cultural chauvinism in TESOL; *Intercultural Communication*, with Hyde and Kullman, Routledge, 2004; *Appropriate Methodology and Social Context*, Cambridge, 1994. He began his career as a British Council teacher in Iran in the 1970s. During the 1980s he set up the ESP Centre at Damascus University, Syria, and was a curriculum consultant at Ain Shams University, Cairo. He is currently writing a book for Sage on Centre–Western chauvinism in intercultural communication.

Sadia Ali has been teaching ESL/EFL for over 11 years and currently teaches English Composition at the Zayed University in Abu Dhabi. Sadia has also worked as an IELTS examiner for several years and has taught teacher education courses. She has an MA in Linguistics and an MEd in Educational Technology and ELT. She is currently pursuing a PhD in Education at the University of Stirling, Scotland. Sadia has written several articles and papers related to ELT. Her research interests include teacher education and educational technology.

Marko Modiano is currently a Senior Lecturer of English at Gävle University, Sweden. He received a PhD in English from Uppsala University in 1987. His research interests include the evolution of EIL and World Englishes paradigms, the conceptualization of 'Euro-English,' as well as the development of ELT in Sweden and the European Union. Issues such as Europeanization, globalization and multiculturalism are central concerns. Previously, Dr Modiano extensively studied the manner in which mainland Europeans mix phonological and lexicogrammatical features of British and American English, work which has acted as the basis for his understanding of the development of EIL, Euro-English and Mid-Atlantic English. He is currently focusing on how culture and identity can be incorporated into mainland European ELT so as to promote intercultural communicative competence and the ideals of multiculturalism. He has published widely in these fields in international journals such as *English Today; World Englishes* and Swedish journals such as *Moderna Språk*.

David C.S. Li is an Associate Professor at the Department of English, City University of Hong Kong. He obtained his BA (English) in Hong Kong, MA (Linguistics and Applied Linguistics) in France and PhD (Linguistics) in Germany. He has published in three main areas: Cantonese-English codeswitching and bilingual interaction, the place of 'Hong Kong English' in World Englishes, and common errors among Hong Kong Chinese EFL learners and effective remedial instruction. He is currently working on two funded research projects: one compares the motivations of Chinese-English codeswitching in Hong Kong and Taiwan; the other investigates the preferred norms and pedagogic model(s) of English in Hong Kong.

Enric Llurda is a Lecturer (*Profesor Titular*) in English and Applied Linguistics at the University of Lleida (Catalonia, Spain), where he is also a member of the Cercle de Lingüística Aplicada, and is currently co-ordinating the undergraduate degree in English Studies. He is the author of several research papers and book chapters in national and international publications, as well as the editor of a book on non-native language teachers, *Non-Native Language Teachers: Perceptions, Challenges and Contributions to the Profession* (Springer, 2005), and the co-author (with J.M. Cots, L. Armengol, E. Arnó and M. Irún) of a recent book on the development of language awareness in the language classroom, *La conciencia lingüística en la enseñanza de lenguas* [*Language Awareness in Language Teaching*] (Graó, 2007). His current research interests include non-native language teachers, English as an international language, multilingualism in educational contexts and language attitudes.

Bojana Petrić is a Lecturer in the Department of Language and Linguistics at the University of Essex in the United Kingdom. Previously she has taught at universities in Novi Sad (Serbia) and Budapest (Hungary). She has published in the area of academic writing, on topics such as citation use, plagiarism, writer identity and interdisciplinarity, contrastive rhetoric and 'subjective description' in student writing during WWI. She has also published a book on educational reform (in Serbian). Her research interests include student and published writing as well as cultural and identity issues involved in the teaching and learning of English as a global language.

Vaidehi Ramanathan is a Professor of Socio/Applied linguistics in the Linguistics Department at the University of California, Davis. Her most recent book, *The English-Vernacular Divide: Postcolonial Language Politics and Practice* (Multilingual Matters, 2005), offers a situated account of sociopolitical concerns around English- and vernacular-medium instruction in some settings in Gujarat, India. She has also co-edited a special issue of *TESOL Quarterly* on grounded perspectives regarding language policies around English and the world's other languages. Her other publications include: *The Politics of TESOL Education: Writing, Knowledge, Critical Pedagogy* (Routledge, 2002) and *Alzheimer's Discourse: Some Sociolinguistic Dimensions* (Lawrence Erlbaum, 1997). Her research interests include all aspects of literacy, teacher education, and civic and societal changes as they occur in non-formal educational contexts and her work in this area has appeared in journals such as *TESOL Quarterly, Applied Linguistics, Critical Inquiry in Language Studies, Journal of Second Language Writing* and *Journal of Language, Identity, and Education.* Her research on the sociolinguistic aspects of illnesses and disability issues has appeared in journals such as *Language and Society, Communication Theory, Journal of Pragmatics* and *Critical Inquiry in Language Studies.* Her book *Body Matters and Applied Linguistics* is under contract with Multlingual Matters. She co-edits a book series entitled *Critical Language and Literacy Studies* with Bonny Norton and Alastair Pennycook (Multilingual Matters).

Brian Morgan is an Associate Professor in the Department of Languages, Literatures and Linguistics at York University in Toronto. His academic interests include research and pedagogy on language and identity, particularly from the perspective of various critical theories. Another major research interest relates to critical literacies, multiliteracies and their applications in multilingual settings. Other primary research concerns include second language teacher education, English for Academic Purposes, and Language Policy and Planning. Brian's work has been published in journals such as *TESOL Quarterly*; *Journal of Language, Identity, and Education*; *International Journal of Bilingual Education and Bilingualism* and the *Annual Review of Applied Linguistics*. He is the co-editor with Vaidehi Ramanathan of the 2007 *TESOL Quarterly* special issue on Language Policies and TESOL: Perspectives from Practice. His first book, *The ESL Classroom* (1998), was published by University of Toronto Press.

Aya Matsuda is Assistant Professor of Language and Literacy at Arizona State University, where she teaches graduate courses in Bilingual Education and Teaching English as a Second Language. She also teaches in the PhD Program in Applied Linguistics. Her research interests include the use of English as an International Language, linguistic and pedagogical implications of the global spread of English, integration of a World Englishes perspective into the US education and identity negotiation of bilingual writers. Her work focusing on these issues have appeared in various books and journals including *English Today*, *JALT Journal*, *TESOL Quarterly* and *World Englishes*.

Sarah Zafar Khan is Director of the Effat English Academy at Effat College in Jeddah, Saudi Arabia, where she has been working since 2002. Prior to this, Sarah worked as a teacher educator at Aga Khan University's Institute for Educational Development in Karachi, Pakistan where she also developed and taught academic English courses. Sarah has an MA in Applied Linguistics from University of Karachi, Pakistan, and is currently pursuing a Doctorate of Education (EdD) in TESOL (Teaching English to Speakers of Other Languages) with the University of Exeter, England. Sarah is a member of TESOL (Teachers of English to Speakers of Other Languages), and her research interests include motivation in second/foreign language learning, teacher education and computer mediated communication.

Paul Roberts has worked as an English Language teacher and teacher trainer in eight different countries and has published a handful of ELT books. He was also a contributor to the Cambridge International Dictionary of English. He is currently Head of ELT at the University of Hertfordshire, UK and Seasky Scholar at Dalian University of Technology, China. His doctoral thesis, and current research interest, concerns English as an International Language and curriculum internationalization: he has given several presentations on these themes at international conferences which he has followed up with journal papers and chapters in edited books.

Suresh Canagarajah is the Kirby Professor in Language Learning at Pennsylvania State University. He teaches World Englishes, Teaching and Research in Second Language Writing, Postcolonial Studies and Theories of Rhetoric and Composition in the departments of English and Applied Linguistics. He has previously taught at the University of Jaffna, Sri Lanka, and the City University of New York (Baruch College and the Graduate Center). He has published papers on bilingual communication, learning of writing and English language teaching in professional journals. His book *Resisting Linguistic Imperialism in English Teaching* (Oxford University Press, 1999) won Modern Language Association's Mina Shaughnessy Award for the best research publication on the teaching of language and literacy. His subsequent publication *Geopolitics of Academic Writing* (University of Pittsburgh Press, 2002) won the Gary Olson Award for the best book in social and rhetorical theory. His edited collection *Reclaiming the Local in Language Policy and Practice* (Erlbaum, 2005) examines linguistic and literacy constructs in the context of globalization. His study of World Englishes in Composition won the 2007 Braddock Award for the best article in the *College Composition and Communication* journal. Suresh edits *TESOL Quarterly*. He is currently analyzing interview transcripts and survey data from South Asian immigrants in Canada, United States and UK to consider questions of identity, community and heritage languages in diaspora communities.

Sandra Lee McKay is Professor of English at San Francisco State University where she teaches courses in sociolinguistics, as well as methods and materials for graduate students in TESOL. Her books include *Teaching English as an International Language: Rethinking Goals and Approaches* (Oxford University Press, 2002, winner of the Ben Warren International Book Award), *Sociolinguistics and Language Teaching* (edited with Nancy Hornberger, Cambridge University Press, 1996) and *Researching Second Language Classrooms* (Lawrence Erlbaum Associates, 2006). Her newest book, *International English in its Sociolinguistic Contexts: Towards a Socially Sensitive Pedagogy* (with Wendy Bokhorst-Heng, Routledge, 2008) is an examination of the social and sociolinguistic context of present-day English teaching and learning. Her research interest in English as an international language developed from her Fulbright Grants, academic specialists awards and her extensive work in international teacher education in countries such as Chile, Hong Kong, Hungary, Latvia, Morocco, Japan, Singapore, South Africa, South Korea and Thailand.

Andy Kirkpatrick is Professor and Head of the English Department at the Hong Kong Institute of Education. His first degree is in Chinese Studies from Leeds and he has a Postgraduate Diploma in Modern Chinese

Literature from Fudan University in Shanghai, an MA in ELT and Linguistics (York, UK) and a PhD (The Australian National University) in Chinese Linguistics. His research interests include the development of Asian varieties of English, the implications of World Englishes for English language teaching and the history of Chinese rhetoric. *World Englishes: Implications for International Communication and ELT* was published in 2007 by Cambridge University Press. He is currently working on a description of English in ASEAN and a history of Chinese academic writing.

Eric A. Anchimbe is Assistant Professor of English Linguistics at the University of Bayreuth, Germany. He obtained his PhD in English Linguistics from the University of Munich (2005). His most recent books are *Linguistic Identity in Postcolonial Multilingual Spaces* (Cambridge Scholars Publishing, 2007) and *Cameroon English: Authenticity, Ecology and Evolution* (Lang, 2006). He has also published several papers on World Englishes and linguistic identity in postcolonial contexts. Among his current research interests are: postcolonial pragmatics, linguabridity (hybrid linguistic identities), sociolinguistics and indigenized varieties of English in Africa.

Abbreviations

ALT	Assistant language teacher
EFL	English as a Foreign Language
EIL	English as an International Language
ELF	English as a Lingua Franca
ELT	English Language Teaching
ENL	English as a National (or Native) Language
EPL	English as a Primary Language
ESL	English as a Second Language
ESOL	English for Speakers of Other Languages
ETS	Educational Testing Services
EU	European Union
HK English	Hong Kong English
IELTS	International English Language Testing System
IVEs	Indigenized Varieties of English (also Institutional Varieties of English)
JET	Japanese Exchange and Teaching
L1	First language
L2	Second language
NNEST	Non-native speaking English teachers (also Non-Native English Speakers in TESOL)
NNS	Non-native speaker
NS	Native speaker
TCM	Traditional Chinese Medicine
TEFL	Teaching English as Foreign Language
TESL	Teaching English as a Second Language
TESOL	Teaching English to Speakers of Other Languages
TOEFL	Test of English as a Foreign Language
WBT	West-based TESOL
WE	World Englishes

Chapter 1

English as an International Language: An Overview

FARZAD SHARIFIAN

Background Studies

For better or worse, by choice or force, English has 'traveled' to many parts of the world and has been used to serve various purposes. This phenomenon has created positive interactions as well as tensions between global and local forces and has had serious linguistic, ideological, sociocultural, political and pedagogical implications. Many publications have been devoted to the study of the worldwide spread of English. Processes, implications and consequences have been explored (e.g. Abbott & Wingard, 1981; Bailey & Görlach, 1982; Brutt-Griffler, 2002; Crystal, 1997; Graddol, 1997; Hardin, 1979; Hassall, 2002; Holliday, 2005; Jenkins, 2000, 2006a; Kachru, 1986; Kirkpatrick, 2007; McKay, 2002, 2003; Nakamura, 2002; Smith, 1983; Strevens, 1980). The roles that English has played in the lives of individuals as well as communities range from marginalization and hegemony on the one side to empowerment and upward mobility on the other. As Kachru (1996: 135) puts it, 'the universalization of English and the power of this language have come at a price; for some, the implications are agonizing, while for others they are a matter for ecstasy'. Recent decades have witnessed scholarly inquiry and unprecedented lively debate about these issues (e.g. Burns & Coffin, 2001; Canagarajah, 1999; Pennycook, 1994; Phillipson, 1992; Phillipson & Skutnabb-Kangas, 1996; Rubdy & Saraceni, 2006).

As English rapidly develops more complex relationships within and between communities of speakers around the world, the dialogue addressing its role as a global language needs to continue to expand. Established arguments and positions regarding politics, policies, pedagogies and practices of English as an international language, as well as its socio-linguistic and sociopsychological complexities need to be revisited, raising new sets of questions. Also, in order to explore these issues from a truly global perspective, it is necessary to open the forum further to scholars from underrepresented regions in the world, who would be able to explore yet untouched issues. This volume is a step towards achieving these aims.

But first, there seems to be a need to clarify what EIL refers to. A good number of discussions in the context of the globalization of English have centered around the use of umbrella terminology. While this overview chapter does not intend to engage in a terminological debate within the field, it aims at clarifying what EIL, as a unifying theme for this volume, stands for.

What is EIL?

In general, we can say that English as an International Language refers to a paradigm for thinking, research and practice. It marks a paradigm shift in TESOL, SLA and the applied linguistics of English, partly in response to the complexities that are associated with the tremendously rapid spread of English around the globe in recent decades. My mention of 'thinking', 'research' and 'practice' above is not meant to suggest that research does not include thinking or that practice excludes thinking. In fact, to engage in *practice*, informed by the perspective of EIL, is to engage in critical think-ing and research.

It is important to emphasize that EIL does not refer to a particular variety of English. Some scholars confuse the term 'International English' with EIL. The use of an adjective plus 'English' often suggests a particular variety, such as American English, Singaporean English or Chinese English. Thus 'International English' can suggest a particular variety of English, which is not at all what EIL intends to capture. EIL in fact rejects the idea of any particular variety being selected as a *lingua franca* for international communication. EIL emphasizes that English, with its many varieties, is a language of international, and therefore *intercultural*, communication.

As a paradigm, EIL calls for a critical revisiting of the notions, analytical tools, approaches and methodologies within the established disciplines such as the sociolinguistics of English and TESOL, which explored various aspects of the English language. One of the central themes of EIL as a paradigm is its recognition of World Englishes, regardless of which 'circles' they belong to (Bolton, 2004; Kachru, 1986, 1992). Kachru (e.g. 1986, 1992) described the role and use of English around the world using a model that has three concentric circles: Inner-Circle, Outer-Circle and Expanding-Circle countries. In Inner-Circle countries, English is used as the primary language, such as in the United Kingdom, the United States, Australia and Canada. Countries located in the Outer Circle are multilingual and use English as a second language, such as India and Singapore. In Expanding-Circle countries, the largest circle, English is learned as a foreign language, such as in China, Japan, Korea and Egypt. Some scholars use the term 'World Englishes' in a limited way to refer only to Englishes in the Outer-Circle countries. However, my usage of the term covers all Englishes from all circles.

The EIL paradigm also emphasizes the relevance of World Englishes to ELT (Matsuda, 2002, this volume). EIL contexts are ones in which English is used between speakers coming from different cultural and national backgrounds. In response to the rapid development of new Englishes, in particular in what was termed 'Expanding-Circle' countries, it has become safe to replace terms like 'English speakers coming from different cultural and national backgrounds' with 'speakers of World Englishes'. Again, it should be stressed, this terminology is not restricted to any narrow sense of English used only in Outer-Circle countries.

As Canagarajah (2006) observes, World Englishes can no longer be viewed through the 'three Circles' metaphor for various reasons. These include the spread of Outer-Circle Englishes and Expanding-Circle English into the so-called 'Inner-Circle' countries. As a large number of speakers from the Outer-Circle and Expanding-Circle countries now live in the Inner-Circle countries, even native speakers of English are increasingly exposed to World Englishes. This means revising the notion of 'proficiency' even for the English of native speakers. Canagarajah (2006: 233) maintains that, 'in a context where we have to constantly shuttle between different varieties [of English] and communities, proficiency becomes complex...one needs the capacity to negotiate diverse varieties to facilitate communication.'

I can provide an example of the complexity of World Englishes from Australia, a country that has generally been viewed as an Inner-Circle country. Here, English has developed into a codified variety which has its own dictionary and a recognized 'standard' Australian dialect. However, Aboriginal people in Australia have indigenized English to Aboriginal English, which acts as a *lingua franca* between Aboriginal and non-Aboriginal people as well as among Aboriginal people who speak mutually unintelligible Aboriginal languages. But Aboriginal English has not been viewed as an Inner-Circle variety, even though it was developed in an Inner-Circle country. Also it should be noted that a large number of Australians speak

Multidialectal competence

other World Englishes such as Indian English, Chinese English, Malay English, and so on. In a sense Australia, and countries like Australia, encompass all three circles, hosting many World Englishes. Thus, successful communication for many Australians requires what Canaragajah (2006: 233) refers to as 'multidialectal competence', part of which is 'passive competence to understand new varieties [of English]'. This observation is not just true of Australia. It is gaining global validity.

EIL does not only have implications for mapping the scope of the World Englishes paradigm but it also engages with it at the level of theory. World Englishes can, and have started to, make a significant contribution to the EIL paradigm through the new approaches employed over the last few decades in the study of that field. These include established sociolinguistic approaches as well as more recent approaches such as those from cultural linguistics and cognitive linguistics (Polzenhagen & Wolf, 2007; Sharifian, 2006, this volume). These approaches can provide deeper insights not only into the nature of world Englishes but also about communication *across* Englishes, an issue which lies at the heart of EIL. This area, however, is still in its infancy (see e.g. Wolf & Polzenhagen, 2006).

EIL has also started to develop a close affinity with research in the area of intercultural communication. As said before, EIL recognizes that English is widely used for intercultural communication at the global level today. It is becoming increasingly recognized that 'intercultural competence' needs to be viewed as a core element of 'proficiency' in English when it is used for international communication (see also Sharifian, this volume, for the notion of *meta-cultural competence*).

Given the fact that the bulk of research in the area of intercultural communication has focused on English as a medium of communication, the results can readily be applied in EIL training and teaching. In fact some scholars of EIL have also written in the area of intercultural communication (e.g. Holliday *et al.*, 2004) and many, if not all, have referred to intercultural communication in their discussions of EIL. It should of course be added here that most studies of intercultural communication in English have, up until now, focused on NS-NNS intercultural communication. Henceforth, what is needed in the EIL paradigm is an expansion of the scope of speech communities and interlocutors engaged in intercultural communication, especially as most instances of intercultural communication in English today takes place between its non-native speakers.

It should be mentioned here that while the EIL paradigm does problematize the polarization of the English speaking world into native speaker/non-native speaker, it does include so-called 'native speakers' of

English. There is after all no word in the phrase 'English as an International Language' that would automatically exclude the native speakers of the language. However, in the context of the globalization, or what I have termed *glocalization* (Sharifian, forthcoming) of English, EIL recognizes the fact that the distinction between who is and who is not a native speaker is not always clear-cut. The focus in the EIL paradigm is on communication rather than on the speakers' nationality, skin color, and so on, those factors which in the metaphor of 'Circles' acted as symbolic markers of the politicized construct of 'native speaker' (e.g. Brutt-Griffler & Samimy 2002). However, while it lasts, this construct can serve as a springboard for ELT scholars to criticize fundamental notions that are often assumed to capture realities.

From a methodological perspective, the EIL paradigm draws on the established research approaches within the areas of sociolinguistics and applied linguistics but also welcomes the newer qualitative approaches that have emerged in the social sciences. These include narrative inquiry (e.g. Clandinin & Connelly, 2000) and ethnomethodologically-oriented interviews (e.g. Seidman, 2006). As English has played a multitude of roles in people's lives, and many speakers of English have developed complex relationships with the language, such that it has touched their identities, cultures, emotions, personalities, and so on, so the stories they tell about their relationship with it reveal significant links between language, culture and identity. These stories may best be captured through methods such as narrative inquiry and autoethnography (e.g. Ellis, 2004). English has also come to be used by communities of speakers on the internet, a phenomenon which may best be captured by cyberethnography (e.g. Hine, 2000). Such methods are currently under-utilized in the field, but we are witnessing more and more scholars using methodologies which tap into speakers'/learners'/teachers' lived experiences and the meanings that they make out of these in relation to English. Some chapters in this volume reflect this trend.

This Volume

The topics covered in the volume represent the variety of arguments and research questions that characterize EIL as a paradigm for thinking, research and practice. The volume also represents the diversity of the research approaches and methodologies that have been adopted to address these questions. These include dialogue, discourse analysis, narrative and conversation analysis. In general, the contributions to this volume fall within the scope of the following subthemes, which are used as a basis for structuring the book. It should, however, be noted that most chapters engage with issues that may relate to two or more of these subthemes:

(1) Native/non-native divide: politics, policies and practices.
(2) EIL, attitudes and identity(ies).
(3) EIL, teacher education and language testing: gaps and challenges.
(4) The scope of EIL: widening, tightening and emerging themes.

Native/Non-native Divide: Politics, Policies and Practices

One of the themes that can broadly be associated with the EIL paradigm is research on English as a Lingua Franca (ELF) (e.g. Jenkins, 2006a, 2007; Seidlhofer, 2004). This line of research aims at characterizing communication in English between people from different linguistic backgrounds. For example, it explores the communication strategies employed by non-native speakers of English when they communicate with each other. Holliday's chapter considers the criticism that has arisen in some quarters that the ELF movement has only focused on the linguistic code and has failed to engage with the political ideological dimensions of native/non-native distinction. This involves taking it to task for seemingly ignoring issues of self-image and identity in users of English. He observes that in many cases, the categorization of speakers into native/non-native has a nonlinguistic basis; for example, it may be based on the colour of skin and the racial background of one's parents.

Holliday also explores the ideological and political consequences of labeling speakers using the Centre and Periphery metaphor, which is again closely linked with the native/non-native dichotomy. He reminds us that such classifications are more ideological than geographic or linguistic. Throughout his chapter, Holliday reveals how a native-speaker ideology and, the Centre/Periphery categorization underlie a great deal of discrimination, for example discrimination in hiring practices in the ELT profession.

The issue of native speaker/non-native speaker (NS-NNS) is also explored in the chapter by Ali, but in the context of Gulf Corporation Council Countries (Saudi Arabia, Kuwait, Bahrain, Qatar, the United Arab Emirates and the Sultanate of Oman). She observes that in these countries English is increasingly being used as an international language between the local residents and expatriates who come from many other countries. One of the main themes of Ali's chapter is the prevalence of discrimination against non-native speakers, particularly those from the Outer-Circle countries, in hiring practices in ELT businesses in these countries. She observes that ELT institutions still largely prefer Western teachers of English, mainly due to the learners' assumed preference for native-speaking teachers. Ali explores the experiences of five English teachers from Outer-Circle counties who are currently working in GCC countries. She reports their frustration with the extent to which the native/non-native divide has disadvantaged them career-wise.

Ali also explores the perceptions of a group of students in relation to native/non-native teachers. She observes that the students' perceptions range from unawareness of the native/non-native divide to the attribution of certain linguistic features and teaching approaches, not necessarily positive ones, to native teachers. For example, some students view native teachers as having incomprehensible accents, being less strict or having less experience. Ali observes that when asked about the desirable qualities of an English teacher, none of the student participants in her study proposed a Western/English background. Interestingly, many students in her study expressed a willingness to be involved in the selection of English teachers at their institutions. The findings of Ali's seem to confirm the context-dependability of students' perception of native/non-native, a point which is also acknowledged in Li's chapter. The point is that students do not have a preference for native teachers of English in all countries around the world.

Modiano's chapter discusses the role of English and the current status of EIL in the European Union (EU). He first stresses the overlap between the paradigms of EIL and World Englishes. Both acknowledge the diversity of norms and forms in English which has resulted from its globalization and internationalization. Also, both challenge the traditional approaches to ELT that promoted undue prescriptivism and that denied the sociolinguistic reality of English in today's world. Modiano observes that ELT in EU is yet to be informed by the developments in the EIL paradigm for several reasons. He observes that while some practitioners have come to sense the global force of English, they still feel uncertain about its implications for their classroom practices. As such, Modiano maintains that Native-speakerism is still the dominant ideology in European ELT.

Modiano also critiques the limited view of the notion of 'lingua franca' held by some ELT scholars who exclude native speakers from the scope of ELF. Consistent with the views presented in several other chapters in the volume, Modiano argues that there is nothing in the definition of 'lingua franca' that would exclude native speakers of English from its scope, or from the domain of international communication. What is more important here is the argument that in ELF contexts, native-speaker norms, however defined, do not enjoy undue privilege as prescribed norms. Furthermore, Modiano's chapter substantially engages with a more general discussion of language policy in EU and its implications for the implementation of an EIL-based ELT approach. He observes that the history of events and ideologies prevalent across Europe, combined with the current doctrine of a unified, while diversified, European entity, presents serious challenges and dilemmas for the ELT profession, at the levels of both policy and practice.

EIL, Attitudes and Identity(ies)

One of the issues that has received attention, and has in fact sparked much controversy, within the general paradigm of EIL is the NS-NNS accent, specifically its link to identity and the implications of this for the choice of a pedagogic model. In this debate, views range from a critical appraisal of the NS pedagogic model, to the glorification of the NS model valued for intelligibility and 'standardness'. Unfortunately, such debates often reduce the whole issue of language and language variety to accent. Even then they ignore the significant diversity that characterizes the so-called native speaker varieties of English. A wrong assumption in this context is that native speakers of English have no difficulty understanding each other's accent. Many non-native speakers assume native speakers all speak one 'standard' English. Several chapters in this volume engage with this topic, exploring it from different points of view.

The chapter by Li addresses the abovementioned theme by exploring the views of a group of Chinese-English bilingual speakers on the questions of intelligibility and identity. By administering a semistructured questionnaire, he identified his participants' preference for NS as opposed to local(ized) varieties of English and investigated how they perceive the issue of intelligibility in this respect. He also examined their perception of the link between English and their own identity. Li observes that about 80% of the participants in his study said they preferred to speak English with a native-based accent. He maintains that for the remaining 20%, the issue of intelligibility versus identity seems to have created a dilemma. While they want to project a Chinese identity in their spoken English they are also concerned that this may lead to unintelligibility. That is, they see a tension between the twin goal of speaking English with a local(ized) English accent to enact the speaker's lingua-cultural identity, and aspiring to a native-like accent in an attempt to minimize intelligibility problems.

It seems that in the context of Li's study, the issue of identity is predominantly linked to local(ized) varieties, not to native speaker varieties. Secondly, it seems that the issue of intelligibility is only seen as a problem for local(ized) varieties. It should be noted that the issue of the link between language and identity is more complicated than that.

First of all, those who appeal to native-speaker accent may do so to project an identity that is linked to that of the native speakers of English. ELT materials construct particular images of native speakers, mostly with highly positive characteristics, so it would not be surprising to see non-native speakers attempting to assimilate those identities by imitating NS accents in their English. The author of this chapter well remembers the case where a visiting academic to Australia from an East Asian country was shocked to see a homeless Australian on the street and remarked, 'Oh, a native speaker of English like that! So dirty! I can't believe it!'

It should also be added that some learners of English may resort to NS accent to distance themselves from their L1 identity. This may happen for example where the L1 dialect is considered 'nonstandard' within the speaker's home country. Many speakers around the world are stigmatized for their L1 accent within their country of origin, or even outside it. There are cases where a language is spoken in more than one country, such as in the case of Arabic. In those cases what is considered to be a 'standard' dialect in one country may be viewed as 'nonstandard' in another, and so people may wish to erase their L1 accent from their English to avoid stigma. The point here is to avoid overgeneralization by drawing attention to the complexities that may be involved in any link between identity and accent in English.

Another point that deserves to be taken into consideration here is how NSs feel about their language and identity when NNSs try to mimic their accent. In Australia I have witnessed how uncomfortable some Anglo-Australians feel when non-native speakers, or even native speakers who look 'foreign', attempt an Australian accent. These issues deserve closer scrutiny in terms of research within the paradigm of EIL and the results of such research need in turn to inform EIL pedagogy and curriculum development. In particular, there seems to be a need for exploring how speakers' identity is constantly shaped and reshaped when their English comes to play different roles throughout their life.

Writing from a European perspective, Llurda engages with attitudes towards native and non-native norms in ELT in his chapter. He observes that the divide between native and non-native speakers, with discrimination against non-native English speaking teachers (NNESTs), is still dominant in most ELT contexts. Llurda partly attributes this to non-native speakers' subordination to native speaker norms, which leads, among other things, to a lack of self-confidence on the part of NNESTs. This continues despite the fact that research has shown an absence of a clear-cut division between the categories of 'native' and 'non-native'. Llurda observes that there has been minimal comparative research on the performance of non-native/native teachers, and it seems that most research in this area has been limited to the exploration of 'perceptions' and 'attitudes'. It should be noted that perceptions and attitudes are often formed and informed by factors other than those which matter most when it comes to facilitating the learning process: teachers' skills and performance.

Llurda also explores the link between NNESTs and the EIL paradigm. He maintains that this group of ELT teachers would, in fact, be in the best position to promote EIL, given the diversity of their linguistic and cultural experiences. He also views an opportunity for NNESTs to engage with the EIL paradigm to increase their critical awareness of teaching an international language as well as to boost their self confidence.

Closely associated with the above-mentioned topic of identity and EIL is teacher's identity construction in the ELT classroom. Petrić's chapter explores this topic in the case of teachers, who she calls 'migrant English teachers', who seek employment in non-English speaking countries other than their own. Drawing on a language and identity framework (e.g. Norton, 2000), she examines how migrant English teachers construct multiple identities, which reflect the different social and linguistic groups to which they belong. By interviewing four migrant EIL teachers in Hungary, Petrić reveals how the teachers' background and history of contact with English has impacted on how they view their identity in relation to English, in particular vis-à-vis the notion of 'native speaker'. She explores how, in the face of the battle with the ideology of 'native-speakerism' which dominates these teachers' professional life, they highlight aspects of their lived experiences they believe useful for teaching and accepted and appreciated by their students.

Petrić observes that each migrant teacher's identity is a by-product of, and shaped by, a host of personal, interpersonal, institutional and sociopolitical factors. She rightly argues that migrant teachers are well-positioned to promote and teach English as an International Language, due to their multicultural competence and experiences. This is also so because in migrant teachers' classes, English is used as the medium of interaction between teacher and students who come from different national and cultural backgrounds, making such contexts truly EIL ones. As Petrić suggests, such contexts should be studied for their potential contribution to the development of EIL pedagogy.

EIL, Teacher Education and Language Testing: Gaps and Challenges

The chapters in this section engage with the gaps in the traditional TESOL paradigm and some of the challenges that face the EIL paradigm.

The chapter by Ramanathan and Morgan, which takes the form of a dialogue between these two scholars, presents a critique of West-based TESOL (WBT) and the ways in which its dominant discourse makes issues that are central to non-Western contexts irrelevant. Ramanathan focuses on the notion of 'class' and maintains that despite its significant relevance to many societal contexts, such as India, it has not surfaced as a topical issue in WBT. Morgan observes that it is the sociohistorical 'baggage' associated with the notion of class, chained to the former Soviet Union, that makes it rather a 'taboo' topic for WBT. On the other hand, it seems that it is not so much that the notion of 'class' is ignored, but rather that it is taken for granted in WBT, due to the fact that the whole profession is mostly a middle class exercise associated with middle class values. So, it might be argued, why then bother talking about 'class' as a variable?

Ramanathan and Morgan also address the issue of globalization processes, such as the outsourcing of jobs to call centers in countries like India, and their implications for educating ELT teachers in the West. It seems that outsourcing call centers is currently contributing to the stigmatization of certain World Englishes, such as Indian English, while conversely glorifying and promoting Inner-Circle varieties such as British English. Drawing on a training website for call center job seekers, Ramanathan and Morgan show how such websites, which are supposed to provide 'advice', in fact stigmatize speakers of varieties such as Indian English. One would hope that outsourcing jobs to non-Western countries could provide more chances for international communication and the recognition of intercultural communication across many world Englishes, but it seems that the industry is currently continuing to foster the hegemony of the Inner-Circle varieties.

Ramanathan and Morgan also reflect on their difficulties in implementing critical pedagogies for novice TESOL teachers, a central challenge for the EIL paradigm in general. Many ELT teachers and teacher trainees still see their role as that of teaching the language and could not be bothered about 'the stuff' that they do not view as relevant to their immediate, classroom-focused concern. However, a pivotal theme in the EIL paradigm is that issues such as identity, ideology and power *are* directly relevant to and do have a determining role on the content as well as the approach in ELT.

As mentioned earlier in this chapter, pivotal to the paradigm of EIL is the recognition that international communication in English is taking place across all World Englishes. This extends the relevance of studies of World Englishes to EIL teacher education, a topic which is addressed in Matsuda's chapter. Matsuda correctly maintains that Teaching English as an International Language entails a mindset different from previous approaches to ELT. This includes the development of a curriculum that takes into account the sociolinguistic reality of English across the globe, rather than settling for a skewed one in which only select groups of native speakers are represented. EIL teacher preparation programs should aim at graduates who can teach others to communicate successfully with all sorts of speakers no matter which World English they use.

Matsuda reports on the empirical study she conducted in order to explore the degree to which, as well as how, the perspectives of EIL and World Englishes have already been incorporated into ELT teacher preparation in Japan. Overall, her findings suggest that there is an increasing interest in the perspectives of EIL and World Englishes among teacher educators in that country. However, Matsuda observes that these perspectives are generally still considered supplementary. They are not the 'default' content of the courses. She rightly maintains that the EIL paradigm still has a long way to go when it comes to introducing the fundamental change in ELT education that will swing it from a monolithic view of English to a pluralistic one which reflects the complex nature of English today. EIL curriculum research, as Matsuda points out, is still in its infancy and much further research and curriculum development is needed.

One of the areas of ELT that has significant implications for teaching and learning is language testing. In the wake of the emergence of EIL as a paradigm, a number of scholars have questioned the validity of traditional approaches to English language testing. These tests largely measured proficiency against the so-called 'native-speaker' norm on the assumption that L2 speakers would use English only to communicate with native speakers (e.g. Brown, 2004; Jenkins, 2006b). In the present volume this topic is addressed by Sarah Zafar Khan, with a special focus on the context of Saudi Arabia. She approaches this topic from the perspective of linguistic imperialism and notes how standardized tests such as the TOEFL still serve to preserve the hegemony of the Inner-Circle varieties. Khan notes that in Saudi Arabia, rather than assessing the use of English as an international language, tertiary colleges widely use the TOEFL for placement and advancement purposes even though that test has little relevance to the communicative needs within the local context. She observes that one of the uses of English in Saudi Arabia is for communication between locals and expatriates who come from several countries including the UK, the United States, the Philippines, South Africa, India and Pakistan. This means that English is serving as a truly international communication tool in Saudi Arabia. However, as Khan points out, when it comes to the assessment and placement of students, TOEFL is still widely popular, even though it is largely biased towards American English.

Khan also reports on the results of a study that she conducted with a group of teachers and students in a higher education institution in Saudi Arabia on the intersection of TOEFL, their own needs and English as an

International Language. In general, the participants in her study attributed the popularity of the TOEFL in Saudi Arabia to factors such as its international *recognition* rather than its ability to effectively assess proficiency in international communication. Some participants in Khan's study also raised their concerns about the cultural content of the TOEFL in terms of its narrow representation, as well as its irrelevance to the context of Saudi Arabia. Overall, as Khan argues, 'in order to lead to effective pedagogy and to promote English as an international language, assessment practices must be linked to cultural and contextual realities' (p. 204).

The Scope of EIL: Widening, Tightening and the Emergent Themes

One of the central questions for an emerging paradigm is its scope, in terms of its themes, approaches, analytical tools, and so forth. The chapters in this section either directly address the question of scope or engage with emerging themes, approaches, and so on, within the paradigm of EIL. The chapter by Roberts and Canagarajah focus on the scope of ELF research. They note that ELF research has thus far excluded native speakers of English, and they make an attempt to broaden the scope of this line of research in that direction. Their main question is how English is used as a contact language, regardless of whether or not it is an L1 or L2. By analyzing cases of communication within a group of non-native speakers, both in the presence and absence of a native speaker, and by drawing on data from Roberts (2005), Roberts and Canagarajah attempt to clear away some of the stereotypes that have often been held about communication between native and non-native speakers. In general, they observe that 'grammatical forms are negotiated by individuals within ELF processes and are not shared by all interacting users' (p. 225). They maintain that success in the international use of English does not so much hinge upon a particular variety or lexico-grammar, but is instead tied to the nature of the negotiation skills and strategies interlocutors adopt.

Roberts and Canagarajah observe a large number of instances that could be identified as cooperative behavior in conversations. These included strategies such as the use of hedging and downtoners, as well the use of laughter to mitigate a negative response. Finally, in terms of topic management, the study could not find any particular rules of topic management that were consistently followed. It should be mentioned here that the chapter by Roberts and Canagarajah is one among a number of other chapters in the volume that marks a step towards establishing a balance between theoretical-speculative and empirical studies of EIL. Hitherto most studies of EIL have remained speculative and theoretical.

One of the emerging areas of EIL that merits a great deal of research is the pragmatics of its interactions. Sandra Lee McKay deals with this topic in her chapter. McKay challenges the conventional perspective of ELT pragmatics, which placed an emphasis on a native-speaker model, on several grounds. Firstly, there is now widespread recognition that the majority of interactions in EIL are between two or more L2 speakers, which makes the native-speaker model mostly irrelevant. McKay notes the hybridity of interactions in English and promotes a context-sensitive view of EIL pragmatics, in which the norms of social interactions are open to negotiation. She also challenges the native-speaker model of pragmatics on the ground that native speakers of English do not form a homogenous speech community and they too draw, at least partly, on different sets of pragmatic norms when communicating in English.

McKay discusses the need for a new pedagogical model for EIL pragmatics. For example, she maintains that the diversity of the socio-cultural backgrounds of EIL speakers requires teachers to focus strongly on communicative strategies that aim at negotiation, comity and avoidance of misunderstanding. These include repair strategies and conversational gambits that enhance international communication.

Sharifian's chapter focuses on the exploration of English as an International Language using the framework of *cultural conceptualizations* (Sharifian, 2003, 2008). The framework, which has been developed by drawing on the analytical tools of cognitive science and cognitive anthropology, views conceptual units such as schemas, categories and metaphors as existing not only at the level of individual minds but also at the level of cultural groups. These units emerge from the interactions between the members of the group across time and space. From the perspective of cultural conceptualizations, World Englishes, both native and non-native varieties, are not only characterized by differences in grammar and phonology but also by the different cultural conceptualizations that underpin their use. Thus, in EIL communications, speakers may use the same English words and sentences to instantiate different cultural schemas, categories and metaphors. This phenomenon is likely to lead to instances of 'hidden' miscommunication.

The above observation calls for conscious attempts on the part of EIL communicators to minimize assumptions of shared cultural conceptualizations, which characterize their intracultural communications. On the contrary they should make explicit and 'negotiate', wherever possible, any conceptualizations that may be culture-specific. The key notion here for successful communication in EIL settings is what I have called *meta-cultural competence*. This competence is tied to speakers'/learners' familiarity with a variety of systems of cultural conceptualizations, ideally achieved through exposure to a range of different World Englishes. The pivotal component of this competence is the understanding that a language and its components such as its lexicon can be used to communicate different systems of cultural conceptualizations. Although this may sound like a scenario for a great deal of miscommunication, in practice the competence gained through familiarity with different cultural conceptual systems can significantly enhance interlocutors' intercultural communication skills.

One of the themes that has received some but as yet insufficient attention, in the context of English as an International Language, is the impact on the language of the dissemination of knowledge and scholarship through English. For example, does the encoding of indigenous knowledge in English change and distort its content and structure? This topic is addressed by Kirkpatrick in his chapter which focuses on the case of Chinese medicine, exploring whether or not it is altered as a result of its dissemination in English. By drawing on literature on the history of the development of Traditional Chinese Medicine (TCM), he highlights the complexity involved in making firm generalizations about the role of English in this respect.

Kirkpatrick observes that TCM is not a purely indigenous system of knowledge originating from one particular ethno-medical system. It appears that TCM is characterized by diversity, both in terms of its original sources and also in terms of the medical traditions, including Western medicine, that have influenced it. Ethnomedical traditions have interacted over the history of human knowledge. Thus, Kirkpatrick maintains that it would be unreasonable to consider Chinese and Western medicine as two completely distinct and unrelated systems. He further observes that the Westernization of TCM is not so much the result of its dissemination in English but of conscious efforts, for example on the part of the Chinese government, to make it conform to Western 'scientific' principles.

Worthy of note, Kirkpatrick observes that Chinese medicine, including acupuncture, is more popular in Inner-Circle countries such as the United States or Britain than in China. He attributes this to the plurality of cultures in these countries, which allows for plurality of medical practice. As Kirkpatrick notes, this is also due to 'an increasing distrust of "scientific" methods and the resultant need for people to seek out what are known as alternative methods' (p. 267). Whatever the cause, Kirkpatrick concludes that Chinese medicine seems to have been modified or 'reshaped' before its dissemination in English. In general, he maintains that indigenous knowledge systems, such as TCM, should not necessarily be viewed as static entities that have now come, through English, into a sudden contact with Western knowledge traditions. It is hoped this line of research lays new ground for much further research into the effect of dissemination-through-English on other knowledge systems.

Reinforcing the main theme of this volume, Anchimbe calls for the pluricentricity of the definition of EIL. He challenges any versions that look for an 'international monochrome standard'. As he puts it, 'if English as an international language has to maintain its currency and vitality then it will have to be spoken by different voices yet understood by different ears' (p. 284). In particular, Anchimbe objects to the exclusion of Indigenized Varieties of English (IVE) from the scope of EIL, and also to the labeling of the norms of these varieties as *degenerate*.

Anchimbe presents a critique of what he calls 'a naming disease' in the field. He maintains that a majority of the terms, such as 'non-native Englishes' and 'New Englishes' are deficient on various grounds. For example, many of the so-called 'non-native Englishes' now have native speakers of their own. Anchimbe also reminds us of the thorniness of the notion of a 'standard' and the way it tends to be monopolized by native speakers of the so-called Inner-Circle varieties. He argues that 'standards' naturally develop according to the needs of communities of speakers. They should not be imposed upon them by speakers of other varieties. Anchimbe discusses the implications of these observations for the teaching of English as an International Language.

Concluding Remarks

Collectively, the chapters in this volume show a great deal of promise. They expand the paradigm and establish new grounds for thinking and research in relation to the role of English as an International Language. Currently, a fair amount of discussion appears to be focusing on terminological clarification. This is natural and necessary in any emerging paradigm. Most importantly, it appears that the EIL paradigm is providing a greater chance for scholars and practitioners to engage in critical thinking and perhaps to develop a sense of empowerment in relation to language and identity. As most chapters in this volume suggest, there is much more to be done, both in terms of research and in changing attitudes of teachers, teacher training institutions, institutions employing English teachers, textbook producers and bodies that develop curriculum and assessment materials.

References

Abbott, G. and Wingard, P. (1981) *The Teaching of English as an International Language*. Walton-on-Thames: Nelson.

Bailey, R.W. and Görlach, M. (eds) (1982) *English as a World Language*. Ann Arbor, MI: University of Michigan Press.

Bolton, K. (2004) World Englishes. In A. Davies and C. Elder (eds) *The Handbook of Applied Linguistics* (pp. 369–396). Oxford: Blackwell.

Brown, J.D. (2004) Comment 1: What do we mean by bias, Englishes, Englishes in testing, and English language proficiency? *World Englishes* 23 (2), 317–319.

Brutt-Griffler, J. (2002) *World English: A Study of its Development*. Clevedon: Multilingual Matters.

Brutt-Griffler, J. and Samimy, K. (2002) Transcending the nativeness paradigm. *World Englishes* 20, 99–106.

Burns, A. and Coffin, C. (eds) (2001) *Analysing English in a Global Context*. London: Routledge.

Canagarajah, S. (1999) *Resisting Linguistic Imperialism in English Language Teaching*. Oxford: Oxford University Press.

Canagarajah, S. (2006) Changing communicative needs, revised assessment objectives: Testing English as an International Language. *Language Assessment Quarterly* 3 (3), 229–242.

Clandinin, D.J. and Connelly, F.M. (2000) *Narrative Inquiry: Experience and Story in Qualitative Research*. San Francisco, CA: Jossey-Bass.

Crystal, D. (1997) *English as a Global Language*. Cambridge: Cambridge University Press.

Ellis, C. (2004) *The Ethnographic I: A Methodological Novel about Autoethnography*. Walnut Creek: AltaMira Press.

Graddol, D. (1997) *The Future of English?* London: The British Council.

Hardin, G.G. (1979) English as a language of international communication: A few implications from a national point of view. *English Language Teaching* 34 (1), 1–4.

Hassall, P.J. (2002) TEIL: English as an international language and the needs of Pacific Rim countries. *Asian Englishes* 4 (2), 72–101.

Hine, C. (2000) *Virtual Ethnography*. London: Sage.

Holliday, A.R. (2005) *The Struggle to Teach English as an International Language*. Oxford: Oxford University Press.

Holliday, A., Hyde, M. and Kullman, J. (2004) *Intercultural Communication: An Advanced Resource Book*. London: Routledge.

Jenkins, J. (2000) *The Phonology of English as an International Language: New Models, New Norms, New Goals*. Oxford: Oxford University Press.

Jenkins, J. (2006a) Current perspectives on teaching World Englishes and English as a Lingua Franca. *TESOL Quarterly* 40 (1), 157–181.

Jenkins, J. (2006b) The spread of EIL: A testing time for testers. *ELT Journal* 60 (1), 42–50.

Jenkins, J. (2007) *English as a Lingua Franca: Attitude and Identity*. Oxford: Oxford University Press.

Kachru, B.B. (1986) *The Alchemy of English: The Spread Functions and Models of Non-Native Englishes*. Oxford: Pergamon.

Kachru, B.B. (ed.) (1992) *The Other Tongue: English Across Cultures*. (2nd edn). Urbana and Chicago: University of Illinois Press.

Kachru, B.B. (1996) World Englishes: Agony and ecstasy. *Journal of Aesthetic Education* 30 (2), 133–155.

Kirkpatrick, A. (2007) *World Englishes: Implications for International Communication and English Language Teaching*. Cambridge: Cambridge University Press.

Matsuda, A. (2002) International understanding through teaching world Englishes. *World Englishes* 21 (3), 436–440.

McKay, S. (2002) *Teaching English as an International Language*. Oxford: Oxford University Press.

McKay, S. (2003) Toward an appropriate EIL (English as an International Language) pedagogy: Re-examining common assumptions. *International Journal of Applied Linguistics* 13 (1), 1–22.

Nakamura, K. (2002) Cultivating global literacy through English as an International Language (EIL) education in Japan: A new paradigm for global education. *International Education Journal* 3 (5), 64–74.

Norton, B. (2000) *Identity and Language Learning. Gender, Ethnicity and Educational Change*. Harlow: Pearson Education.

Pennycook, A. (1994) *The Cultural Politics of English as an International Language*. New York: Longman.

Phillipson, R. (1992) *Linguistic Imperialism*. Oxford: Oxford University Press.

Phillipson, R. and Skutnabb-Kangas, T. (1996) English only worldwide or language ecology? *TESOL Quarterly* 30 (3), 429–452.

Polzenhagen, F. and Wolf, H. (2007) Culture-specific conceptualisations of corruption in African English: Linguistic analyses and pragmatic applications. In F. Sharifian and G. Palmer (eds) *Applied Cultural Linguistics: Implications for Second Language Learning and Intercultural Communication* (pp. 125–168). Amsterdam: John Benjamins.

Roberts, P. (2005) English as a world language in international and intranational settings. PhD thesis, University of Nottingham.

Rubdy, R. and Saraceni, M. (eds) (2006) *English in the World: Global Rules, Global Roles*. London: Continuum.

Seidlhofer, B. (2004) Research perspectives on teaching English as a lingua franca. *Annual Review of Applied Linguistics* 24, 209–239.

Seidman, I. (2006) *Interviewing as Qualitative Research*. New York: Teachers College Press.

Sharifian, F. (2003) On cultural conceptualisations. *Journal of Cognition and Culture* 3 (3), 187–207.

Sharifian, F. (2006) A cultural-conceptual approach to the study of World Englishes: The case of Aboriginal English. *World Englishes* 25 (1), 11–22.

Sharifian, F. (2008) Distributed, emergent cognition, conceptualisation, and language. In R. M. Frank, R. Dirven, T. Ziemke and E. Bernárdez (eds) *Body, Language, and Mind (Vol. 2): Sociocultural Situatedness* (pp. 241–268). Berlin/New York: Mouton de Gruyter.

Sharifian, F. (forthcoming) Glocalization of English in World Englishes: The case of Persian English. In M. Saxena and T. Omoniyi (eds) *Contending with Globalisation in World Englishes*. Bristol: Multilingual Matters.

Smith, L.E. (ed.) (1983) *Readings in English as an International Language*. Oxford: Pergamon Press.

Strevens, P. (1980) *Teaching English as an International Language*. Oxford: Pergamon Press.

Wolf, H. and Polzenhagen, F. (2006) Intercultural communication in English–Arguments for a cognitively-oriented approach to intercultural pragmatics. *Intercultural Pragmatics* 3 (3), 285–321.

Part 1

Native/Non-native Divide: Politics, Policies and Practices

Chapter 2

English as a Lingua Franca, 'Non-native Speakers' and Cosmopolitan Realities

ADRIAN HOLLIDAY

Introduction

In this chapter I shall argue that the recent interest in English as a lingua franca cannot be considered on sociolinguistic grounds alone. The English as a lingua franca movement has a lot of relevance to what we now understand about the changing ownership of English. There are, however, the claims from some quarters that it represents yet another ploy for domination from the Center. This needs to be looked at because these claims connect with unresolved political aspects of the native–non-native-speaker issue. I shall suggest that the English as a lingua franca movement, although it searches for a cosmopolitan solution to the hegemony of 'native speaker' English, may not connect with other sorts of cosmopolitan realities that underpin some of the experiences of so-called 'non-native speaker' educators.

This chapter is not intended to be a critique of the English as a lingua franca movement, and will not address its linguistic or sociolinguistic aspects. It is instead an observation of possible reasons for conflict. There is, however, a deeper note of caution to Center academics, like myself, who may be seduced into thinking they can 'solve the problems' of a Periphery to which they do not belong and cannot speak for. My argument will also interrogate the concepts of Center and Periphery and 'native speaker' and 'non-native speaker'.

On a technical note, I refer to English as a lingua franca as a specific category within the far broader notion of English as an international language, the latter of which I see as an alternative terminology to ESOL (English for speakers of other languages).

Background to the Issue

An outcome of the English as a lingua franca movement is the idea that there might be a reduced code which is sufficient for the purposes of communication between 'non-native speakers' in international settings. Its major proponents claim that the research which has produced this idea is doing no more than describing an existing linguistic phenomenon (Seidlhofer, 2006: 45), is based on principles of 'tolerance for diversity' (Seidlhofer, 2006: 44), and that there is an interest in establishing the possibility of an international English which is 'negotiated and developed by ELF speakers themselves rather than imposed from "above" by native speakers' (Jenkins, 2006: 36), and will 'present a counterweight to hegemonic Anglo-American dominated English' (Jenkins, 2006: 38, citing Phillipson). Despite continued claims that there is no intention to impose a preferred model for non-native speakers (Jenkins, 2007: 19–22), there are accusations that the English as a lingua franca movement is yet another device to maintain Center dominance (Holliday, 2005a: 9). An example of this can be seen in this comment by Kuo, a Taiwanese teacher:

> Although I did feel comfortable to be told that I did not have to be native-speaker like, I would definitely feel upset if I could not reach my own expectation in pronunciation ... I just wanted to draw attention to the psychological part, the feeling, how people feel about themselves in terms of speaking ... If we take Jenkins's view and tell them to stay where they are – you don't need to twist your tongue this way and that and it's perfectly all right to keep your accent – at some point, we would terribly upset the learners because they might want to ... It's been clear that I'm a language learner from the periphery and – listen to this – I prefer to speak for myself! (Holliday, 2005a: 9, citing email interview)

The force of this comment is also present in Kuo's later statement that the English as a lingua franca movement fails to address the self-image and identity of users of English (Kuo, 2006: 216).

Center and Periphery

The placing of the conflict within the Center-Periphery dimension, exemplified by Kuo's statement, in her email interview (Holliday, 2005a: 9), that she is 'a language learner from the periphery', is a complex matter. The dimension traditionally relates to a regional or global inequality in affluence and power. I have, however, not in the past felt comfortable with this geographical aspect of Center and Periphery because it can so easily be an over-generalization. However, looking at the distinction again helps me to get to the bottom of the English as a lingua franca issue. If the Center and the Periphery are ideas rather than geographical locations, rather like 'the West' as an idea, they represent uneven power relations or qualities of life, and can be applied strategically or emotionally to different groups of people, events or attitudes at different times. What is important is that they are meaningful to the people who use them. I find it useful here to use Hannerz's (1991) explanation that the relationship between the Center and the Periphery is one of giving and taking meaning within an unequal world.

It is therefore not a simple matter to 'fix' the issues of the Periphery. One has to live the ideas and emotions of the Periphery condition to understand both the Periphery and the Center as ideas. It is the lack of appreciation of this principle which underlies the long-standing problems encountered when well-meaning Center educators try to tamper with the professional lives of others. Such problems can be seen in relation to Center imaginations in that they can be stakeholder-centered or that they can apply appropriate methodology in settings where there are unequal power relations (Holliday, 2005a), which imply the same missionary imagina-tions of 'freedom and democracy' as those implicit in US foreign policy. The plot thickens when the Center's desire to 'help' is more to do with professional, institution, political or cultural self-affirmation than with a profound desire to understand (Holliday, 2005a: 157–177, citing Edward Said). Maley (2006: 5) relates this issue of who has the right to occupy 'the higher moral ground' specifically to the English as a lingua franca movement, which he perceives as setting out to 'emancipate the repressed learning masses from the stifling coils of "Standard English"'.

For this reason, as a Center academic, I cannot presume to speak *for* the Periphery. However, I have a responsibility to make sense of how I am implicated in being viewed by the Periphery as Center (see also Holliday, 2005a: x, 2005b on how it is possible for a Center academic to write about the Periphery).

Linguistic or Political?

The native–non-native-speaker distinction is also central to the com-plexity of the English as a lingua franca issue, especially as both 'native' and 'non-native speakers' are included amongst English as a lingua franca researchers and those opposing them. On the one hand the distinc-tion has been largely discredited, especially by English as a lingua franca researchers themselves (e.g. Jenkins, 2000), or treated with ambivalence (Davies, 2006: 432). On the other hand it is sustained as a basic means for labeling English users throughout the TESOL profession. Kuo (2006: 214) herself considers 'native' and 'non-native speakers' as being straight forwardly corresponding to users of English from Kachru's 'inner circle' (the English-speaking West) and 'expanding circles' (where English is acknowledged as a foreign language) respectively. Davies (2006: 435) sustains six criteria for 'native speaker' status – to do with childhood L1, grammatical intuition and capacity for fluent spontaneous discourse and creative communicative range, and presents the category as a major measure of who is best able to provide a good model in the *teaching* of English (Davies, 2006: 445).

Perhaps surprisingly, the 'non-native speaker' label has also been sustained by the people who most decry it – the NNEST Caucus, whose goal is 'to create a nondiscriminatory professional environment for all TESOL members regardless of native language and place of birth' (http://nnest. moussu.net/purpose.html). Ryuko Kubota explains that sustaining the 'non-native speaker' label in this way offsets the 'blindness' to inequality that might arise from a 'liberal' desire to do away with it (Holliday, 2005a: 7, citing email interview).

What I feel is however particularly significant about the way in which the NNEST Caucus deals with the native–non-native-speaker issue is that it is *political* rather than largely *linguistic*. While language is still the prime focus, it is the *politics* of English as a potentially imperialist force, rather than concerns with linguistic models, which occupies critical applied linguists (e.g. Canagarajah, 1999a; Edge, 2006; Kubota, 2001; Kumaravadivelu, 2003, 2007; Pennycook, 1994, 1998; Phillipson, 1992). The mythic nature of the 'native speaker', as a mainstay of the dominant TESOL ideology is much discussed (e.g. Holliday, 2005a; Kumaravadivelu, 2003; Phillipson, 1992: 193; Rajagopalan, 1999a, 2004).

This NNEST Caucus's political usage of 'non-native speaker' resonates with what I have already noted about the concepts of 'Center' and 'Periphery' – that its full meaning for people who connect it with discrimination can only really be understood by the people who have experienced this discrimination. *I* prefer to keep 'native speaker' and 'non-native speaker' in inverted commas throughout because *I* consider them the products of a particular native-speakerist ideology which I believe inaccurately considers 'non-native speakers' inferior; but I am not someone, perhaps like Kuo (2006), for whom they have high stakes in relation to self-image and identity.

This qualitative difference between the linguistic and political adds to the reason why the linguistic 'liberation' presented by the English as a lingua franca movement might indeed be construed as somehow bypassing the deeper issues of speakerhood discrimination.

Instrumental Division of Labor or Discrimination

The 'non-native speaker' discrimination issue is also complex. Again, there is a traditional linguistic and pedagogic interpretation of the difference between 'native speaker' and 'non-native speaker' educators in terms of what they are expert in. 'Non-native speakers' teachers have been traditionally recognized as having the alternative attributes of 'local' knowledge of their students as 'L2' learners within a particular 'L2' context that they share (e.g. Medgyes, 1994). The distinction has thus been recognized as one of division of labor which provides a *diversity* of roles and expertise (Holliday, 2005a: 167, citing email interview with Chinese academic).

In contrast, the discrimination issue arises out of *competition*. 'Non-native speakers' having to compete for teaching jobs with 'native speakers' who are professionally less well qualified but have the advantage of speakerhood is now well known (Holliday, 2005a: 13 citing interviews; Kamal, 2006; Mora Pablo, 2006; Shao, 2005). This has become more apparent in recent years because of the increasing mobility of 'non-native speaker' educators and the acknowledgement that they do travel outside their traditional 'home' settings to become 'world' educators alongside 'native speakers' (Holliday, 2005a: 159; Kubota, 2001; Petrić, this volume).

Most worrying is the fact that much of this discrimination is on *ideological* rather than linguistic grounds, which can be traced to the way in which 'native speaker' superiority has been *constructed* as part of the grand plan for English superiority all along (Phillipson, 1992). Being acknowledged as a 'native speaker' is thus to do with 'acceptance by the group that created the distinction' (Braine, 1999: xv, citing Kramsch), where the 'native speaker' represents the in-group. This form of acceptance is not a linguistic matter, of sounding or writing like a 'native speaker'. There is growing evidence that the populist notion of 'native speaker' is connected with the 'white Anglo-Saxon' image of people who come from the English speaking West, and that 'non-native speaker' educators are excluded from 'native speaker' status because they do not fall neatly into this image. This is exemplified in this statement which was collected to demonstrate the range of popular student understandings of 'native speaker' when applied to their teachers:

> I'd prefer to have a teacher who is definitely a native English speaker. I'm not satisfied with Mr ***** – well, maybe he was born in England

but he doesn't *look* English, so I think maybe he doesn't have a good
accent and he doesn't really speak proper English. (QuiTE, 2006,
student statement, their emphasis)

Indeed, 'fair skinned', northern Europeans from countries where
English is not considered a mother tongue, can manage to escape this
discrimination because of how they look. Kubota *et al.* make this very clear
with biographical examples of what it takes for 'non-native speaker' educators working in the United States to 'pass' as 'native speakers':

Ulla Connor, who is White, and Xiaoming Li, who is Chinese ... both
face common challenges in acquiring the native speaker voice. Connor
succeeds in achieving this identity. Li doesn't. She revises her trajec-
tory of progression and chooses to develop a hybrid voice, positioned
between Chinese and American. I posit that ... Connor's Finnish identity provides her with possibilities of passing, while Li's Chinese identity encounters more difficulties ... More specifically ... the invisible
and normative nature of Whiteness is associated with the notion
of NS and ... the NNS construct is combined with 'coloredness' or
'Asianness'. (Kubota *et al.*, 2005, citing Connor and Li)

Discrimination of this type also seems rife in the traditional 'home'
setting of the 'non-native speaker'. Shao's (2005) informants connect pro
'native speaker' job discrimination in China with the language learning
public's association between 'non-native speaker' Chinese and being
'colored'; and Amin (1999) makes the connection with gender issues. The
range of the locations in which these types of discrimination occur suggests
a widespread phenomenon.

The incidence of discrimination questions the 'liberal humanist' intentions of what Kubota (2002: 84) describes as 'a nice field like TESOL', which
denies its role in 'the persistent racism of contemporary society' (Kubota,
2001: 28; see also Holliday, 2005a: 24–25, 33). The extent of this populist
image is demonstrated in Shuck's (2002) study of US high school students'
attitudes towards each other and their teachers.

The native-speakerist ideology underlying this discrimination can,
I argue, be traced to a chauvinistic Center perception that 'non-native
speaker' 'cultures' lack critical thinking, autonomy, the ability to plan and
manage, individuality, and so on, necessary to do the job of successfully
carrying an English-speaking Western vision of English across the world
(Holliday, 2005a, 2006; Kumaravadivelu, 2003; Nayar, 2002). It also resonates with Latour's (2006) view of modernism, which establishes 'them'
as 'prisoners inside the narrow confines of their cultures'. Exclusion of an
imagined 'non-native speaker' Other thus becomes a general pattern.

It is in addressing these *political* aspects of discrimination that I think the *linguistic* philanthropy of the English as a lingua franca movement may be construed as failing. It may well be that the establishment the existence of a bland international code, which in some aspect claims a reduction in linguistic difficulty and cultural rootedness, would appear undesirable to a group of people for whom it is largely designed, if they are at the same time suffering from prejudiced perceptions of their linguistic and cultural ability.

Different Cosmopolitan Realities

The concept of a lingua franca that transcends or escapes from national linguistic restrictions of speakerhood to some degree connects with cosmopolitan realities which are becoming increasingly apparent in a globalized world. However, discrimination against 'non-native speaker' educators indicates more complex and problematic aspects of cosmopolitanism. There are cases where the cultural and racial prejudice attached to the label place people in the 'non-native speaker' group when they have no linguistic reason to be there. These cases suggest that not simply *being* a 'non-native speaker', but being *called* a 'non-native speaker' is itself a form of discrimination.

Despite fulfilling all of the 'native speaker' criteria cited by Davies (2006), Pakistani British teacher Aliya (pseudonym) is labeled as a 'non-native speaker' while working in the UAE. She explains that 'It's more than language; it's a little more racial – the colour of the skin that matters' (Holliday, 2005a: 34, citing interview) and that this 'silently robs' people like her 'of the rights to speak in the language they may know best' (Holliday, 2006: 7, citing interview). Bangladeshi Kamal, born and brought up in Kuwait, and with primary and secondary education in an American international school, followed by university in the United States, does not quite meet the childhood L1 category cited by Davies (2006). She nevertheless 'passes' easily as a 'native speaker' in writing and on the phone when applying for teaching posts. However, when she presents herself physically for job interviews, and shows her Bangladeshi passport, in a country where she will always be expatriate, she is confirmed a 'non-native speaker' (Kamal, 2006). Sounding like a 'native speaker' is not sufficient.

Even if these are just eccentric cases, it is 'marginal' fragments of life that help us question our perceptions of the 'normal' (Holliday, 2004: 286; Honarbin-Holliday, 2005: 36, citing Norris; West, 2001: 29–30); and it is for this reason that such stories 'reveal themselves to us' and 'insist on being told' (Roy, 2002: Track 3). However, I would like to suggest that Aliya and

Kamal's narratives are *not* eccentric, but present a cosmopolitan *normality* in which large numbers of people no longer live in the places where they or their parents were born and where there is a blurring of traditional national and cultural identities. This is recognized generally in social science (e.g. Ahmad & Donnan, 1994; Delanty, 2006; Grande, 2006), but represents a relatively new awareness in applied linguistics (Kumaravadivelu, 2006; Rajagopalan, 1999a).

A cosmopolitanism awareness has had to fight hard against a more traditionally dominant methodological nationalism found in social science which stems from a 19th century vision of European nation states that goes back to the classic functional sociology of Durkheim and 'blinds' us to 'the multi-dimensional process of change' (Beck & Sznaider, 2006: 2; also Bhabha, 1994; Crane, 1994; Schudson, 1994). Rajagopalan (1999a, 1999b) suggests the same preoccupation has existed in applied linguistics where one-nation-language-culture has blinded us to the realities of 'speakers' who are 'transplanted' to new environments, and, I would say, is behind the nation-based cultural definitions that underlie the negative othering of 'non-native speakers' referred to above (Holliday, 2005a: 18), and also the 'native speaker' criteria cited by Davies (2006).

There is a significant twist in the discussion at this point. There is also a cosmopolitan awareness which is promoted by the Center, which Homi Bhabha expresses in the following way:

> This kind of *global* cosmopolitanism...configures the planet as a concentric world of national societies extending to global villages. It is a cosmopolitanism of relative prosperity and privilege founded on ideas of progress ... Global cosmopolitans of this ilk [that] frequently inhabit 'imagined communities' that consist of silicon valleys and software campuses ... call centres ... sweat shops ... readily celebrates a world of plural cultures and peoples located at the periphery, as long as they produce a healthy profit margin. (Bhabha, 1994: xiv, my emphasis)

I am not suggesting that the English as a lingua franca movement is necessarily falling into the global cosmopolitan trap, but that it might be construed as such because it appears to have the 'convenience of a uniform language' produced by the Centre. If it *is* construed as such, it is understandable why it would considerably anger the Periphery. Kumaravadivelu (2006: 22) connects Centered globalization with the 'self-marginalization' of 'non-native speaker' educators, where 'the periphery surrenders its voice and vision to the centre' and 'knowingly or unknowingly' they 'legitimize the characteristics of inferiority attributed to them by the dominating group'. Resonant with Kubota's comment, above, about how the removal of the native–non-native-speaker distinction can lead to a liberal color-blindness, Canagarajah, in his critique of Rajagopalan (1999a), warns us that a romanticized cosmopolitanism can lead to an irresponsible 'apathy ... or even playfulness' which is in danger of allowing the Center to imagine that inequalities do not really exist (Canagarajah, 1999b: 207). Global cosmopolitanism also prescribes what constitutes 'proper' social life, resulting in the rhetoric of 'you are with us or against us' (Bhabha, 1994: xvi) which we are familiar with in current US foreign policy concerning the militaristic spear of 'democracy'.

Decentered Cosmopolitanism

To counter global cosmopolitanism, Bhabha (1994: xv–xvi) suggests 'another ... *vernacular* cosmopolitanism which measures global progress from the minoritarian perspective' which connects with a globalization that 'begins at home'. Canagarajah (1999b: 208–209) considers this to be the cosmopolitanism which 'has always been there in non-Western communities' with villagers dealing easily across small linguistic boundaries, and which was destroyed by the 'greater globalization and homogeneity' that was imposed when 'colonial powers divided these communities arbitrarily into nation-states for their convenience, and imposed on this seemingly chaotic diversity the efficiency and convenience of a uniform language'.

The idea of 'beginning at home' resonates with Kuo's already cited statement that she 'prefers to speak for herself' about the sorts of linguistic standards she finds meaningful (Holliday, 2005a: 9, citing email interview). It helps me to understand what she means here by looking at recent work on young Iranian women, who, after years of isolation, are appealing to recover their place in a broader world that transcends the régime they feel represses them. Honarbin-Holliday (2005) describes art students who wish to claim European art as part of their own heritage. Alavi (2005) describes the way they use weblogs to express their desire for modernity in their own terms, in the face of what they see as a repressive theocratic régime in their own country. This example suggests a cosmopolitan defiance which is not defined by the Center and which attempts to explain a state of affairs more complex than that assumed by the Center: 'We are no different from the free men and women of the world. We know how to think, how to educate ourselves' (Alavi, 2005: 175, citing weblog posted in May 2002).

There is a sense here of the Periphery claiming ownership of Center territory – which is very different to having ownership bestowed under the aegis of a Center-led cosmopolitanism. This sense of claiming ownership is evident in Kuo's description of how 'native speaker' models can be manipulated creatively and owned as a commodity at the local level. She is speaking here about what it takes to make a model of English attractive:

> Generally speaking, you have to make an investigation of the target market and you satisfy the needs of the local people, rather than imposing some strange offer. However, sometimes people will choose to have the original American flavour for its exotic and exciting attraction. Then, why not sell the originals? If the students are fascinated with the exotic flavour of English and prefer to learn it the way it is, then teach it that way. There is really no need to encourage some sort of awkwardly regional standard, particularly where English is not used within the society, as in Taiwan. (Holliday, 2005a: 166, citing email interview)

While the commodification of a range of things, such as education, is considered the bane of late modern society, Kuo is demonstrating here how this might be turned to an advantage.

Conclusion

In this chapter I have placed alongside each other two important phenomena in current applied linguistics – that of the English as a lingua franca movement, and that of the Periphery voice of 'non-native speakers'. The two are connected in that 'non-native speakers' have critical things to say about an English as a lingua franca movement which aims, at least partly, to offer them a liberation from 'native speaker' models of English. The arising conflict deals directly with issues of Center and Periphery, with different perceptions of cosmopolitanism derived from these positions, and with the often unrecognized discrimination leveled at 'non-native speaker' educators. On one side, the English as a lingua franca movement is concerned with linguistic aspects of ownership and models of English, and with representing 'non-native speakers' in terms of the technical features of their linguistic performance. On the other side, 'non-native speakers' present a more qualitative set of issues which concern politics, identity, status and freedom of choice. It is important here to repeat Seidlhofer's principled statement that English as a lingua franca research is *emic* in that it is 'from the participants' perspectives' (Seidlhofer, 2006: 44). However, there may be perspectives that are important to other people, that purely linguistic research does not include, which are to do with the cultural richness that make people *choose* linguistic products. In the words of Chácon and Girardot:

> We believe that NNESTs need to position themselves in their contexts, contest social inequity, and express their 'voice' to gain empowerment and promote change in their own realities. This transformation demands a 'conscientization' so that individuals become aware of their contextual realities and the actions that alienate them. (Chácon & Girardot, 2006, citing Freire)

References

Ahmad, A.S. and Donnan, H. (1994) Islam in the age of postmodernity. In A.S. Ahmad and H. Donnan (eds) *Islam, Globalization and Postmodernity* (pp. 1–20). London: Routledge.

Alavi, N. (2005) *We Are Iran*. London: Portobello Books.

Amin, N. (1999) Minority women teachers of ESL: Negotiating white English. In G. Braine (ed.) *Non-Native Educators in English Language Teaching* (pp. 93–104). Mahwah, NJ: Erlbaum.

Beck, U. and Sznaider, N. (2006) Unpacking cosmopolitanism for the social sciences: A research agenda. *The British Journal of Sociology* 57 (1), 1–23.

Bhabha, H. (1994) *The Location of Culture*. London: Routledge.

Braine, G. (1999) *Non-Native Educators in English Language Teaching*. Mahwah, New Jersey: Erlbaum.

Canagarajah, S. (1999a) *Resisting Linguistic Imperialism*. Oxford: Oxford University Press.

Canagarajah, S. (1999b) On EFL teachers, awareness and agency. *ELT Journal* 53 (3), 207–214.

Chácon, C.T. and Girardot, L.C. (2006) NNES teachers' and prospective teachers' perceptions of English as an international language: An exploration in an EFL context. *NNEST Newsletter* 8 (1).

Crane, D. (1994) Introduction: The challenge of the sociology of culture to sociology as discipline. In D. Crane (ed.) *The Sociology of Culture* (pp. 1–19). Oxford: Blackwell.

Davies, A. (2006) The native speaker in applied linguistics. In A. Davies and C. Elder (eds) *The Handbook of Applied Linguistics* (pp. 431–450). Oxford: Blackwell.

Delanty, G. (2006) The cosmopolitan imagination: Critical cosmopolitanism and social theory. *British Journal of Sociology* 57 (1), 25–47.

Edge, J. (ed.) (2006) *(Re)locating TESOL in an Age of Empire: Language and Globalization*. London: Palgrave.

Grande, E. (2006) Cosmopolitan political science. *The British Journal of Sociology* 57 (1), 87–111.

Hannerz, U. (1991) Scenarios for peripheral cultures. In A.D. King (ed.) *Culture, Globalization, and The World-System* (pp. 107–128). New York: Palgrave.

Holliday, A.R. (2004) The value of reconstruction in revealing hidden or counter cultures. *Journal of Applied Linguistics* 1 (3), 275–294.

Holliday, A.R. (2005a) *The Struggle to Teach English as an International Language.* Oxford: Oxford University Press.

Holliday, A.R. (2005b) How is it possible to write? *Journal of Language, Identity, and Education* 4 (4), 304–309.

Holliday, A.R. (2006) Native-speakerism. *ELT Journal* 60 (4), 385–387.

Honarbin-Holliday, M. (2005) Art education, identity and gender at Tehran and al Zahra Universities. Unpublished PhD thesis, Department of Art and Design, Canterbury Christ Church University.

Jenkins, J. (2000) *The Phonology of English as an International Language: New Models, New Norms, New Goals.* Oxford: Oxford University Press.

Jenkins, J. (2006) Global intelligibility and local diversity: Possibility or paradox? In R. Rudby and M. Saraceni (eds) *English in The World* (pp. 32–39). London: Continuum.

Jenkins, J. (2007) *English as a Lingua Franca: Attitude and Identity.* Oxford: Oxford University Press.

Kamal, A. (2006) The challenges and experiences of teaching in Kuwait. Unpublished paper presented at the Cutting Edges: Classrooms, People and Cultures, Department of Language Studies, Canterbury Christ Church University.

Kubota, R. (2001) Discursive construction of the images of US classrooms. *TESOL Quarterly* 35 (1), 9–37.

Kubota, R. (2002) (Un)ravelling racism in a nice field like TESOL. *TESOL Quarterly* 36 (1), 84–92.

Kubota, R., Bashir-Ali, K., Canagarajah, S., Kamhi-Stein, L., Lee, E. and Shin, H. (2005) Race and (non)nativeness in English language teaching: A brief report. *NNest Newsletter* 7 (2).

Kumaravadivelu, B. (2003) Problematizing cultural stereotypes in TESOL. *TESOL Quarterly* 37 (4), 709–719.

Kumaravadivelu, B. (2006) Dangerous liaison: Globalization, empire and TESOL. In J. Edge (ed.) *(Re)locating TESOL in an Age of Empire: Language and Globalization* (pp. 1–26). London: Palgrave.

Kumaravadivelu, B. (2007) *Cultural Globalization and Language Education.* Yale: Yale University Press.

Kuo, I-C. (2006) Addressing the issue of teaching English as a lingua franca. *ELT Journal* 60 (3), 213–221.

Latour, B. (2006) War of the worlds – what about peace? On WWW at http://www.btgjapan.org/catalysts/bruno.html. Accessed 21.07.08.

Maley, A. (2006) Questions of English. *English Teaching Professional* 46, 4–6.

Medgyes, P. (1994) *The Non-native Speaker Teacher.* London: Macmillan.

Mora Pablo, I. (2006) Power, identity, and language learning in Mexico. Unpublished paper presented at the Cutting Edges: Classrooms, Cultures and People, Department of Language Studies, Canterbury Christ Church University.

Nayar, B. (2002) Ideological binarism in the identities of native and non-native English speakers. In A. Duszac (ed.) *Us and Others: Social Identities Across Languages, Discourse and Cultures* (pp. 463–480). Amsterdam: John Benjamins.

Pennycook, A. (1994) *The Cultural Politics of English as an International Language.* London: Longman.

Pennycook, A. (1998) *English and the Discourses of Colonialism.* London: Routledge.

Phillipson, R. (1992) *Linguistic Imperialism.* Oxford: Oxford University Press.

QuiTE (2006) QuiTE Quotes: Native Speaker Teachers. On WWW at http://www.
quality-tesol-ed.org.uk/2006_seminar.html. Accessed 21.07.08.
Rajagopalan, K. (1999a) Of EFL teachers, conscience and cowardice. *ELT Journal*
53 (3), 200–206.
Rajagopalan, K. (1999b) Reply to Canagarajah. *ELT Journal* 53 (3), 215–216.
Rajagopalan, K. (2004) The concept of "World English" and its implications for
ELT. *ELT Journal* 58 (2), 111–117.
Roy, A. (2002) Come September: In conversation with Howard Zinn. Audio record-
ing, Lensing Performing Arts Centre, Santa Fe, Lannan Foundation.
Seidlhofer, B. (2006) English as a lingua franca in the Expanding Circle: What it
isn't. In R. Rudby and M. Saraceni (eds) *English in The World* (pp. 40–50).
London: Continuum.
Schudson, M. (1994) Culture and the integration of national societies. In D. Crane
(ed.) *The Sociology of Culture* (pp. 21–43). Oxford: Blackwell.
Shao, T. (2005) Teaching English in China: NNESTS need not apply. *NNEST
Newsletter* 7 (2).
Shuck, G. (2002) Constructing the non-native speaker in everyday discourse. Paper
presented at the AAAL Annual Conference, *(Re)Interpreting Applied Linguistics*,
Salt Lake City.
West, L. (2001) *Doctors on The Edge: General Practitioners Health and Learning in The
Inner City.* London: Press Association.

Chapter 3

Teaching English as an International Language (EIL) in the Gulf Corporation Council (GCC) Countries: The Brown Man's Burden[1]

SADIA ALI

Introduction

I will first briefly explain the role of English as an International Language (EIL) in the Gulf Corporation Council (henceforth GCC) countries before describing how English teachers from the Outer Circle are not offered equal employment possibilities in these countries. I will present the reflections of five English teachers (with origins in the Outer Circle who work in the GCC) on the hiring practices of English teachers in the GCC. Later I will also share accounts of 31 university students who discussed their perceptions of the difference between 'native' and 'non-native' teachers of English through email interviews. It could be concluded from the interviews and survey that teachers from the Outer Circle face discrimination in the hiring process of English teachers in the GCC while students, who are also stakeholders, cannot always differentiate clearly between a 'native' and a 'non-native' English teacher. Furthermore, when discussing which qualities students desire in an English teacher, none of the surveyed students identified 'Westerner' or 'native speaker' as a desirable quality. Finally, more than half of these students indicated that they would like to be involved in the employment process of English teachers at their university. These results could be beneficial as a springboard for future research on the pedagogy of EIL in the GCC countries. For further research, using a larger data pool would produce more compelling results.

We Are Not There Yet

> I was working in an institution where a no-smoking policy was enforced. In order for teachers in this institution to continue to smoke without being perceived as not abiding by the regulations, they would switch off the light of their offices, lock them, and smoke inside. There were approximately a total of thirty teachers, seven of whom were native speakers of other languages. One native English speaker colleague invariably knocked on the door of his smoking colleagues and introduced himself thusly: 'NATIVE SPEAKER'. The response of course was that the colleague inside would open the door and welcome him. In the same institution, a native speaker of Arabic adopted a somewhat similar tactic. Whenever he needed to talk to someone smoking in his office, he told me he would knock, saying in unmistakably educated English: 'NEAR-NATIVE SPEAKER'. (Raddaoui, 2005: 116)

The above quote from Raddaoui, which he uses as anecdotal evidence to show the 'native/non-native'[2] divide, has more serious implications on English language teaching practices than perhaps he intended to indicate. Not only does this anecdote signify the innate sense of superiority of the teachers from the 'English speaking West' (while also pointing towards the realization of speakers of other languages that they can always only be 'near-native' speakers of English) as has been pointed out by Raddaoui, it also suggests a metaphorical 'only native speaker allowed' zone – the English language classroom. In the GCC countries (Saudi Arabia, Kuwait, Bahrain, Qatar, the United Arab Emirates and the Sultanate of Oman) the English language classrooms/institutions/program can be seen as the locked office where only certain 'privileged' teachers can gain entry.

In this section I will offer a brief overview of the division between 'native' and 'non-native' teachers with special reference to the teaching of EIL by first discussing very briefly the role of English language and the history of higher education in the GCC.

The official language of the GCC is Arabic but English is widely spoken because of the presence of large expatriate communities and the importance of English as the language of business. English can be considered a truly international language used for communication amongst people from various cultures in the GCC, particularly as the expatriate population outnumbers the local population in most of the GCC countries. Therefore English, along with Urdu/Hindi, has became an indispensable lingua franca. As EIL expands, bilingual speakers use English on a daily basis within their own countries (McKay, 2002: 49). This is also happening in the GCC and due to this process, English as an international language cannot be linked to any single country or the culture of any single group of expatriates working in the GCC. Thus, English in these countries allows for the expression of the individual cultural identities of its users while at the same time preserving the convenient collective benefit of a language which is intelligible nationally and internationally (De Kadt, 1997: 162).

The history of institutions of higher education in the GCC is just as interesting as the colorful expatriate communities which live in these countries. Once the oil boom established generous resources in the oil-producing, tax-free GCC, attention shifted from sustenance to maintenance, a project which can be achieved successfully when the local population is skilled and educated enough to carry forward the development of their country. This belief has led to the proliferation of colleges and universities in the GCC. In recent years, several major American and Canadian universities have opened branch campuses in Education City, Qatar. The cities of Sharjah and Dubai in the UAE each have university cities (Sharjah University City and Dubai Academic City) which house several colleges and national universities (Dubai has a few branch campuses of international universities as well). In 2006, the Sorbonne opened its first campus outside France in Abu Dhabi while MIT is also entering into partnership to set up a college in the Emirate. Similarly, other GCC countries also have reputable colleges and universities which offer quality higher education to the local and expatriate population.

When these institutions of higher education were being established in the GCC, their management and supervision was outsourced to American and Canadian professionals. For example, several educational institutions in Kuwait, Oman, Qatar and the UAE have established partnership with AMIDEAST whereby AMIDEAST assists in human resource development through recruitment and training. Whether it is a precondition of the local authorities or a wish of the outsourced management, English teachers from the Outer and Expanding Circles[3] have never filled teaching positions in well-established private schools, colleges and universities in the GCC. A cursory reading of these educational institutions' catalogs reveals that all but only a very few of the English language teaching staff are English speakers from the Inner Circle. This is the case despite TESOL's vehement opposition to discrimination in hiring practices (Braine, 1999: xvi; TESOL Member Resolution Against Discrimination on the Grounds of Nationality, 1999). One of the major goals of TESOL's NNEST (Non-native English Speakers in TESOL) caucus is 'to create a nondiscriminatory professional environment for all TESOL members regardless of native language and place of birth' (Braine, 1998) but this resolution has hardly taken effect in the GCC.

Institutions of higher education in the GCC are perpetuating 'linguistic elitism' (Nayar, 1994) by continuing to hire only Western teachers of English, consequently marginalizing an entire group of teachers from non-Western countries even though they form the majority of English language teachers in the world (Canagarajah, 1999). In Nayar's words,

> ... the native-nonnative paradigm and its implicational exclusivity of ownership is not only linguistically unsound and pedagogically irrelevant but also politically pernicious, as at best it is linguistic elitism and at worst it is an instrument of linguistic imperialism. (Nayar, 1994)

On a global level, the ELT profession is perhaps the world's only occupation in which the majority faces discrimination.

In the rest of the chapter I will present the reflections of five English teachers on the employment practices of English teachers in the GCC. These teachers have their origins in the Outer Circle and are currently working in the GCC. Forty-three teachers, who were part of a mailing list for English teachers in the GCC countries, were initially contacted via email inviting them to participate in the study. Five teachers eventually accepted the invitation and were interviewed via email over a period of two months.

I will also discuss the results of an email survey, presented as excerpts of interviews, conducted on 31 randomly selected university students from the GCC countries. These respondents are students of the five teachers being interviewed for the study and willingly agreed to participate in the study.

The Native/Non-native Divide: 'Only Native Speakers Will be Hired'

> Five languages
> five different worlds
> yet English
> shrinks
> him
> down
> before white men
> (Dreaming Gujurati, Shailja Patel)

Braine (1998) offers two main excuses for discrimination against 'non-native' teachers. First is the most commonly used excuse that English language learners prefer 'native-speaker' teachers. Another frequently cited reason for not hiring NNS English teachers is the complex legal process that employers must go through in order to recruit foreigners. For instance, the Immigration and Naturalization Service requires proof that by hiring a foreigner ('alien', in immigration jargon), the employer is not depriving an American citizen of employment. Braine explains this as an excuse offered by employers in the United States. However, in the GCC, while employers may sometimes mention the first excuse as a reason not to hire 'non-native' teachers, the second justification is not relevant since there are hardly any GCC citizens in the English language teaching profession in higher education and the process for hiring all foreigners is the same.

Nevertheless, in the GCC, where the expatriate population is a highly colorful mix, the great majority of English language teachers are white. Raddaoui cites an actual job advertisement in his article that blatantly announces the requirement for 'native English speakers with *western faces* and neutral accent' (Raddaoui, 2005: 120, his emphasis). Raddaoui's reference supports two incidents that were reported to me by colleagues in their email interviews.

Aisha, an English language teacher with several years of teaching experience from a leading institution of higher education in Pakistan, tells the experience of her long and fruitless search for ESL/EFL jobs in the Gulf. She shares an anecdote that shows the injustice:

> Four years ago as I sat waiting to be called for an interview outside an employer's cubicle during TESOL Arabia's annual conference job fair I realized that I was the only 'brown' candidate and the only one not called by any employer. I sat for four hours. Finally a friendly Caucasian woman came to sit next to me and casually explained that she had already received two job offers but wanted to try her luck with the university of her choice. She asked me how many interviews I had had and much to my own dismay I had to tell her that I was not interviewed at all. I presume she pitied me because eventually she let me in on her secret that she was not a native speaker of English, German being her first language. Then she looked at me with a very serious face and pointed out that I could not even claim to be a native-speaker because I am 'brown'. Funnily her observation had some truth to it because although my first language is English I was not called for any interview that day. (email interview)

Asiya, a second generation American of Asian origin, is a teacher of English married to an Omani national. She lives in the UAE and teaches in a private school. She reports:

> Once I sent an application via email for the post of an EFL instructor to a reputable English language institute in the UAE which claims to 'teach English to the world'. With the email I attached my photograph and carefully highlighted my academic and professional qualifications in the resume while also highlighting that I am American. I received a prompt reply from the EFL programme's head addressing me as 'Dear Mr Ahmed' and stating that he had found a 'more suitable candidate' since the job strictly required a 'female, native-speaker (citizen of UK/USA/Canada/Australia) with at least a BA'! It was very obvious from his unashamedly prejudiced response that he had not bothered to take even a perfunctory look at the email's attachments. On another note I wonder how much he himself knew about the Arab Muslim culture to be working in the UAE since he failed to *guess* my gender from my Arab Muslim name! (email interview)

These are only two anecdotes from two different professionals but there may be many other teachers who face similar discrimination in recruitment everywhere. According to Red-Baer (1995, in Sahin, 2005) 'an inexperienced Caucasian will be chosen over a much better qualified foreigner' because English teachers are more often than not selected 'by their looks than their qualifications'. Conversely, 'for many NNS English teachers, qualifications, ability, and experience are of little help in the job market' (Braine, 1998). Many migrants in English speaking countries give birth to children who grow up as native speakers of English but with foreign names. However, if these children want to become English teachers, they would be treated as the 'generalized Other' (Holliday, 2005: 19) by some countries recruiting English teachers because they have origins in the Outer/Expanding Circles.

This means that some trained teachers who are in effect 'native-speakers' (by virtue of being born and brought up in the Inner Circle) like Asiya, and as such are linguistically not different at all from the 'unproblematic Self' will still be seen to belong to the perceived monolithic 'non-native' group which is characterized as people who are described as 'dependent, collectivist, passive, docile, lacking in self-esteem, easily dominated, traditional, static, rigid, need to be trained, and empowered', and so on (Holliday, 2005: 19–20). These perceived notions about the 'generalized Other' are so strong that many times candidates that seem to belong to the 'Other' camp are disqualified much before the interview stage. This can be terribly frustrating for an entire group of people who are 'denied what they have been trained to do' (Braine, 1998).

Mahboob (2007) believes that several 'concrete steps' can be taken by teachers from the Outer Circle to 'create a more professional and non-discriminatory atmosphere' in English language teaching. He suggests that 'non-native' teachers should 'become familiar with literature on World Englishes' and that they should 'question the native-speaker-as-model in SLA research'. I believe that these are the first few steps that a teacher from non-English speaking countries may take to gain self-confidence and argue their position in the job market. However, I do not see how self-confidence and sense of worth can be useful if a teacher is not even given the chance to discuss their expertise by being invited for an interview. As illustrated in the two anecdotes above, these teachers with foreign names (regardless of whether or not they are actually from Outer Circle) were not short-listed and so had no way of discussing their potential face-to-face with an employer.

The 'Native' Teacher in Alien Culture: Crusoe Meets Man Friday

> The trouble with the Engenglish is that their hiss hiss history happened overseas, so they dodo don't know what it means. (*The Satanic Verses*, Salman Rushdie, 1988)

There are several English teachers from the Outer Circle who would like a career in language teaching in the GCC and these teachers also often share the culture of the students. When teachers have knowledge of their students' culture it can be extremely rewarding as it enables student empowerment rather than an insistence on assimilating the learners into the target language culture (Pennycook, 1990, in Phillipson, 1992: 15).

A common problem in the GCC is that 'where cultural difference is connected with nationality' it is assumed that all people of that nationality will behave similarly. This is an assumption Holliday warns against by stating that 'we must therefore be wary of not to use these differences to feed chauvinistic imaginations of what certain national or ethnic groups can or cannot do – as exotic, "simple", "traditional" Others to our complex, "modern" selves'. (Holliday, 2005: 23).

In 'Western-Educated Faculty Challenges in a Gulf Classroom', Sonleitner and Khelifa (2005) investigated the challenges for new Western/Western-educated faculty as they started teaching at an Arab university located in the Gulf. Their paper is based on the accounts of several teachers who participated in the study and it is quite interesting to note the words participants used to describe the university students and their culture:

- *not* having opinions about issues that do not directly affect them (p. 4)
- *not* having experience of expressing what is on their mind (p. 4)
- *eerie* feeling (p. 7)
- *funny* feeling (p. 7)
- bit *problematic* (p. 8)
- non-verbal behavior ... was *lacking* in the students (p. 8)
- *difficult* to understand (p. 13)
- seeming *disinterest* in obtaining specific employment (p. 14)
- *never* been truly engaged by teaching (p. 16)
- *not* there yet (p. 16)
- *non*-emotiveness (p. 16)

(Sonleitner & Khelifa, 2005, all emphasis mine)

In numerous places the writers use the words 'frustration' 'disappointment', 'difficulty', and 'struggle' to refer to the teaching experiences of the Western faculty when teaching the Arab students at the university. Clearly the hired faculty had no prior experience of teaching Arab students, even though most universities and colleges in the GCC advertise that experience of teaching Arab students and knowledge of Arab Muslim culture is highly desirable in a candidate.

A reader cannot help but notice how fittingly the teachers' accounts, aims and practices match the native-speakerist attributes oriented to 'Our' system which Holliday (2005: 142) mentions in his remarkable book *The Struggle to Teach English as an International Language*. These attributes relate to the teachers' aim to change 'their' educational environment through necessary cultural engineering to fit 'our' system and are in turn related to 'the unspoken problem that some English-speaking Western ESOL educators have ... not been "trained", "corrected", culturally "civilized"' (Holliday, 2005: 124).

However, the ESOL educators from non-English speaking countries, although called 'non-native', have indeed been 'trained' and 'corrected' and culturally 'civilized'. The educators who possess a 'deep understanding of the language and cultures of the learners' are the 'bilingual and bicultural' teachers whom Phillipson (2005: 27) calls 'a sine qua non for valid English teaching'. These teachers possess knowledge of their learners' culture which can positively affect 'study habits, order and method of presentation, practice and retention of information' (Raddaoui, 2005: 129). In most instances, they share the culture of students from GCC and would not find the students or their culture 'problematic', 'lacking', 'difficult' or 'non-emotive'. Unfortunately, such educators are not employed by 'Our' system.

Classification of English Teachers: Near-native, a New Divide

> Excuse me
> standing on one leg
> I'm half-caste
> (Half Caste, John Agard)

Braine (1999: xvi) emphasizes that 'no issue is more troubling than that of discrimination in employment' but it 'is rarely mentioned in the popular literature in ELT'. On the one hand, we have some 'native teachers' who are hired whether or not they are trained because their 'nativeness' can compensate for their lack of qualification and experience, on the other hand, there are several 'non-native teachers' who are fortunate enough to be trained but, because they are not 'native speakers', are not employable at all.

In the last few years, many job advertisements requiring English language teachers in the GCC do not clearly invite 'only native-speakers'. However, there are several other ways to indicate that only English speakers from the English-speaking West need apply.

Figure 3.1 is part of an actual job advertisement for teachers in a GCC country which highlights what is required of an English teacher.

New recruitment practices in almost all GCC require that educational institutions do not accept degrees earned through distance learning programs if the candidate is not a 'native-speaker' of English from the English-speaking West. Employers insist on hiring English teachers from American/Canadian/British cultures, ensuring that teachers have thorough knowledge of these cultures by either being born into the culture or

---

> *MA in TESL/TEFL. Faculty should have native-speaker proficiency in English, demonstrated either through being a native of an English-speaking country or by a score of 8.5 or above on the IELTS test. Non-native speakers of English: must have near-native proficiency in English; both degrees must be from an English-speaking country and earned while residing in that country.*

Figure 3.1   Part of a job advertisement in a GCC country

having spent considerable time in the West. This is one reason why educational qualifications gained through distance learning programs are not *recognized* by employers. Thus, teaching candidates from the Outer Circle must prove their 'near-native' proficiency in the IELTS test by securing a band score of 8.5 or above in all four skills and must possess teaching qualifications from an English-speaking country 'earned while residing in that country'.

In contrast, English teachers who belong to the English speaking West are not required to meet such demanding criteria. The screen shot in Figure 3.2 of an authentic job posting clearly illustrates this disparity (more examples are attached in Appendix 1a–e).

Mahboob notices a similar trend in other countries as well:

> ... the discriminatory discourse in job ads has shifted from requiring 'native speaker' to requiring candidates from a list of specified inner circle countries; interestingly, these are all White Anglo-English dominated countries. This change in the lexicon is a thin veil that attempts to hide the racial and L1-based discrimination in the field. (Mahboob, 2007)

When a person uses English for international purposes, the speaker's ability to communicate across a number of World Englishes is more important than the skill in a particular World English (Hassall & Ganesh, 2005). However, 'colonization of the mind' (Tsuda, 1997: 26) is encouraging employers to replace the requirement for a 'native speaker' with the prerequisite of 'near-native proficiency' thereby demanding that teachers from the Outer Circle 'stand on one leg' so they can model hyphenated identities. If English has now become an 'international language', then questions such as who is a native speaker and who should a *near-native* speaker try to emulate can no longer be taken for granted.

Figure 3.2 Screen shot of an authentic job posting

Smith, argues that English, since it is an international language, does not belong exclusively to the 'native English speaker' any longer:

> We in ELE [English Language Education] need to find redundant ways to point out that English belongs to the world and every nation which uses it does so with a different tone, color, and quality ... [Many nationalities] speak with accents when they speak English, but so do Canadians, Australians, and all the rest. English is an international language. It is yours (no matter who you are) as much as it is mine (no matter who I am) ... No one needs to become more like the Americans, the British, the Australians, the Canadians or any other native English speaker in order to lay claim on the language. To take the argument a step further, it isn't even necessary to appreciate the culture of a country whose principal language is English in order for one to use it effectively. (Smith, 1976, in Pack, 1977: 2)

What Smith reveals is the fact that people from the English speaking West will always be called 'native' English speakers. However, those English speakers who belong to non-English speaking countries should not be treated like the 'generalized Other' because globalization is ensuring that English no longer belongs to any one kind of people; it is an international language and belongs to everyone who uses it.

Basim is an English teacher from Iraq who is 'tired' of the 'native/non-native' divide and how it affects the hiring practices in the UAE where he works. Basim was born in Iraq and moved to Yorkshire when he was six years old. He lived there for 10 years before moving to the UAE with his family. He has a Masters degree in TESL earned through a distance learning program which is not recognized by many leading colleges and universities in the UAE. Currently, Basim teaches in a public school which pays him less than half the salary he could make in a college or university. When asked if he would call himself a 'native' English teacher or a 'non-native' English teacher, he said:

> I don't understand this distinction! I regard myself as an English language teacher. Native and non-native are terms more relevant to race and nationality. I don't like to mix that with my professional activities. (email interview)

Basim's frustration is evident from his response. He is experienced and qualified, and has spent a considerable amount of time living in the UK, but his passport prevents him from benefiting from a well-paying career which can be advertised like a working holiday – 'Native speaker: teach English & see the world' (Reid, 1996).

It is interesting that with the spread of English as an international language, and a somewhat necessary global language, English speakers from Outer and Expanding Circles are also beginning to identify themselves as 'native' speakers. They are refusing to stand on one leg and define their English proficiency as 'near-native' anymore. Susan, an Indian teacher of English, takes pride in being multilingual:

> Well, since I am an Indian and speak more than four languages which include English, and since I have been brought up right from my childhood in an English speaking atmosphere, I can be called a native English speaker too!!! (email interview)

The use of the word 'too' and the triple exclamatory marks are significant in that they explain how she sees herself (a 'native' speaker of English) although perhaps she is not always identified as one. Her 'nationality' has no influence on her linguistic abilities and she is aware of her strengths: that she is a multilingual, fluent speaker of four languages.

Students' Perceptions: A 'Native' Teacher is 'One Who Has a Very Strong Accent that I Cannot Understand'

> I understand X,
> but cannot speak Y.
> Possessive phrases: he has,
> she has, I don't have.
> Look, I lack,
> says my language.
> (Primer for Non-Native Speakers, Philip Metres)

Justifying the bias in hiring decisions by referring solely to students' preferences is 'seen as one of outright discrimination' (Raddaoui, 2005: 119). Nonetheless, many institutions do continue to make this claim when hiring teachers exclusively from the Inner Circle. On the contrary, teachers I interviewed think that in many cases students are not even aware of the 'native'/ 'non-native' divide. Mona teaches English in Saudi Arabia and feels that

> ... students are not really sure about the difference between native and non-native teachers. This is a distinction that we (as English language teachers) have created. My students 'think' they know what the distinction is. To them, teachers who speak with an American accent that they can't understand and who are white and blonde and come from the US are native teachers. In fact, my students don't even

know these terms, they call all white blonde teachers 'American Miss'. (email interview)

Susan thinks that students can distinguish between a 'native' and a 'non-native' teacher. She says that her students

'think that native will not give them the information they ask because they might not be able to communicate with them. (email interview)

Definitions of a 'native' teacher and a 'non-native' teacher

Many students offer similar responses when asked to differentiate between a 'native' and a 'non-native' teacher of English. Ahmed, an engineering student from Oman, describes a 'native' English teacher as:

the one who has a very strong accent that I can not understand. Yet, as long as the teacher can communicate, has a good English and do not misuse word she or he is good English speakers and do not need to born in UK to be native English speakers. (I find them harder to understand and they have an accent.) (email interview)

Ahmed's definition corroborates Mona's assumption that students describe 'native' speakers as those with 'very strong' and incomprehensible accents. However, Ahmed goes on to categorize other teachers who 'can communicate' and who 'do not misuse words' as native English speakers, adding that they do not have to be born in the UK to be called 'native' speakers.

An interesting definition of 'native' English teachers is offered by Eiman, a baccalaureate student in the UAE:

A native English teacher is a teacher whose first language is English, or a teacher who's so fluent in English and speaks better than people whose first language is not English. (email interview)

To Eiman, a 'native' speaker is not one who is native by virtue of accident of birth but is one who is 'fluent in English' which she does not qualify as *any one type* of English. Both Eiman and Ahmed are perhaps inadvertently pointing towards speakers who use English as an international language.

Hajar, a medical student from Qatar, writes in her email that a 'native' English teacher 'has less experience and she might try to be good with the students like she won't tell them their mistakes and she will just let them pass'. Respondents of other researchers have also differentiated 'native speaking' teachers and 'non-native speaking' teachers by their different approaches towards correction of students' errors (Lasagabaster & Sierra, 2005; Medgyes, 1994; Üstünlüoglu, 2007).

Ibrahim, a Saudi student, also mentions this in his definition of a 'non-native' English teacher:

> She is strict with language rules and does her job without expecting any benefits from her students. She never has anything against the student. Which will allow her to be clear and fair in what she is marking. (email interview)

Ibrahim sees 'strict(ness) with language rules' as a desirable quality in an English teacher as he combines it with other positive qualities like clarity, fairness, and sincerity.

Students defined 'non-native' English teachers through a variety of other different terms. For instance, Mohammed, an Omani student, thinks that even non-native English teachers speak English as a first language

> A non-native English teacher is a teacher whose first language is English, but he/she does not know how to teach English. (email interview)

Mohammed's definition shows that he is not clear about the distinction between the two types of teachers as created by those in the teaching profession. This supports what teachers who were interviewed for the study mentioned in their emails, that not all students know the difference between 'native' and 'non-native' teachers of English.

Mohammed's friend Saif, defines a 'non-native' English teacher as

> the one who finds a very hard time when he or she want to explain something. they can not find the right words to communicate and they seem to use some words in wrong situations. But such people don't become English teachers, they teach Maths or science or something. (email interview)

According to Saif, a 'non-native' teacher is one who struggles with the English language and perhaps he is referring to speakers for whom English is a third or foreign language. Such teachers, according to Saif, become teachers of subjects other than English.

On the other hand, Eiman gives a very different definition of a 'non-native' English teacher. She says that a 'non-native' English teacher is

> someone who speaks English very well but he is not originally from an English speaking country. (email interview)

It is worth mentioning that the students who were interviewed do not see 'non-native' teachers as incompetent speakers of English. For instance, for Mohammed, even 'non-native' English teachers speak English as a first language. Saif, on the other hand, thinks that those teachers who are not proficient English speakers do not become English teachers in the first place; 'they teach Maths or science or something'. Eiman thinks that even 'non-native' English teachers 'speak English very well' but they do not belong to the English-speaking West.

Desirable qualities in an English teacher

The 31 students who kept contact with me through email offered a wide range of desirable qualities in an English teacher which are listed in Table 3.1. Interestingly, none of them said that they wanted their teacher to be someone from the English-speaking West.

Student involvement in the employment process of English teachers

I also wanted to enquire from the students whether they would like to be involved in the employment process of English teachers at their university. Seventeen out of the 31 students who responded to my emails said they would very much like to have a say in what type of English teachers they want. I particularly found Eiman's response quite enlightening:

> I would love it if I am asked what type of English teacher I want. I have suffered from being taught by an unqualified teacher for two years and if I had been taught by another teacher my learning experience would have been so rewarding. Teachers should be selected because of their skills, qualification, and dedication, not the university they studied in, or English country they lived in. (email interview)

Eiman seems confident that she can differentiate between a qualified teacher and an 'unqualified' English teacher. From her earlier responses it appears that she has a fair idea about the nature of division between teachers from the Inner Circle and those from the Outer and Expanding circles, and she defines the former as 'native speakers' and the latter as 'non-native speakers'.

Fatima, Eiman's friend, is not too sure about wanting to be involved in the employment process of English teachers at her university. When asked

Table 3.1   Desirable qualities in an English teacher

• Cares about the students and their progress
• Challenges them to do better
• Develops their self esteem
• Develops student's opinions and views
• Evaluates me according to my work and effort
• Enthusiastic
• Just
• Motivating
• Has excellent qualifications
• Kind
• Sweet
• Has a sense of humor
• Patient
• Optimistic
• Always smiling
• Caring
• Smart
• Innovative
• Active
• Fair
• Honest
• Knowledgeable
• Hard working
• Helps each student individually on their weak points
• Patience
• Constant feedback
• Creative
• Flexible

if she would like to be involved in the hiring process of English teachers at her university, she said:

> Yes and no. Yes, because students are the ones who will be interacting with the teachers the most, so they should have a voice in choosing their teachers. No, because some students might be unfair in their judgments (for example if a teacher is really good but is strict and fair – students might not like that). Besides, the university has done a good job so far in selecting English teachers. If the university decides to involve students in the employment process, I suggest that only the best students should be selected to represent the student body. (email interview)

However, Amani, a student from Bahrain, feels she is not qualified enough to think what type of English teacher is best for her and presents compelling reasons for it. What Amani proposes instead is a sound system of teacher evaluation to ensure that only good teachers are retained:

> As students we might not have enough experience and qualifications to choose a teacher and most of the students might not take the process seriously and choose the teacher according to the way he/she looks or from the country they come from. I think it would be better if there is a method or a person between the students and the teacher who would listen to their complaints about the teacher or any comments about his way of teaching or evaluation without any conflicts. (email interview)

Conclusions: Are We There Yet?

> You taught me language, and my profit on't
> Is I know how to curse. The red plague rid you
> For learning me your language. (*The Tempest*, Shakespeare)

Many universities and colleges in the GCC are around 20 years old which is infantile compared to the universities with histories going back several centuries that can be found in some countries. However, 20 years is a long time if you happen to be an English teacher from the Outer Circle and have been constantly 'shoved in the back of a segregated ELT bus' (Raddaoui, 2005: 129). Despite years of protests from ELT professionals from the Outer Circle asking for and making recommendations through scholarly research that 'hiring practices should be conducted on the basis of professional expertise and personal attributes rather than on native speaking background' (Inbar, 2001), the vast majority of institutions of higher education in the GCC insist on hiring 'only native speakers'. By doing so, they define 'people negatively, in terms of what they are not' rather than celebrating their 'multiple linguistic competence' (Phillipson, 2005: 14).

The aim of this chapter is not to suggest that English teachers from the Inner Circle should be replaced by those from the Outer Circle. All I am asking for is balance. English teachers from the Outer Circle should *also* be allowed to act as 'inter-state actors' (Phillipson, 1992: 54). While I understand that some teachers who apply for employment in educational institutions may not be well qualified or suited for the job, I think it is discriminatory not to consider the applications of an entire group of teachers on the basis of race. Generalizing the 'Other' must stop and when applications for ELT posts are being screened, under-qualified or inexperienced teachers should be identified irrelevant of the country in which they were born. Not all teachers from the Outer Circle are incompetent and in all fairness not all teachers from the Inner Circle are hired only on the basis of their skin color.

Some countries do recognize English teachers from non-English speaking countries as valuable professionals committed to the English language and to its teaching. Hungary is an example where 'it is not uncommon for non-native speakers to occupy positions traditionally reserved for native speakers only' (Bojana, in Holliday, 2005: 159). In the GCC, we are clearly not there yet.

While many students from GCC may insist on being taught by 'American Misses', as Mona thinks, there are also those, like Eiman, who may feel they 'suffer' when an unqualified teacher is hired to teach them only because they happen to be from the English speaking West. Students desire an array of qualities in their English teachers and 'native speaker' is not always one of them. Thankfully, 'the inevitable trickle-down effect of the native speaker fallacy' (Maum, 2002) has not affected many students in the GCC *yet*. The voices of students who are also stakeholders, after all, should be heard instead of supposing that all students want to be taught by 'native speakers'.

What can be done to ensure fairness in the hiring process?

A series of steps need to be taken to guide the future of the pedagogy of EIL in the GCC. Governments of the GCC countries are trying to create knowledge economies and have turned to the 'best' institutions of learning to build centers of excellence in education. However, these efforts need to be continuously monitored and evaluated to ensure their effectiveness and relevance to local culture. Qualified teachers from countries outside and *within* the English-speaking West need to educate employers in institutions of higher education in the GCC that the 'native speaker fallacy' is 'linguistically anachronistic' (Canagarajah, 1999, in Lasagabaster & Sierra, 2005: 136), 'old-fashioned' and 'even nonsensical' (Lasagabaster, 1999, in Lasagabaster & Sierra, 2005: 136). One way this can be achieved is by conducting research in the area of 'native/non-native' divide, and publishing literature on the topic.

On a global level, IATEFL (International Association of Teachers of English as a Foreign Language) like TESOL International can help (as an *international* association) by standing up for English teachers from the Outer Circle. TESOL Arabia (http://tesolarabia.org/), which is a proud affiliate of TESOL International and operates to 'establish a network of communication among professionals who use English as a medium of instruction' in Arabia, can also help by openly recognising, supporting and promoting English teachers from the Outer Circle.

English is an international language and when a language becomes international, the English language speaking regions do not exist as individual Inner, Outer and Expanding Circles; they unite to create intersects where English is spoken not as it is spoken by Circle A or Circle B but as an amalgam of A and B. GCC countries are 'intersects'. Teachers with the willingness to make a long-term commitment to the International Language and its teaching should be hired and hiring should not be based on whether or not the degrees and work experience they have earned are from the English-speaking West. This is what Carol Renner from University of Regensburg explains in her response to Nayar's article:

> The point shouldn't be so much whether a person has been born in this or that country or whether he or she is monolingual, or belongs to a particular ethnic group, but whether s/he is willing to make a long-term commitment to the language. When this kind of commitment to the language becomes the measure, it becomes clear that the native speaker who makes no effort to improve, who rests on his/her native speaker laurels, who stagnates in the sluggish waters of native-speakerdom does more harm to the language and to language teaching than the one who dedicates him/herself to the language for 25 years whatever the country or culture of his or her origin. (http://www-writing.berkeley.edu/TESL-EJ/ej01/f.1.html#R2)

Notes

1. This part of the title is a reference to Henry Labouchère poem 'The Brown Man's Burden' (1899) written in response to Kipling's 'The White Man's Burden'.
2. Like Holliday (2005) I too do not like to use the terms 'native' and 'non-native' to refer to teachers who are all struggling together to teach English that is truly an International language. Calling an English teacher a *non-native speaker* automatically makes them a deviant from the norm and I personally believe that no teacher deserves to be recognized by a hyphenated identity. I will therefore put the terms within quotation marks to refer to how they are used by other writers/researchers.
3. According to Kachru (1985) Outer Circle refers to countries where English has spread in non-native settings and has become part of the countries' main institutions (example of Outer Circle countries are India and Singapore). English is used as a second language in such multilingual countries. The Expanding Circle includes countries that recognize the importance of English as an International Language but which were not colonized by the English-speaking West. English is usually taught as a foreign language in these countries.

References

Agard, J. (c. 2007) Half Caste. On WWW at http://www.intermix.org.uk/poetry/poetry_01_agard.asp. Accessed 15.1.07.

Braine, G. (1998) NNS and Invisible Barriers in ELT. On WWW at http://nnest.moussu.net/history.html. Accessed 2.2.07.

Braine, G. (1999) *Non-Native Educators in English Language Teaching*. Mahwah, NJ: Lawrence Erlbaum Associates.

Canagarajah, S. (1999) Interrogating the 'native speaker fallacy': Non-linguistic roots, non-pedagogical results. In G. Braine (ed.) *Non-native Educators in English Language Teaching* (pp. 77–92). Mahwah, NJ: Erlbaum.

De Kadt, E. (1997) McWorld versus local culture: English in South Africa at the turn of the millennium. In L.E. Smith and M.L. Forman (eds) *World Englishes 2000* (pp. 146–168). Honolulu: College of Languages, Linguistics and Literature.

Hassall, P.J. and Ganesh, S. (2005) Correspondence analysis in attitudinal research: The case of world Englishes and teaching English as an international language. *Learning and Teaching in Higher Education* 2 (1). On WWW at http://www.zu.ac.ae/lthe/vol2no1/lthe02_06.pdf. Accessed 15.01.07.

Holliday, A. (2005) *The Struggle to Teach English as an International Language*. New York: OUP.

Inbar, O. (2001) Native and non-native English teachers: Investigation of the construct and perceptions. PhD thesis, Tel Aviv University, Israel.

Kachru, B.B. (1985) Standards, codification and sociolinguistic realism: The English language in the outer circle. In R. Quirk and H.G. Widdowson (eds) *English in the World: Teaching and Learning The Language and Literatures* (pp. 11–30). Cambridge: CUP.

Lasagabaster, D. and Sierra, J.M. (2005) What do students think about the pros and cons of having a native speaking teacher. In E. Llurda (ed.) *NonNative Language Teachers: Perceptions, Challenges and Contributions to the Profession* (pp. 217–241). New York: Springer.

Mahboob, A. (2007) The native model fallacy in SLA: What can we do about it? *TESOL NNEST Newsletter* 9 (1). http://www.tesol.org//s_tesol/article.asp?vid=151&DID=8552&sid=1&cid=718&iid=8545&nid=2982. Accessed 31.3.2007.

Maum, R. (December 2002) Nonnative-English-speaking teachers in the English teaching profession. *Center for Applied Linguistics Digests.* On WWW at http://www.cal.org/resources/Digest/digest_pdfs/0209maum.pdf. Accessed 18.12.06.

McKay, S. (2002) *Teaching English as an International Language.* Oxford: Oxford University Press.

Medgyes, P. (1994) *The Non-Native Teacher.* London: Macmillan.

Metres, P. (2007) Primer for non-native speakers. From the Fishouse: An audio archive of emerging poets. On WWW at http://www.fishousepoems.org/archives/philip_metres/primer_for_nonnative_speakers.shtml. Accessed 15.1.07.

Nayar, P.B. (1994) Whose English is it? *TESL-EJ* 1 (1). On WWW at http://www-writing.berkeley.edu/TESL-EJ/ej01/f.1.html. Accessed 18.12.06.

Pack, A.C. (1977) Man and God's gift of languages. On WWW at http://w2.byuh.edu/academics/domckay/Speeches/Mckay/A_Pack.htm. Accessed 2.2.07.

Patel, S. (2006) Dreaming Gujurati. Imagining ourselves: A global generation of women. On WWW at http://imaginingourselves.imow.org/pb/Story.aspx?G=1&C=0&id=443&lang=1. Accessed 15.1.07.

Phillipson, R. (1992) *Linguistic Imperialism.* Oxford: Oxford University Press.

Phillipson, R. (2005) New contexts of English use in globalization: New learning norms? In Z. Syed (ed.) *Culture, Context, and Communication in English Language Teaching.* Abu Dhabi: Military Language Institute.

Raddaoui, A.H. (2005) Bridging the native non-native gap in ELT. In Z. Syed (ed.) *Culture, Context, and Communication in English Language Teaching.* Military Language Institute: Abu Dhabi.

Reid, E. (1996) *Native Speaker: Teach English and See the World.* Caldwell: In One Ear Publications.

Rushdie, S. (1988) *The Satanic Verses.* New York and Harmondsworth: Viking Penguin.

Sahin, I. (April 2005) The effect of native speaker teachers of English on the attitudes and achievement of learners. *Journal of Language and Linguistic Studies* 1 (1). On WWW at http://www.jlls.org/Issues/Volume1/No.1/ismetsahin.pdf. Accessed 15.01.07.

Shakespeare, W. (n.d.) *The Tempest.* The complete works of William Shakespeare. On WWW at http://shakespeare.mit.edu/tempest/tempest.1.2.html. Accessed 17.2.07.

Sonleitner, N. and Khelifa, M. (2005) Western-educated faculty challenges in a Gulf classroom. *Learning and Teaching in Higher Education* 2 (1). On WWW at http://www.zu.ac.ae/lthe/vol2no1/lthe02_02.pdf. Accessed 02.02.07.

TESOL Member Resolution Against Discrimination on the Grounds of Nationality (1999) On WWW at http://www.tesol.org/s_tesol/sec_document.asp?CID =87&88DID=244. Accessed 17.2.07.

Tsuda, Y. (1997) Hegemony of English vs. ecology of language: Building equality in international communication. In L.E. Smith and M.L. Forman (eds) *World Englishes 2000* (pp. 21–31). Honolulu: College of Languages, Linguistics and Literature.

Üstünlüoglu, E. (2007) University students' perceptions of native and non-native teachers. *Teachers and Teaching Theory and Practice, The Journal of the International Study Association For Teachers and Teaching* 13 (1), 63–79.

Appendix 1A

Screen shot of an advertisement for 'native English speakers' with a passport from: Canada, New Zealand, Australia, US or UK' in Kuwait

English Language Instructors – Based Kuwait

Opportunities to teach English to trainees and employees of major companies in the oil, gas and petrochemicals industries.

Kuwait, occupies nearly 500 kilometres of coastline along the Arabian Gulf. It's friendly & family orientated, enjoys lovely weather for many months of the year, immense diversity and a booming economy make it an interesting place to work. In addition, Kuwait is also a tax free state.

Due to our continued business expansion, enthusiastic & energetic English Language Instructors are required to join our team, dedicated to delivering the best possible service to our clients.

To meet business objectives we are looking for candidates, able to take up employment in June/July 2007.

Teaching takes place in training centres at various locations throughout Kuwait. Normal working hours are from Saturday to Wednesday, 7am to 3pm.

Qualifications:
Applications from male and female instructors with a good first degree from a recognised University as well as a CELTA/TEFL certificate and five years experience are welcomed. Applicants must be native English speakers, with a passport from: Canada, New Zealand, Australia, US, or UK.

Appendix 1B

Screen shot of an advertisement for 'native speakers' born in England, America, Canada or Australia (British, American, Canadian or Australian passport holders) in Saudi Arabia

Exciting Opportunities in Kingdom of Saudi Arabia

Brief Job Description:

Male native speakers born in England, America, Canada or Australia (British, American, Canadian or Australian passport holders).

Applicants other than American citizens must reside in Saudi Arabia at the time of application and be prepared to transfer their Iqama at the end of their present contract.

American citizens outside Saudi Arabia must reside in the United States at the time of visa processing or if they are residents of Saudi Arabia must be able to transfer their Iqama from within the country.

Qualifications:
(In order of Preference)
Masters degree in Applied Linguistics,
Masters in TESOL, TEFL or ESL
Masters in Education (ESL)
Masters in Education (Mainstream)
Bachelors with a Grad. Dip. in TESOL, TEFL or ESL
Bachelors with a Grad. Cert. in TESOL, TEFL or ESL

Appendix 1C

Screen shot of an advertisement for 'native English speakers' with no necessary work experience required in the UAE

Qualifications: 6 experienced TEFL teachers are required to work in primary schools in Abu Dhabi from September. You must have the following:

* At least 1 year experience teaching TEFL
* CELTA/DELTA or equivalent
* Due to shared accomodation, must not have any dependents to accompany you
* Due to local customs/regulations, only female teachers are required
* Native english speakers

Successful candidates will be contacted.

Minimum Education: Diploma/Certification

Languages :
• English

Languages Used as a Medium of Teaching:
• English

Experience Required: no

This Program is open to American, Australian, Canadian, European, Kiwi and South African Participants.

Appendix 1D

Screen shot of an advertisement for 'English native speaking university graduates' in Qatar, Oman, Bahrain, Lebanon, Syria, Jordan, Saudi Arabia, Egypt, United Arab Emirates. No 'formal education/certification in teaching' required. Experience is 'not compulsory'

Employer: ساحة شاتة في المدينة العربية المتحدة

Location: UAE, QATAR, OMAN, BAHRAIN, LEBANON, SYRIA, JORDAN, SAUDI ARABIA, EGYPT, United Arab Emirates
Deadline: Tuesday 31. July 2007
Experience: No experience required

Details:
Would you like to teach in the Middle East or the Gulf region?
Would you like to continue your career as a senior administrator or school director?

is an international, college-preparatory education system with roots in the 19th century and a vision for the 21st century. This system is currently being successfully implemented in 41 schools in 14 countries

Applications invited for August 2007 from English native speaking university graduates to teach:
a) Kindergarten & Primary English & Social Studies, Maths, Science.
b) Secondary English & Social Studies, Maths, Computer science, Economics and Business.
Graduates of all disciplines are invited to apply. Formal education/certification in teaching not required. Experience and training is helpful but not compulsory. We provide in-service training.

Appendix 1E

Screen shot of an advertisement for 'English teacher with native English accent' in Bahrain

Job Title:	English Teacher
Job Category:	Electronics
Job Location:	Manama – Bahrain
Job Ref. Number for your records:	
Job Description:	English Teacher with Native English Accent for elementary Students. Highly Motivated, Talented, Leadership Skills.
Skills Required:	Should be a university graduate in english, love children, good & clear english accent.
Language Requirements:	• English-Very Good • French-Good
Employment Type:	• Full Time
Yearly Salary:	Unspecified
Posting Date:	Mar 31 2007
Education & Experience	
Education level required:	Bachelor
Experience (in years):	3 to 5 Years

Chapter 4

EIL, Native-speakerism and the Failure of European ELT

MARKO MODIANO

Introduction

Kachru (1988), as noted in Brown (2006), established a number of precepts which have bearing on how English can be conceptualized in educational programs which transcend 'foreign-language' ELT. One of these is the 'belief that there is a "repertoire of models for English" as opposed to one best model' (Brown, 2006: 688). The work carried out by Kachru, Smith and others working in world Englishes has influenced the manner in which English is taught and learned in first and foremost the outer circle. Here, there has been a strong emphasis on envisioning English in its multiplicity, on recognizing the utility of local varieties and on the formation of identity in the use of English as an L2. EIL (developed in part by Smith [1981, 1983]), while very much associated with the basic tenets of Kachruvian sociolinguistics, differs significantly however in some respects (see Crystal, 1999 and Modiano, 1999a, 1999b, 2000). EIL has developed as a concept which is relevant to the teaching and learning of English in the new era, and here, this is especially germane to L2 users of English in the expanding circle. Many are now envisioning EIL as a basis for teaching cross-cultural communicative skills on a global scale. For expanding circle learners (where English has traditionally been taught as if it were a 'foreign language'), more and more practitioners are introducing English as a global language, one which exists in many different forms. One result of this is that one can no longer claim that English is simply Standard English in its two forms, Standard American English (AmE) and Standard British English (BrE), with all other varieties relegated to subservient positions in a 'self-evident' hierarchy.

An understanding of the diversity of English, for production as well as for comprehension, makes one a better communicator. This is where EIL and world Englishes ideologies overlap. Both the EIL and the world Englishes paradigm position English as having local as well as global dimensions. Both approaches challenge conventional ELT protocols that promote English as a foreign language and which define divergence from Standard English as non-standard and thus worthy of being eradicated from the speech of learners. One can claim that the world Englishes/EIL fraternity is opposed to those who cling to outmoded prescriptivism. Those committed to traditional ELT are for the most part solely focused on Standard English and show little interest in other varieties (for examples, see Prator [1968], Quirk [1988], and more recently, Kuo [2006]). However, despite the fact that the world Englishes/EIL perspective is more in line with current sociolinguistic and applied linguistic thought, it is nevertheless difficult to define how ELT in the European Union (EU) is informed by EIL ideologies. For example, it is hard to differentiate between conventional prescriptivism and contemporary descriptivism. The two often overlap. It is also challenging to distinguish between curriculum intended to foster the general development of English language skills, and programs designed to promote the teaching and learning of English for international purposes. When turning to the actual classroom, what we find across Europe is the utilization of eclectic methodologies, as well as a good deal of uncertainty. Practitioners are finding it difficult to come to terms with the internationalization of language teaching and learning.

There are, nevertheless, a few things which unite ELT practitioners across the EU. One is a commitment to *communicative competence*, often also referred to as *cross-cultural communicative competence* (see Halliday, 1978; Hymes, 1972; Savignon, 1997). The other is the understanding that learners are no longer learning English because it is used primarily to communicate with native speakers, but are acquiring English because it will be required of them in a wide range of work related, educational and social activities, many of which will not include native speakers. Thus, while there is agreement that English is now 'global' and as such is best defined as a heterogeneous entity, few practitioners have as yet been able to devise methods and curricula that can act as a basis for teaching with such an understanding as the guiding principle. There is a lack of consensus as to how English should be taught and learned, and certainly less agreement over which educational norm is best suited to represent English in the new era. If we are to understand how EIL has impacted on language education in the EU, we must look at two things; one: how other conceptualizations, such as English as a lingua franca, Mid-Atlantic

English and Euro-English, have influenced the manner in which English is appropriated in this part of the world, and two; how contemporary educational theory and subsequent governmental policy is impacting on classroom practice.

English is used across mainland Europe on a daily basis in many different capacities. For more than 50 years now it has been vigorously pursued on a large scale in education in Western Europe, and this tradition, after the collapse of the Soviet Union in the early 1990s, has extended across Eastern Europe. In countries like Romania and Bulgaria, which became member states in 2007, we see indications that English is taking root there and is now an important component of education at all levels. The dissemination of English across Europe, which people like Phillipson want to define as a form of *linguistic imperialism* (see Modiano, 2004a; Phillipson, 1992, 2003), has until recently been perceived as a decidedly British endeavor, with teachers and pupils adhering to the understanding that the goal of the instruction is the attainment of native or near-native proficiency in BrE. *Native-speakerism*, steeped in an Anglophile tradition, is the dominant paradigm in European ELT. Yet, while it is the case that native-speakerism and conventional 'prescriptive' ELT are dominant in language education in the EU, there are a number of developments which are challenging this order. Because of the advent of linguistic Americanization, for example, one can no longer claim that Europe's lingua franca is unequivocally a British commodity. English is emerging in Europe, not only as a universal language, but also as a potential norm-generating variety. Before we go further with this line of reasoning, however, it is prudent, I think, to look closer at the term *lingua franca*.

Lingua Franca

According to Longman's *Dictionary of Contemporary English* (2003), the term lingua franca succinctly denotes 'a language used between people whose main languages are different'. In *A Dictionary of Linguistics & Phonetics*, by David Crystal (5h edn, 2003: 271) the term is defined as 'an auxiliary language used to enable routine communication to take place between groups of people who speak different native languages'. *Longman Dictionary of Language Teaching & Applied Linguistics* (Richards & Schmidt, 2002: 309) defines a lingua franca as

> a language that is used for communication between different groups of people, each speaking a different language. The lingua franca could be an internationally used language of communication (e.g. English),

it could be the **native language** of one of the groups, or it could be a language which is not spoken natively by any of the groups but has a simplified sentence structure and vocabulary and is often a mixture of two or more languages. (Bold present in the original as indicator of cross reference)

The ambiguity over whether or not the 'simplified' usage among non-native speakers is 'always' or 'sometimes' the case is an unfortunate slip. Nevertheless, these understandings of the term are certainly that which most people would subscribe to, and there is consensus that languages such as English, Spanish, Russian and Arabic have lingua franca status which transcends local or regional functionality. We also find in the literature the inference that the term lingua franca designates a universal language used by non-native speakers. For example, Jenkins (2006: 160) notes that 'ELF researchers specifically exclude mother tongue speakers from their data collection. Indeed in its purest form, ELF is defined as a contact language used only among non-mother tongue speakers'. While this line of reasoning may mesh well with research methodology targeting the linguistic behavior of non-native speakers, its does not, in my opinion, reflect a pragmatic conceptualization of how an auxiliary language actually functions as a medium of communication in various regions around the world. For example, because there are over 60 million native speakers of English in the EU (of a total of nearly 500 million people), the idea that native speakers are ignored in a definition of English as a European lingua franca is counterproductive (see Table 4.1). When a native speaker of English uses his or her English with a group of people for whom English is an L2, it is used in that capacity as a lingua franca by the native speaker as well. Thus, the idea of a language having considerable utility in multicultural settings, among people with differing linguistic profiles, brings us closer to how English actually operates as an auxiliary language in the postmodern era. To exclude the L1 speaker from this fraternity is to limit our understanding of how English operates globally as Europe's and the world's primary lingua franca.

Seeing as the movement to bring forth the conceptualization of English as a lingua franca is gaining momentum worldwide, and more specifically for Europe, it is imperative that an analysis is made of the implications of the two differing approaches (for comprehensive discussion see Jenkins, 2006). One is the (traditional) idea that English is a lingua franca for a non-native speaker constituency which should pursue knowledge of the language as if it were a foreign language. The other, upheld by those who have bought into the world Englishes paradigm, is to see English as

Table 4.1   Population figures for the EU

The 27 Member States with population figures	
Austria 8.2 m	Latvia 2.3 m
Belgium 10.4 m	Lithuania 3.4 m
Bulgaria 7.3 m	Luxembourg 500,000
Cyprus 700,000	Malta 400,000
Czech Republic 10.2 m	Poland 38.2 m
Denmark 5.4 m	Portugal 10.5 m
Estonia 1.3 m	Romania 22.3 m
Finland 5.2 m	Slovenia 2 m
France 59.9 m	Spain 43 m
Germany 82.5 m	Sweden 9 m
Greece 11.1 m	The Netherlands 16.3 m
Hungary 10.1 m	The Slovak Republic 5.4 m
Ireland 4.1 m	The United Kingdom 60 m
Italy 58.5 m	Total: 493.2 million. (According to EU statistics, approximately half of all EU citizens are capable of speaking English.)

Source: 2005 *Eurostat*

a lingua franca for interlocutors who use it with others in multicultural settings (and thus see English in its diversity as opposed to viewing English as a prescriptive entity defined by idealized inner-circle speakers). It should be made clear, moreover, that my own position here is that a lingua franca must be *inclusive* as opposed to *exclusive*. That is to say, it is imperative that our understanding of how English is used in Europe is integrated with a vision of a communicatively viable use of the language internationally. Applied linguistic concerns, as well, are also relevant. It is this applied linguistics dimension which informs the development of EIL in the EU.

While research which targets discourse strategies and the pragmatics of intercultural communication need not necessarily take into consideration the concerns of language teaching and learning, that which is studied, and the results of such study, inevitably come to the attention of those who teach learners the English language in formal educational settings. For example, in contemporary descriptive sociolinguistics there is a reevaluation of how we come to terms with the culture-specific 'idiosyncrasies' of the L2 speaker. Such lines of reasoning call into question educational practices which have been harshly defended by prescriptivists for some time (often referred to as *negative interference* and instead in my work as *positive transference* when examples of transference show promise of evolving into practical features of communication and thus of identity, and moreover show signs of becoming systematic in a speech community). That which sociolinguists do in their pursuit of a better understanding of how English operates as an auxiliary language will have grave bearing on the manner in which educational authorities, writers of dictionaries, grammars, language-learning materials and practitioners carry out their professional duties.

Our understanding of 'the ways in which local values, identities, and interests are negotiated in the new role of English as a global contact language' has greatly improved as a result of the work of ideologues such as Canagarajah (2006: 197). In his seminal paper, 'Negotiating the local in English as a lingua franca' Canagarajah (2006) anchors our understanding of the concept 'lingua franca' within the parameters of the non-native speaker and the multicultural social order. The juxtaposition of *localization*, which puts emphasis on the importance of local identity markers, and the idea of English as a language 'conceived as a transnational contact language', challenges the ELT community in that these two notions are apparently difficult to negotiate in many expanding circle contexts. Nevertheless, Canagarajah has been able to conceptualize an ELT platform based on multiculturalism. He speaks of those who 'are adopting the position that English is a heterogeneous language with multiple norms and diverse systems' (Canagarajah, 2006: 199). This understanding of how we define the trope *lingua franca* for Europe is certainly much more in tune with that which is inferred in national curriculums issued by governments across the EU, namely, that pupils are engaging the English language as a contact language which has utility in local (European) as well as global contexts. It is here, in this contemporary understanding of the term *lingua franca*, that we find the greatest challenges for ELT in the new era. As a lingua franca, one possessed by competent users of the language across Europe, the notion of *identity* has become much more important. It is apparently the case that Canagarajah's postcolonial insights, which emphasize the importance of identity for speakers of second-language varieties, are also relevant for L2 users of English living and working in the EU. Thus, if one abandons the claim that English is to be taught and learned as a foreign language in the EU, and instead take on board Canagarajah's more contemporary definition of the term *lingua franca*, English suddenly becomes something quite different when compared to what English has entailed in traditional ELT. It is no longer sufficient to see a lingua franca as merely a universal language. It is now something much more, and is taking on new properties.

It is also the case that there is a great deal of misunderstanding. For instance, as an example, we can see in the work of Kuo a general attitude which is a misrepresentation of the ideals of the lingua franca movement. Kuo sums up her understanding of the term *lingua franca*:

> The description of English as a lingua franca has, from the outset, restricted its focus down to the very instrumental function of English as the language for international communication. It is primarily and ultimately concerned with enabling learners to carry out international communication in various global contexts, reflecting a view of English as entirely and fundamentally an instrument of communication. It has largely overlooked aspects of language such as literacy, register, style, and various aesthetic concerns and has made no reference to a language's social functions, such as to project self-image, to establish self-identity, and to develop personal voice. (Kuo, 2006: 215)

Kuo, after presenting the results of a small-scale study, comes to the conclusion that '[a] native-speaker model ... would appear to be more appropriate and appealing in second-language pedagogy than a description of English which is somewhat reduced and incomplete' (Kuo, 2006: 220). As to Kuo's description of what she feels 'English as a lingua franca' embodies, I do not feel that it does the literature justice. In my view, what distinguishes English as an international language and 'English as a lingua franca' is the notion that both represent an attempt to gather English-language users into an all encompassing 'cross-cultural communication' taxonomy. They denote the use of English in multicultural forums (where native as well as non-native speakers participate, although it is also relevant to forums where only non-native speakers interact). EIL, moreover, emphasizes that for those who communicate in international forums, the primary focus should be placed on situational adaptation, and it is this pragmatic aspect of communication which is targeted in educational programs designed to promote an EIL vision of English as opposed to a foreign language orientation.

I am not convinced that either conceptualization suggests that individuals who pursue competency in the English language will not have access to the full range of English-language expression. If we speak of

lexicogrammatical complexity, the use of a broad range of idiomatic constructions and other embellishments which make language usage more
erudite, rich and complex, there is nothing in the ideologies of EIL and
EFL which indicate that non-native speakers should be limited in such
respects. Learners may decide that they do not want to make the investment required to acquire a 'native-like' accent. Nevertheless, if and when
they decide that they want to have a comprehensive command of the language, there is every reason to believe that these conceptualizations of
the English language embody all that is needed to develop high levels of
proficiency, and this includes fluency comparable to that of a native
speaker (albeit with the understanding that native-like proficiency in
phonological terms is not required). Moreover, seeing as Kuo has mentioned 'literacy, register, style, and various aesthetic concerns ... [as well
as] ... a language's social functions, such as to project self-image, to establish self-identity, and to develop personal voice' it must be noted that this
is exactly what EIL and ELF promote. The point is simply that these
things mean something entirely different when one envisages such
aspects of language within the frame of reference which the non-native
speaker represents. If one attempts to mimic an idealized native speaker,
such notions become, by default, once removed from the true essence of
individual identity. Non-native speakers must be provided a space where
such dimensions of language usage can come into being as manifestations of the non-native speaker's own sociocultural and thus linguistic
realities. On the other hand, when discussing EIL with respect to the
native speaker's speech performance in multicultural forums, here EIL
entails the conscious effort to avoid culture-specific features which flourish in native speaker to native speaker interaction when such features are
potentially obscure to non-native speakers involved in the communicative act. This notion of situational adaptation across varieties, moreover,
is always relevant to communication between individuals who do not
have similar linguistic profiles.

A Nordic Perspective

It must also be made clear that the discussion in this chapter is based on
experiences from working as a professional ELT practitioner in Sweden
and as such reflects a Nordic take on English in the EU. It is possible that
those working in Southern and Eastern Europe will see things differently.
People residing in the Nordic countries and in other member states such
as Holland have had a considerable head-start when it comes to English,
and in this respect are perhaps experiencing that which is soon to take

place in other parts of the continent. Basically, what we have is a traditional basis for ELT, one centered in BrE, on the teacher as model, on British and American social studies, and on the goal of mimicking the idealized native speaker, evolving into a platform for ELT which constitutes a radical departure from such beliefs and practices. Instead, linguistic Americanization, the mixing of BrE and AmE which suggests a kind of Mid-Atlantic accent and a rich blend of lexical usage, the idea of a variety labeled 'Euro-English', the use of postcolonial texts in cultural studies modules, and the desire to develop cross-cultural communicative skills, is on the upswing, while BrE, prescriptivism, and traditionalist positioning are declining. One can claim that Europe is moving toward defining English as an international language, and that the concept 'Euro-English' is simply an extension of this conceptualization, with the addition of idiosyncratic features characteristic of the English spoken in the EU (mainly local esoteric lexical usage, and idiomatic phrases and expressions) (see Jenkins *et al.*, 2001). It is also the case, naturally, that the accent of many mainland Europeans will reflect their geographical positioning. Euro-English is based on EIL, but includes lexical, grammatical, and phonological features which are characteristic for the English used in continental Europe by non-native speakers, and here there is, and will always be, a great deal of regional variation.

The official basis for English language teaching in Sweden has gone through a radical transformation. While it was previously the case that the national curriculum for primary and secondary education stated that proper British English was to be the sole educational norm (and finally either AmE or BrE), this changed in 1994 when the call for intercultural communicative competence was stressed (later, in 2000, additional reinforcement of the international framework was introduced). There is no longer reference to a culture specific educational standard, only that English is to be learned for international contacts. Noted instead are the 'English speaking countries' and the 'growing English speaking world'. It is also the case that this widening of the conceptualization of English is to be integrated into a broad curriculum interned to promote multiculturalism. An intercultural understanding is to run across several disciplines, and is especially relevant to language and cultural studies (see *Skolverket*, 2000). The emphasis on multiculturalism and on language learning for international contacts can be seen in national curriculums across Europe. Like the Swedish example, educational authorities are eager to see language education as a stepping stone toward an increased awareness of Europeanization and globalization. But when the actual implementation of multiculturalist ideologies is delegated to the local school district, and even to the school level, without proper guidelines, teachers find it difficult to transform the intentions of official policy into viable educational methodology.

It is possible to find rather elaborate explanations of pedagogies suitable for the multicultural classroom. Here, Byram (1997), Byram and Fleming (1998), Kramsch (1993) and McKay (2002) have carried out pioneer work in the field. As such, one can formulate a framework for teaching practices which actually do establish a basis for ELT that is multicultural, international and which promotes the teaching and learning of English as an international language. Teachers can promote awareness of the many varieties of the language for use in multicultural settings without presupposing that AmE and BrE are the standards by which all other varieties are measured. They can, as well, select texts and language-learning materials from cultures throughout the world and in this way promote cultural diversity as something normative. For this to be done in an orderly manner, EIL needs to be legitimized, not necessarily as a variety in its own right, but as a pedagogically functional conceptualization of the English language. This would benefit practitioners in many ways. Why is it the case then that EIL is continually dismissed when educational norms for ELT are discussed?

The European Union: An EIL Paradox?

The new pedagogical theories, strategies and methods which are altering the course of ELT across the EU, in order to be viable, require an educational platform which is multicultural in its orientation, as opposed to culture specific (Anglo-American-centric). English in mainland Europe has been in the clutches of the Anglo-American sphere of influence since the war because of political, economic and cultural forces emanating from the UK and North America. This post-war legacy is now coming to an end. At the same time, Europe has changed considerably in the last decades as a result of unification and is now searching for a new identity for a new era. It is especially well equipped for this endeavor. Europe is the most ambitious, advanced and developed region worldwide for language learning. Nowhere else do we find so many pupils and students studying languages in formal educational settings, so many people reaching high levels of competence, and such a broad range of L2 language usage in social interaction. While it may seem to be an illogical supposition, it is perhaps the tradition of excellence in language education which has held back the development of EIL in this part of the world. There are a number of historical reasons for the apparent reluctance to transform English from a language best defined by an idealized inner-circle native-speaker, to a communicative tool for international contacts based on the usage of proficient speakers. And while much is currently in place which supports an international language-learning program – pedagogy based on intercultural communicative competence, knowledge of the forms and functions of English around the world and learner-centered learning – the very basis for English language instruction, the model or norm, remains inner-circle, native-speaker oriented and this reinforces the ideology that teachers are cultural ambassadors responsible for introducing the Anglo-American worldview to students eager to become auxiliary members of that alliance. This tension between traditionalist views of ELT, and the current call for an international approach, requires the attention of all who are involved in language education.

ELT Across the European Union

Perhaps one needs to first conduct a wide-scale survey of the entire EU, and chart central, regional and local language policy regulations and pedagogical practices before one can begin to understand how various ELT ideologies impact on classroom instruction at the elementary, secondary and tertiary levels. Such an inventory is beyond the scope of this chapter. We do, nevertheless, have a good understanding of how English is taught and learned in European schools. This in turn can be juxtaposed with the current wave of critical pedagogical initiatives which have the potential to radically alter ELT in this part of the world. Moreover, it will become apparent that the way in which language policy is implemented and carried out is not furthering the ideals of plurilingualism but is in fact acting to promote English (for discussions of plurilingualism, see Cenoz & Jessner, 2000; Coulmas, 1991). English, for the EU, because of the power of the prescriptivist lobby, has not been able to fully benefit from the implications of the world Englishes paradigm and evolve into a legitimate second language variety as it has done in other regions when it has achieved status as an important if not primary lingua franca. Nevertheless, while BrE hegemony is fast being dismantled, no new program for ELT has been seen as an obvious replacement. It should also be noted that the reluctance to regulate the language within the parameters of the EU has allowed English to impose itself on lesser used languages as well as on dominant European languages in an uncontrollable manner. This disinclination to come to terms with English allows a kind of pedagogical anarchy to flourish as well, with educators bewildered as to how they can make ELT *international* while promoting primarily BrE, but also AmE (or both) as the target model. EIL and perhaps the idea of a Euro-English variety have the potential to bring a modicum of logic to what is at present a basis for language education poorly designed to handle the demands of Europeanization and globalization. At stake is the very identity of the mainland L2 user of English.

Nation State Ideology

Nation state ideologies as well as standard language ideologies grew in stature during the 19th century when the vision of the unified and homogenous political entity reached its zenith. It was believed that a nation was most sovereign, progressive and defensible if the people shared a common heritage, language, religion and sense of culture. Communal belonging was fostered, it was believed, by instilling in the minds of people the notion that their allegiance was first and foremost to the state. This was demonstrated by investing in the normative behaviors which constituted the ideal vision of the national character. Conformity was (and is) rewarded and unwillingness or inability to conform was (and is) punished by various forms of stigmatization. It became apparent (and is still apparent) that success in social and economic respects is best achieved by assimilating into the mainstream, something which props up the myth of the homogenous community. This is the true nature of nationalism. Europe was one of the first regions to make this sense of nation-state building its mantra (a similar process transformed the United States into a unified nation state), and Europe has succeeded, through colonialism, in importing this concept of the nation state to much of the developing world. While this narrative is now being challenged by the current postmodern drive to celebrate diversity, multiculturalism, linguistic multiplicity and the pluralistic society, the belief in unification, both politically, culturally and linguistically, still operates locally at the member state level, and on the pan-European level, as the extended arm of monoculturalism. What we are witnessing is an effort to superimpose faith in the pluralistic society onto a world order which is dependent on the creation of singularities.

The EU is one nation composed of diversified member states. There, many languages are spoken and pursued in education, but one language, English, is the most utilitarian when speakers with different languages interact. As border crossing intensifies, with English operational as the primary code, unification, in and through English, becomes superimposed upon the diverse communities which make up one unified whole. Pluilingualism falls into the linguistic trap, with hierarchies constructed that make continental European languages subordinate to English. The singularity emerges, social life becomes divided between the private sphere where local languages thrive while public life is conducted in the lingua franca. Europe becomes unified under the banner of Anglo-Americanization and the old order is made redundant. Ancestral languages become museum pieces. English triumphs. If an effort is made to challenge that which now seems inevitable, the best we can do at this point in time is to insist that the educational norm, the model learners attempt to mimic, reflects the international functionality of the language, so as to provide L2 speakers an opportunity to engage the issue of identity at some distance from the hegemonic Anglo-American mindset. Here EIL and perhaps also Euro-English promise not only to provide such an opportunity, they can also bring order to what has become a chaotic system.

This scenario of Anglo-American linguistic domination is not a projection of something which potentially casts a dark shadow over Europe's linguistic future. English has already come to dominate an increasing number of domains. To take just a few examples, those working in higher education, as well as those conducting scientific research in the private sector, are now required to have knowledge of English. One could also argue that the entertainment field, which occupies much of our time, is dominated by English-medium programming, as is the Internet. As work becomes increasingly transnational, the use of English for business will be even more dominant. (It should be noted as well that the vast majority of Europeans are exposed to the American, British and continental European varieties of the language, and Asian and African varieties of English are not prevalent in mainland European society.) As English continues to make headway in these respects, the status of the language increases considerably. It is also showing signs of spilling over onto the social sphere, which is a natural consequence when English comes to dominate more and more domains. If this is the case, and I think it is, one must wonder what inspires the leaders of the EU to conveniently sidestep the issue when devising language policy and planning initiatives.

EU's Failed Language Policy

The answer is found in the initial decrees upon which the EU was organized in the first place. After the devastation of World War II, the leaders of Europe were desperate to devise a political strategy which would not only unite Europe but would also secure a viable peace. It was a delicate balancing act, acknowledging the prerogatives of the victors, respecting the rights of those in Germany and elsewhere who survived the war, and protecting Europe from Soviet expansionism. One basic tenet of unification was that each member state in the EU would enjoy the same rights and privileges. One in particular was the right to an official language, one not subordinate to a more powerful language which could operate as the primary auxiliary language of the EU. This set into play the kind of Darwinian conditions which have made it possible for English to emerge as the champion utilitarian language across Europe. Without an official language, Europe, which was intended to develop as a plurilingual society, has been allowed to evolve freely, and in such conditions the cultural, economic, military and technological power of the United States, backed up by British interests, has been able to make gains which are now irreversible. That the rest of the world is developing along similar lines is further solidifying the role English maintains in Europe, and the fall of the Soviet Union in the early 1990s has made this development even more apparent (see Table 4.2).

Europeans are now faced with this linguistic dilemma. Will Europeans resign and accept that EU is headed toward the one nation–one language–one culture form of societal organization envisioned in the classic development of the nation state, because it is an historical inevitability? What is Europe to do with this English? Is it to be adopted lock, stock and barrel in the standardized forms promoted in Britain? Are we to bring the American tongue to Europe and teach it here as it is used in North America? Who is in control of this process? Up to now many regulatory authorities in a number of member states have sanctioned, or at the very least, not opposed the belief that the British version of the language should

Table 4.2   Official EU languages

The 23 Official EU Languages, as of 1 January 2007		
English	German	Polish
Bulgarian	Greek	Portuguese
Czech	Hungarian	Romanian
Danish	Irish	Slovak
Dutch	Italian	Slovenian
Estonian	Latvian	Spanish
Finnish	Lithuanian	Swedish
French	Maltese	

'EU legislation is published in all the official languages, and you may use any of these languages to correspond with the EU institutions ...'
Source: http://europa.eu/abc/eurojargon/index_en.htm

be the norm for school education. On what basis is this decision made? What English is actually being spoken and written in Europe today? While one may imagine that there are easy answers to questions such as these, it is in fact the case that we do not have any convenient responses at this point in time. Moreover, when looking for solutions we need to keep in mind that they should be based on two fundamental principles: (1) that the English targeted in education accommodates the European sense of identity; and (2) that it is a form of the language which operates well in communicative terms locally in Europe as well as globally. This is what is meant by *integrated* as opposed to *exclusionary*. Previously, the primary principle governing ELT was faith in the British version of the language because it was thought to be esthetically superior to all other varieties, was well suited for education, social life and the work place, and for these and other reasons was worthy of mimicking. Such beliefs are no longer viable. In postmodern Europe, the ideology underpinning the lingua franca must support the vision of a common European culture, the European commitment to 'unity through diversity' and multiculturalism. Here, there are reasons to suspect that both the British as well as the American version of the language do not live up to the requirements which mainland Europeans will want to place on their lingua franca. Identity, as well as multiculturalism, must be central to our understanding of ELT for Europeans.

EIL in a European Union Context

There are a number of things which the vast majority of Europeans share, such as a common history and the legacy of Christianity. For these and other reasons, a somewhat similar epistemological and ideological framework is operational in the majority of European cultures and speech communities. As a result, Europeans do not 'border cross' when speaking English in a manner characteristic for L1 speakers of Asian and African languages. Nevertheless, English does represent, for mainland Europeans, a 'somewhat' foreign understanding of the world. When using English, many mainland Europeans mold English into something more appropriate for continental culture than for the sociocultural contexts associated with inner-circle speakers. English has become a mainland European language, and has adapted to new social and cultural conditions. In fact, the dissemination of English across the EU is linguistically unique. Never before has one language been so widespread among the general population, taken such a prevalent place in education at all levels, had such presence in information services such as printed media, film, radio and television, been so prominent in music and entertainment, as well as the Internet, and also serve as a contact language with people from throughout the world.

It is true that both German and French hold prominent positions in Europe, but English is the primary lingua franca. Unfortunately, it is a borrowed language for mainland Europeans, something possessed and defined by others. This has not as yet been perceived to be a problem. Instead, the EU has been more concerned with the promotion of European languages in addition to English. Initiatives which support multilingualism in the EU, such as the Bureau for Lesser Used Languages, work to protect endangered languages from encroachment from the dominant national and regional languages. Now however, there is also pressure from English, which is demanding more and more resources. Moreover, educational schemes intended to increase student exchange between member states, which support the intentions of Brussels, namely plurilingualism, inadvertently fuel the spread of English because more and more educational establishments are offering instruction in English for the explicit purpose of attracting foreign students. Thus, this policy, that EU citizens should speak at least three EU languages, while promoting foreign language learning throughout the EU, has not made any noticeable dent in the current drive across Europe to learn English. It has in fact contributed to the upswing in English proficiency by growing numbers of Europeans.

Language Policy and Planning, when contextualized within the EU, has three distinctive levels of operation. The first, a macro-perspective, encompasses efforts made at the EU level to regulate official languages. Secondly, there is the member state level of engagement (with Spain, for example, in the emergence of linguistic rights for speakers of Catalan), and finally, there are regional and local centers of activity. A great deal can be gained by studying the manner in which language policy is carried out in the EU. There is a need to evaluate the effectiveness of the work being done, as well as the larger political implications of language policy. Apparently, the manner in which the entire enterprise is being conducted is not based on a firm theoretical foundation. If it is the case that the EU is committed to supporting linguistic diversity as well as the linguist rights of EU citizens, it is possible to argue that what is actually taking place does not support this vision. One can imagine the three tiers of activity to be, in many respects, contradictory and ill designed to further the ideals claimed in the many policy documents drawn up by EU legislators to support plurilingualism. Other basic problems exist as well, concerns which address the very nature of the nation state building project currently

taking place in Europe. For example, how can Foucault's notion of 'gover-
mentality' impact on language issues in Europe (Foucault, 1991), or what
does Bourdieu's 'habitus' mean for European language policy? (see e.g.
Bourdieu, 1991; Habermas, 1987). Globalization, (the blurring of borders
and the interaction now taking place between peoples throughout the
world), is also an issue which in many important respects impacts on the
development of language and on interaction through language. What I
want to propose here is that Europe is currently entangled not only in its
own history, in the epistemology of nation state building, standard language ideology, in monocultural self-perceptions and in unification as a
Eurocentric foundation for social development, it is also challenged by its
inability to determine the linguistic makeup of the EU.

The vision of plurilingualism needs to be deconstructed to see what
centers of power benefit by its implementation as well as to better understand the ideological foundation upon which this policy rests. Europe has
always been multilingual and culturally diverse. What EU policy brings to
this diverse world of lived realities is the institutionalization of a vision of
multiculturalism which presupposes that official action is both required
and necessary in order to bring some structure to the diversity already in
place. And while one may want to believe that such initiatives are based
on human rights and on the promotion of a common European unity, there
is much which now indicates that Europe is in fact becoming less linguistically diversified as a result of the very program intended to secure linguistic pluralism in the first place. The emergence of English as the unchallenged
auxiliary language, and its dissemination in virtually all walks of life, is
thwarting efforts to preserve diversity, and here, the leaders of the EU
seem to be both incapable and unwilling to come to terms with this unex-
pected development. Efforts to stimulate the learning of other languages,
while successful to a considerable extent, nevertheless fall short in competition with English. It is perhaps the case that it is the embedded belief in
monoculturalism, in the notion that nation states inevitability gravitate
toward one centralizing sociocultural and linguistic system, which drives
English forward as the unchallenged first language of the EU (see Modiano,
2004b). It is not unreasonable either that the citizens of the EU demand
that Europe exercises greater willingness to allow this to be publicly discussed. Up to now the role which English is playing in European affairs
has been ignored. Instead the call for plurilingualism is sounded.

One must keep in mind that it is possible that Europe, on its own, is
incapable of altering the course of events. The success of English is a global
phenomenon. It is driven, not only by events in Europe, but also by what
is taking place in Africa, Asia and elsewhere. My concern, however, is with

ELT in Europe and with the educational standards and pedagogical practices deployed in the teaching and learning of English in the EU. If mainland Europeans are committed to acquiring competence in English because they need it locally, when interacting with other Europeans, and internationally, when inhabiting the global village, what English best serves their purposes? The sociocultural realities which come into being when English is used as an auxiliary language in Europe are something different if the framework for the use of the language is governed by inner-circle standards, as opposed to the ideological basis for English in the EIL paradigm. This has an impact not only on actual language behavior but also on the manner in which our understanding of a common European culture comes into being. Europe is moving steadily toward a prevailing order which is monocultural, and this is taking place despite efforts to ensure that all European citizens have knowledge of more than one additional European language. Seeing as English is threatening to become the basis for a monocultural social order, policy-makers, educational authorities, as well as language practitioners, must reappraise the benefits and drawbacks of Standard English ideologies for ELT. EIL, as an alternative, has advantages which 'foreign' culture-specific educational norms lack, and these benefits are both ideological as well as utilitarian. The new Europe, under the banner of 'unity through diversity', requires an internationally orientated lingua franca which has the potential to support the acquisition of cross cultural communicative competence, act as a counterweight to Anglo-Americanization and operate as a carrier of a common European culture.

It has not been my intention to debate the pros and cons of a European variety of English (which I have done elsewhere, see Modiano, 2006). Suffice it to say that the concluding point here is that if we are to take heed of the advances that have been made in theoretical thinking in the post-modern/postcolonial era, it is evident that language, which always reflects identity, inevitability adapts to the socio-cultural conditions in which the language is used. In this instance, English is adapting to mainland Europe in a plethora of ways. It is here, in this new vision of the language, that Europeans can rally behind the tongue as a complementary language, one not intended to be the voice of a monocultural and monolingual Europe, but to have currency as a second language for Europeans when the other languages they have at hand are not shared by those with whom they interact. As the need for a common language is becoming increasingly apparent, and as English becomes more and more a living language in continental Europe, there is every reason to believe that such matters will be more directly addressed by the leaders of the EU, and that measures will be taken for a European variety of English to be submitted to the linguistic scrutiny, policy development, and planning which it deserves. The basis for this should be to set ELT in Europe within an EIL framework. Not only does such posturing offer Europeans an opportunity to learn an English which is viable throughout the world, it also counteracts, to some extent, the ontological domination of the Anglo-American sphere of influence and in this sense furthers the idea of mainland European identity. One, so to speak, kills two birds with one stone. Cross-cultural communicative competence is stressed, as is the development of 'identity' in the use of the lingua franca, something certainly appropriate for the new Europe, as well as for globalization.

References

Bourdieu, P. (1991) *Language and Symbolic Power*. Oxford: Polity.

Byram, M. (1997) *Teaching and Assessing Intercultural Communicative Competence*. Clevedon: Multicultural Matters.

Byram, M. and Fleming, M. (eds) (1998) *Language Learning in Intercultural Perspective*. Cambridge: Cambridge University Press.

Brown, K. (2006) Models, methods, and curriculum for ELT preparation. In B. Kachru, Y. Kachru and C.L. Nilson (eds) *The Handbook of World Englishes* (pp. 680–693). Oxford: Blackwell.

Canagarajah, S. (2006) Negotiating the local in English as a lingua franca. *Annual Review of Applied Linguistics* 26, 197–218.

Cenoz, J. and Jessner, U. (eds) (2000) *English in Europe: The Acquisition of a Third Language*. Clevedon: Multilingual Matters.

Coulmas, F. (ed.) (1991) *A Language Policy for the European Community*. Berlin: Mouton de Gruyter.

Crystal, D. (1999) The future of Englishes. *English Today 58*, 15 (2), 10–20.

Crystal, D. (2003) *A Dictionary of Linguistics and Phonetics* (5th edn). Oxford: Blackwell.

Foucault, M. (1991) Governmentality. In G. Burchell, C. Gordon and P. Miller (eds) *The Foucault Effect: Studies in Governmentality* (pp. 87–104). Chicago: University of Chicago Press.

Habermas, J. (1987) *The Theory of Communicative Action* (Vol. II). Boston: Beacon Press.

Halliday, M.A.K. (1978) *Language as Social Semiotic: The Social Interpretation of Language and Meaning*. London: Edward Arnold.

Hymes, D. (1972) On communicative competence. In J.B. Pride and J. Holmes (eds) *Sociolinguistics* (pp. 269–285). Harmondsworth: Penguin.

Jenkins, J., Modiano, M. and Seidlhofer, B. (2001) Euro-English. *English Today 17* (4), 13–19.

Jenkins, J. (2006) Current perspectives on teaching World Englishes and English as a lingua franca. *TESOL Quarterly* 40 (1), 157–181.

Kachru, B. (1988) *ERIC/CLL News Bulletin*. September, 12 (1), 1, 3, 4, 8.

Kramsch, C. (1993) *Context and Culture in Language Teaching*. Oxford: Oxford University Press.

Kuo, I-C. (Vicky) (2006) Addressing the issue of teaching English as a lingua franca. *ELT Journal* 60 (3), 213–221.

McKay, S.L. (2002) *Teaching English as an International Language.* Oxford: Oxford University Press.

Modiano, M. (1999a) International English in the global village. *English Today* 15 (2), 22–34.

Modiano, M. (1999b) Standard English(es) and educational practices for the World's lingua franca. *English Today* 15 (4), 3–13.

Modiano, M. (2000) Rethinking ELT, and Mid-Atlantic English: A communicative strategy. *English Today 62,* 16 (2), 28–34, 56, 62–63.

Modiano, M. (2004a) Review of *English-Only Europe?* By Robert Phillipson. *Applied Linguistics* 25 (1), 119–123.

Modiano, M. (2004b) Monoculturalization and language dissemination. *Journal of Language, Identity, and Education* 3 (3), 215–227.

Modiano, M. (2006) Euro-Englishes. In B.B. Kachru, Y. Kachru and C.L. Nelson (eds) *The Handbook of World Englishes* (pp. 223–239). Oxford: Blackwell Publishing.

Phillipson, R. (1992) *Linguistic Imperialism.* Oxford: Oxford University Press.

Phillipson, R. (2003) *English-Only Europe?* London: Routledge.

Prator, C. (1968) The British heresy in TESL. In J.A. Fishman, C.A. Ferguson and J. Das Gupta (eds) *Language Problems of Developing Nations* (pp. 459–476). New York: John Wiley.

Quirk, R. (1988) The question of standards in the international use of English. *Georgetown University Round Table in Languages and Linguistics 1987* (pp. 278–341). Washington DC: Georgetown University Press.

Richards, J.C. and Schmidt, R. (eds) (2002) *Longman Dictionary of Teaching and Applied Linguistics* (3rd edn). London: Longman.

Savignon, S.J. (1997) *Communicative Competence: Theory and Classroom Pratice: Texts and Contexts in Second Language Learning.* New York: McGraw-Hill.

Skolverket (2000) *Kursplaner och betygskriterier. Grundskolan.* Stockholm: Skolverket.

Smith, L.E. (1981) *English for Cross-Cultural Communication.* London: Macmillan.

Smith, L.E. (ed.) (1983) *Readings in English as an International Language.* Oxford: Pergamon.

Part 2
EIL, Attitudes and Identity(ies)

Chapter 5

Researching Non-native Speakers' Views Toward Intelligibility and Identity: Bridging the Gap Between Moral High Grounds and Down-to-Earth Concerns

DAVID C.S. LI

Introduction

In the debate concerning the most appropriate pedagogic model in the outer and expanding circles, many scholars are critical of the hegemony of the native speaker (NS)-based model (e.g. Jenkins, 2000, 2006a, 2007; Kirkpatrick, 2006, 2007; McKay, 2002; Seidlhofer, 2001, 2004, 2006; *cf.* Rubdy & Saraceni, 2006). Being an international lingua franca, English is now learned and used by millions of non-native speakers (NNSs) as an additional language, outnumbering NSs by an ever-widening margin. Research in second language acquisition has shown that relatively few NNSs can develop native-like competence in English (Cook, 1999). For the majority of NNSs, a NS-based pedagogic model is simply unattainable and thus impractical as a learning goal (Kirkpatrick, 2006, 2007). In terms of functions, English is used primarily as a nativized language for intra-national communication in the outer circle, and as a local or regional lingua franca in the expanding circle, often with no NSs present. A monolithic or monocentric NS-based pedagogic model is thus irrelevant. Instead, it has been argued that pluricentricity should be the norm, following local(ized) linguistic and discourse-pragmatic patterns of innovation and creativity.

Amidst this critique of the global hegemony of English, ideological assumptions are made, often tacitly, about what is in NNSs' best interest, in particular ownership of English and their concern for linguacultural identity. When English is learned by millions of bilingual speakers as an additional language for international communication, it is necessarily denationalized and acculturated to local specific needs. Hence it is unacceptable that NS-based norms should prevail and serve as the yardstick for measuring NNSs' phonological accuracy, lexicogrammatical correctness and discourse-pragmatic appropriacy. At the same time, language being intimately linked to speaker identity, it is generally believed that NNSs are naturally inclined to diverge from NS-based norms and to be in favor of local(ized) linguistic features. The unrivaled prestige of NS-based pedagogic models is generally regarded as a direct result of their uncontested standardness and correctness, leading to a 'grassroots practice' of an '(unquestioning) submission to native-speaker norms' (Seidlhofer, 2005, cited in Jenkins, 2006a: 172). Likewise, in her analysis of the survey results of 1251 returned questionnaires from students in a mainland Chinese university, Hu (2004: 31) found that 100% of the respondents regarded British English and American English to be the only two standards, and claims that '[t]his belief has been inculcated into them, and their teachers before them, by all the language books that they use'. Commentaries such as these portray NNSs as uncritical victims of the global hegemony of NS-based pedagogic models. Until recently, NNSs' views toward the most desirable pedagogic model of English were not subjected to rigorous scrutiny. There is little empirical evidence of the extent to which the researchers' assumptions are matched by NNSs' own perceptions (but see Jenkins, 2005, 2007). Indeed, it has been pointed out that in a debate involving what is supposed to be in the best interests of NNS learners and teachers, it is curious that the views and voices of millions of real 'consumers' of ELT are seldom consulted and represented in research (Kirkpatrick, 2006: 72).

Timmis (2002) is one of the more recent studies investigating what NNS teachers and learners think about the most appropriate pedagogic model of English – a 'classroom perspective'. Based on 580 completed questionnaires (400 responses from students from 14 countries, and 180 teacher responses from 45 countries) and 15 interviews with students, he found that over two-thirds (67%) of all students preferred NS pronunciation to accented NNS pronunciation. The native-like accent ('sometimes people think I am a native speaker'), however, does not seem to apply to students from three inner- or outer-circle countries: South Africa, Pakistan and India, where 64% of participants indicated a wish to retain 'the accent of my country'. This led Timmis to conjecture that the research question, whether NNS learners of English would like to conform to NS norms of pronunciation, is probably context-sensitive (Timmis, 2002: 242). Very similar findings were obtained for grammatical norms, where 68% of all students preferred to be able to 'use all the grammar rules that native speakers use, even the informal grammar native speakers use when they speak to each other' (Timmis, 2002: 244).

Using a questionnaire and tape-recorded story extracts, Luk (1998) elicited 66 Hong Kong Secondary Three students' reaction to a native speaker's received pronunciation (RP) accent and a local speaker's marked Cantonese accent. Luk's working hypothesis was that students would empathize with the local speaker's Hong Kong accented English out of such concerns as group solidarity and linguacultural identity. This hypothesis, however, was not supported. Instead, the findings showed that '[a] much greater preference for the RP speaker was in evidence' (Luk, 1998: 98). Luk believed that the students' lack of empathy toward Hong Kong accented English could be attributed to its stigmatization in class and oral exams, as well as the prestige of the RP accent in teaching materials (see Bolton, 2003: 290 ff for a discussion).

Kirkpatrick and Xu (2002) conducted a similar survey with 171 mainland Chinese college students (88 English and 83 engineering majors). They were asked to indicate to what extent they agreed or disagreed with 14 statements, of which three are particularly relevant to our discussion. The statement 'only native speakers can speak standard English' was strongly rejected by 124 students (60 English majors and 64 engineering majors; 72.5%). This suggests that most Chinese students considered Standard English to be an attainable goal for NNS learners like themselves. To the statement 'when I speak English I want people to know I'm from China', a total of 104 students (60.8%) disagreed, especially female students (60 out of 64). As for the statement 'one day there will be a variety of English called Chinese English', 78 disagreed (45.6%), 48 agreed (28%), the rest were neutral. These findings led Kirkpatrick and Xu to conclude that few educated Chinese, especially female English majors, appeared 'happy to sound Chinese' when speaking English, and that 'China English' did not seem to be 'socially acceptable' (Kirkpatrick & Xu, 2002: 277).

The brief review of the relevant literature above shows that, whatever one's inclination regarding the appropriate choice of pedagogic model in the outer and expanding circles, not enough has been done to research NNSs' views. Do they share the concern of WE and EIL/ELF researchers that NS-based models of English are imposed on them? Do they believe that the local(ized) accent constitutes an 'act of identity'? For those who prefer a NS-based accent, what are their reasons? Is there a widely shared aspiration for the local(ized) variety of English to be recognized as a legitimate variety of English? To date, research on intelligibility between NNSs and NNS identities is either based on analyses of 'performance data' in a purposefully collected corpus featuring NNS–NNS interactions in intercultural encounters, or experimental studies under controlled laboratory conditions (see Pickering, 2006 for a review). In the analysis of performance data, an NNS accent is generally interpreted as being indexical of a preferred NNS identity. This assumption however does not seem to be supported by the dearth of research on NNSs' views about the relationship between accent and identity summarized above. This exploratory study is a modest attempt to research this relationship, with a view to generating sound hypotheses for more in-depth scrutiny.

Methodology

The data of this study were elicited using a survey questionnaire (Appendix 1) administered toward the end of 12 focus group interviews as part of a funded project entitled 'One day with only English'. There were altogether 107 Chinese participants, who were all self-selected by responding to an email invitation to participate in an experimental study. The email invitation was linked to a website where details of the experimental study including research goals, what participants were expected to do, dates of the briefing and experiment and remuneration (HK$300, *c.* US$35, per participant) could be found. Of the 107 participants, 89 were university students from Hong Kong or mainland China; 18 were working adults. Table 5.1 gives an overview of the general profile of all participants.[1]

At the briefing before the focus groups, organized according to academic disciplines ('English', 'Social Science', 'Natural Science', 'Law' and 'Business') and 'Working adults', all participants were requested to fill in a personal 'Participant's Profile' form. In addition to basic information such as self-assessed proficiency levels of English and Chinese in terms of the four skills, and the number of years learning English, the 'language profile' also required them to indicate whether they had lived or studied outside of Hong Kong in an English-speaking country. As expected, the majority of the 77 Hong Kong participants had studied English for over 10 years, which is considerably longer compared with that of the 30 mainland participants (7–9 years). In terms of experience living and/or studying overseas, 30 participants (Hong Kong 24, mainland 6) had lived in an English-L1 country before (eight for over 3 years, two 1–3 years, and 20 less than 1 year), mostly as exchange students. Following Bolton (2003), these 30 participants may be loosely characterized as 'returnees',

Table 5.1   General profile of participants

Participants' general information	HKU participants n = 47	CityU participants n = 42	Working adults n = 18
Gender			
Male	18	9	4
Female	29	33	14
Ethnicity			
Hong Kong Chinese	33	27	17
Mainland Chinese	14	15	1
Educational background			
Foundation/Associate degree	0	4	N/A
Undergraduate	31	33	N/A
Postgraduate	14	5	N/A
First language			
Cantonese	33	28	17
Mandarin	14	14	1
Professions			
Education	N/A	N/A	10
Human resources	N/A	N/A	2
Information technology	N/A	N/A	3
Logistics	N/A	N/A	1
Banking and finance	N/A	N/A	1
Government sector	N/A	N/A	1

whose overseas experience may have some impact on their English proficiency, and possibly on their attitudes towards the national variety of English in the host country as well. All the focus groups were co-moderated by the author and a research assistant, who are both trilingual in Cantonese, English and Putonghua/Mandarin. Language choice varied depending on the language background of participants in the focus group, mainly Cantonese supplemented by some English, with a few conducted mainly in Putonghua/Mandarin (see Appendix 2 for an excerpt of one focus group).

There are three questions in the survey questionnaire (see Appendix 1). The main purpose of the focus group was explained before the survey began. Additional background information was provided as and when necessary. Question 1 asks: 'If possible, I would like to speak English like_____'. Participants were asked to choose one of three categories of role model: (1) speakers of 'HK English'; (2) 'speakers of 'China English'; and (3) native speakers. The latter is illustrated with reference to the typical accent of newscasters in international media such as BBC and CNN. Since most participants were unlikely to be familiar with the terms 'HK English' and 'China English', some prominent bilingual speakers were given as role models ('HK English': Chief Executive Mr Donald Tsang, former Chief Secretary Mrs Anson Chan; 'China English': Foreign Minister Mr LI Zhaoxing, Commerce Minister Mr BO Xilai). Participants were reminded that these examples of 'role models' were meant to be illustrations of highly proficient Hong Kong or mainland Chinese speakers of English, and that if necessary, they could think of the accent of other highly proficient Chinese speakers of English. After selecting their preferred category of role model, participants were requested to briefly state the main reason for their preference. The majority of participants indicated the main reasons for their preference (see analysis below).

Question 2 asks participants to indicate their 'preferred identity when speaking English with Chinese/non-Chinese' interlocutors. They are expected to choose one of three options:

(1) I want to sound like a (HK) Chinese speaker of English, not a native speaker of English – so long as others can understand me.
(2) I want to sound like a native speaker of English.
(3) other (please specify):

Question 3 elicits participants' 'attitudes toward non-native English accents when listening to others speak'. They were asked to choose one of three options:

(1) It's fine when others speak English with a non-native accent – so long as I can understand it.
(2) The non-native accent should be corrected (which accent should be the norm?).
(3) other (please specify):

To contextualize and stimulate group discussion, the words in one sentence 'I think this product is nice' were pronounced using a few phonological features which are typical of NNSs in East Asia. Accordingly, the key words were pronounced as follows:

Target word   Improvised learner pronunciation at the focus group
think   [tɪŋk]/[fɪŋk]
this   [dɪs]
product   [pərɒdʌkʊtə]
nice   [laɪs]

The NNS learner features exemplified here include: the substitution of /f/, /t/ or /d/ for the dental fricatives; underdifferentiation of /l/ and /n/; syllable-timed rhythm, and the use of additional vowels to simplify the structure of a consonant cluster (*cf.* Hung, 2000; Jenkins, 2000, 2003). Upon hearing the improvized NNS learner pronunciation by the author in his capacity as moderator, especially the pronunciation of 'product' [pərɒdʌkʊtə], many participants found it amusing. A few commented that the improvisation sounded 'authentic' (Cantonese: *hou* [35] *ci* [23], '好似').

Results

Data analysis of survey questions 1–3

Q.1 asks participants to indicate their preferred English accent: 'HK English', 'China English' or 'a NS-based standard'. Of the 107 valid responses, 90 (84.1%) would like to speak English with a NS-based accent (see Table 5.2).

The clearest trend is working adults: 17 out of 18 (94.4%) chose 'a NS-based standard' to be their preferred model. Most participants gave some indication of the main reason(s) behind their preference in the space provided. An analysis of these reasons reveals many positive attributes associated with NS-based pronunciation. These attributes, cited verbatim

Table 5.2 Participants' preferred accent

Preferred English accent	*No. of CityU participants*	*No. of HKU participants*	*No. of working adults*	*Total*
HK English	4	8	0	12 (11.2%)
China English	3	1	1	5 (4.7%)
NS-based standard	35	38	17	90 (84.1%)
Total	42	47	18	107 (100%)

from participants' remarks, were collapsed according to their semantic affinity (see Table 5.3).

Apart from these positive attributes, several remarks regarding the preference of a NS-based standard indicate that English is like any other foreign language, suggesting that the participants in question do not feel that English is 'their' own language[2]:

1. Their English is very good. (CBF7)
2. Just like I want to speak Putonghua like native Putonghua speakers. It is like how the language is best spoken. (HSSF5)

Table 5.3 Reasons for preferring a NS-based accent

Attributes of NS-based accent (original in English)	No. of CityU participants (n = 42)	No. of HKU participants (n = 47)	No. of working adults (n = 18)
very good / the best (for learning) / the highest level/(sounds more) fluent / better (than a NNS accent)	8	5	2
the real English / sounds more 'English' / the (most) standard / what 'proper' English is / the prototype	2	3	3
(more) professional / highly educated	4	3	—
more beautiful / nice / pleasant / sweeter	2	4	—
formal / accurate / correct	3	2	2
perfect / perfection / pure / elegant	3	1	2
more easily understood / widely accepted (e.g. foreign businessmen)	3	2	—
(more) comfortable (to listen to)	—	3	—
natural / originated from England / America/their mother tongue /	1	1	2

3. Foreigner should be a better role model as I am learning a foreign language. (HLF4)
4. The final goal of learning one language is speaking like its native speaker. (HSM12)
5. They sound more natural, and English is their mother tongue after all. (WF4)

Of those participants whose preferred English accent is a NS-based standard, some state the preferred native accent explicitly: BBC (9), CNN (6), Australian accent (2) and Canadian accent (1), the last mentioned being preferred for its perceived neutrality. For example:

British accent ('BBC')

6. I'm a pro-British, so I'd like to speak in a BBC accent (in order to be part of the British group). (CEF5)
7. This is the accent I would like to acquire. Sounds clear, original and classic. (CEM10)
8. I speak HK English to Chinese speakers; I want to speak English with native accent to foreigners. I now speak HK Eng. So I want to speak with native accent so that I can switch between them freely. (HSSF4)
9. BBC. Cool with British accent. (HSF11)
10. British English sounds classy, British is the origin of English. (WF6)
11. It's the most standard type of English. After all, Britain uses where the language originated .... (WF19)

General American accent ('CNN')

12. The more native it sounds, the better American accent is clearer and sounds more decisive. (CSSF5)
13. This is an advantage in contemporary competition. I am sound more professional; my career will have more selection. (CEF4)
14. I like American English. American English has great influence throughout the world. (HEM9)

Australian accent

15. Aussie accent. I grow up in Australia, but I end up with HK + US accent (mix with). (HSF5)
16. Aussie accent. I don't like Hong Kong accent and I went to Australia for exchange. I like their accent. (HSF9)

Canadian accent

17. I prefer some 'neutral English' with no regional accent. Ex. Canadian English (not too American or Aussie or British). (HSF2)

There are relatively few participants who prefer the accent of a highly proficient local bilingual speaker of English as their role model: 'HK English' (*n* = 12), 'China English' (*n* = 5). It is perhaps significant that none of the 18 working adults (all Chinese Hongkongers) prefer 'HK English'. Some of the reasons for their respective preferences are as follows:

'HK English'

18. I think the main reason for communication is to understand each other, as the speakers can understand each other, the accent is not important, therefore, I prefer to main[tain] the natural Hong Kong accent which require no more adjustment of accent. (CEM8)
19. They [Anson Chan and Donald Tsang] can speak English fluently and using Hong Kong style English is more suitable in Hong Kong. (CBF8)
20. I think he [Donald Tsang] speaks good English, we are not possible to speak like native speakers since we only learn and speak in HK Environment. (CBF9)
21. Easy to learn and communicate. (HSSF1)
22. Just want to be natural instead of intentionally 'pretentious'. (HEF4)
23. Close to my born culture. (HEF11)
24. Others can understand what I say easily and it is natural for me to have a Hong Kong accent. (HSF1)
25. It's more important to let each other understand than the actual accent / wordings. (HSM7)
26. Most of time I communicate with local people rather than foreigners so HK English. (HSF10)

'China English'

27. I can understand it more easily. (CLF2)
28. It is the most possible thing. (CLF4)
29. I am a mainland student and I live in Beijing. So my English will [be] close to the 'China English'. And I don't think it's bad. (CSSF10)

30. Because it's the symbol of China and others can understand them. (HSF10)

In contrast, four Hong Kong participants make it clear that the typical local English 'intonation' or accent is unacceptable to them as a role model, in part because it has low prestige, sometimes leading to discrimination of its speakers (WF12):

31. I don't like the intonation of HK English. (HSSM8)
32. I really think their English accent is nice to listen to. HK accent is terrible. (HBF7)
33. Aussie accent. I don't like Hong Kong accent and I went to Australia for exchange. I like their accent. (HSF9)
34. NS-based standard, since people discriminate towards non-native accent. (WF12)

Given that the highly proficient role-model English speakers rarely address the Chinese general public in English, it seems safe to assume that when writing these negative remarks about the local intonation or accent (see 31–34), the participants in question were actually making reference to a low-proficiency (basilectal) learner accent which is much more commonly encountered in their daily life than the accent of a fluent (acrolectal) local speaker. As HSF9 puts it in a further remark, 'I really don't like the English with very strong HK accent, so I will try to speak like a native (even I can't).' On the other hand, HEF10 explains that she did not choose 'HK English' because she was unconvinced of the suitability of the two role models, and that she would have done so if a more suitable role model (Audrey Eu, an outspoken legislator and member of Civic Party) had been cited.

Q.2 asks participants to indicate their preferred identity when speaking English to Chinese *and* non-Chinese. They are requested to choose one of three options. Their preferences are summarized in Table 5.4.

At first sight, the patterns of responses to Questions 1 and 2 seem to be fairly consistent. Of all the 107 responses to Q.1, 90 (84.1%) indicate some NS-based standard to be their preferred accent. A very similar pattern of responses was found in Q.2: a total of 84 participants (78.5%) want to sound like a native speaker when speaking English. Upon closer scrutiny of the participants' remarks, however, a number of apparent inconsistencies were detected. First, eight participants who chose a NS-based standard as their preferred model of English for learning and use in Q.1 say they want to be seen as Chinese rather than a NS of English in Q.2. Of these eight participants, six give additional remarks explaining their position.

Table 5.4 Participants' preferred identity when speaking English

Q.2	My preferred identity when speaking English with Chinese/non-Chinese (tick one):	CityU participants (n = 42)	HKU participants (n = 47)	Working adults (n = 18)
(1)	I want to sound like a (HK) Chinese speaker of English, not a native speaker of English – so long as others can understand me.	7 (16.7%)	9 (19.1%)	3 (16.7%)
(2)	I want to sound like a native speaker of English.	34 (80.9%)	36 (76.6%)	14 (77.8%)
(3)	Other (please specify)	1 (2.4%)	2 (4.3%)	1 (5.5%)
Total		100%	100%	100%

Their remarks are strongly indicative of a concern for *both* a native-like English proficiency and their Chinese identity as projected or symbolized by a native-like accent. For example:

35. As long as there is a smooth communication and understanding between each other, I think it is not necessary to speak like a native [speaker]. Because it is ... respect to each other. (CBF2)
36. I want to be seen as Chinese but can speak fluent English in foreign accent. (CSF5)
37. Others feel more comfortable if I speak HK Eng. But I want myself to acquire a native accent .... language is for communication ... To interact with locals I speak HK English; to talk with foreigners I speak with native-accent. (HSSF4)
38. English is like Chinese to me – as a tool for communication. As a person, I feel very strongly that I'm Chinese though I'm fluent in English. (WF18)

The tension between speaking English with a native-like accent and the problems engendered by the speaker identity thus projected when interacting with fellow Chinese is nicely captured by WF19, an experienced teacher of English in her late 20s who has acquired a British accent through education: 'too much [native-like] intonation makes me sound haughty.

Therefore, I don't want to be seen as 媚外 [*mei²¹ ngoi²²*, 'fawn on foreigners']'.

Second, seven participants who choose 'China English' or 'HK English' in Q.1 indicate that they want to sound like a NS of English. As shown in their remarks, this apparent inconsistency may be accounted for by two main factors: (1) a concern for being intelligible to others through a native-like command of English; and (2) a fact of life that most NNSs speak English with a non-native accent. For example:

39. [China English] As an English learner, I want to sound like a native speaker of English in order to communicate with others well, however, when I talk to others, it is impossible to require every speaker to speak like a native speaker so long as I can understand it. It's OK. (CLF4)
40. [China English] I want to sound like a native speaker in order to make more people to understand me. But for others any one [accent] is ok, as long as I could understand them. (CSSF10)
41. [HK English] Since I am a HK people, my English is typical "HK English". Actually, I want my English sounds like a native speaker with proper accent like a foreigner. But I think it's impossible unless I study abroad for several years (...). (CSF4)
42. [HK English] It sounds good if I have a native accent, and it seems that my oral English is good if I talk like a native speaker. (HSSF1)

Q.3 asks participants about their attitudes toward non-native English accents in general. Before the survey began, the contrast between native-like and non-native accents was contextualized with the help of one sample sentence 'I think this product is nice' (for the rationale behind the choice of this sentence and the non-native phonological features targeted, see 'Methodology'). This question received one invalid response (CSSF7) from the CityU group (hence $n = 41$). Table 5.5 gives a summary of their preferences.

In option (a), a total of 76 out of 106 valid responses (71.7%) say that they find nothing wrong when interacting with others who speak English with a non-native accent, provided communication is not impeded. Quite a few participants point out in their additional remarks that non-native accents are unavoidable and therefore should be seen as a natural consequence in foreign language learning. Those who are in favor of seeing non-native pronunciation features corrected (25 out of 106, or

Table 5.5   Participants' attitudes toward non-native English accents

Q.3	*My attitude toward non-native English accents <u>when listening</u> to others speak (tick one):*	*CityU participants (n = 41)*	*HKU participants (n = 47)*	*Working adults (n = 18)*
(1)	It's fine when others speak English with a non-native accent – so long as I can understand it.	30 (73.2%)	36 (76.6%)	10 (55.6%)
(2)	The non-native accent should be corrected. (Which accent should be the norm?)	10 (24.4%)	8 (17%)	7 (38.9%)
(3)	Other (please specify)	1 (2.4%)	3 (6.4%)	1 (5.5%)
Total		100%	100%	100%

23.6%) base their judgment on three factors, in decreasing order of numerical significance as follows:

(a) Like any other foreign language: native-like competence should be the learning target

43. Because I think whenever you learn a language, you should also learn their accent, non-native accent is quite 'ugly'. Even learn Spanish like Spanish, learn Japanese like Japanese. (CSSM4)
44. Native English, for example, British English, is widely accepted as the most standard English among the people. (CEF7)
45. When I speak English, I'd like others to think my pronunciation is good, as good as native speakers. (CSF6)
46. …like grammar structure, listening / reading / writing, every one can do well except accent. [with native-like accent] It's like '完滿地' [*jyun²¹ mun²³ dei²²*, 'satisfactorily'] learned a language. (HBF1)
47. Because I think only native speaker can stand for a standard pronunciation for that language. And non-native accent should be corrected to American English. Because I think USA is the powerest nation in the world, we speak English is just because of this, otherwise we needn't learn English. (HSM3)

(b) non-native accent is less desirable / needs to be improved

48. I have foreign friends who tell me ppl [people] in Hong Kong are not good at English as their accent and their grammar mistakes are so foolish. This makes me ashamed. (CSSF1)
49. Because the non-native accent can be improved and [I'll] try my best to do so. (CBM5)
50. It is less irritating to hear and speak English with native accent (…). (HSF2)
51. I think I want to speak like a native speaker if possible, but if I really need to communicate with those people who have a hard accent, I think it is OK. But I highly recommend that they should try to improve or correct their accent. (HBF7)

(c) Compared with a non-native accent, a native-like accent is more intelligible

52. It would be much easier to be understood. (HLM8)
53. I need to pay much more attention when others speak English with a non-native accent. (HBM8)
54. If people from different countries speak English with different accent and they cannot communicate with each other, then the objective of learning English is not reached. (HSM12)

Of the five participants who choose (c) 'other: please specify', one participant (CEF9) makes it clear that even though she won't correct the non-native pronunciation, she does not like it:

55. I won't like it but I won't correct it either. (CEF9)

In sum, the results show that while the majority of the participants (over 70%) find it unnecessary for non-native pronunciation to be corrected provided communication is not adversely affected, there are nevertheless 20–25% of participants in favor of seeing non-native pronunciation problems corrected for three closely related reasons: (1) native-like pronunciation is the norm and goal of learning; (2) non-native pronunciation is less prestigious; and (3) non-native pronunciation is subjectively more difficult to follow.

However, after the participants' responses to Q.3 were tallied (by a show of hands) and briefly discussed, in all of the focus groups participants were almost unanimous when the context was shifted to classroom teaching: they were asked whether or not teacher correction was necessary if the non-native pronunciation features occurred in English-L2 learners' output during an English lesson. With four exceptions (56–59), the rest of the 103 participants shared the view that the English teacher – in East Asia – should make an effort to point out the pronunciation 'errors' and demonstrate NS-based pronunciation, regardless of whether such corrective feedback would make a difference to the learners' pronunciation. The concerns of these four participants are as follows (original in Cantonese; my translation):

56. I won't suggest correcting students' non-native English accent at the elementary level because they have already put so much effort in learning new things. Correcting their accents will limit or slow down their learning progress. This may also hinder their learning. (CEM8)

57. The choice of accent is a personal decision. I know some people who are very reluctant to speak English with an American accent and who stick to their Hong Kong English accent at all costs because they think 'that's me!'. So there are some people who prefer to speak English with a clear Hong Kong accent. (HSF11)

58. I think it depends. If it is an English lesson, the teacher should correct the learner's pronunciation. If it is not an English lesson, the teacher shouldn't do that. (HLM2)

59. It depends on whether others can follow. Take, for example, 'I think', I can understand. Some friends of mine who're Pakistanis, they say 'I tink I tink', and I understand. So I don't think you should correct their pronunciation. But certainly if someone says, 'I fank', or 'I fong' [to mean 'I think'], when there is no way for me to understand what he/she's talking about, then [correction is needed because] it is completely off the mark and incomprehensible. (WF18)

These four participants' concerns touch upon three main issues:

(1) Pedagogical soundness: Is teacher correction a pedagogically sound decision vis-à-vis other higher-order teaching and learning goals at hand? (CEM8 and HLM2)
(2) Linguacultural identity: Does the learner want to be corrected and learn the 'proper' pronunciation? Could the non-native pronunciation be purposefully intended as an 'act of identity'? (HSF11)
(3) Primacy of communication over accent: As long as communication is not adversely affected, why should we insist on native-like pronunciation? (WF18)

These overriding concerns are shared by a few other participants to some extent, but one thing seems certain: when it comes to the question, whether or not the teacher of English should demonstrate the NS-based pronunciation in an English lesson, there is near unanimity that the teacher should do so and draw the learner's attention to some NS pronunciation model, regardless of teaching effectiveness and possible uptake by the learners.

Qualitative analysis of one focus group discussion

In all of the 12 focus groups, practically all of the points mentioned in the quantitative analysis above were taken up by participants when requested to explain their position with regard to specific Questions 1–3. Owing to space constraints, I will analyze participants' elicited responses to Q.1 (turns 717–748) and Q.2 (turns 749–757) in one focus group: nine students of business studies and one social science student (see Appendix 2).

Regarding their preferred English accent (Q.1), two participants chose proficient speakers of 'HK English' (CBF8 and CBF9), and one participant chose proficient speakers of 'China English' (CSSF10) to be their respective role model. CSSF10, a social science student from Beijing studying in Hong Kong on exchange, found nothing wrong speaking English with a Beijing accent; on the contrary, when interacting with others in English, be they NSs or NNSs, that accent made her feel more comfortable (original in Putonghua; my translation):

60. Eh.. because I live in Beijing / so our English is generally characterized by a Beijing flavor or accent / eh the people around [us] all speak in this way / that is we find it more convenient to communicate in this way.. that is [we can] all understand [each other's English] / and I don't see anything improper about this // (CSSF10, turn 732)

61. [No] that is not imitation / because [all] around [us everyone] speaks in the same way / so it is more comfortable [for us] to communicate [in English with a Beijing accent] // (CSSF10, turn 734)

Similarly, CBF8 chose 'HK English' as her preferred accent mainly out of a concern for her linguacultural identity. According to her, the 'HK English' accent is easier to understand compared with other accents (original in Cantonese; my translation; original English expressions in italics):

62. Because actually.. actually [I] choose *Hong Kong English* because for Hongkongers to speak like foreigners it is already quite difficult / and also the accent [you have] when learning a [foreign] language / some [speech] sounds are really difficult to acquire /

Instead of … I mean spending time correcting our own accent /
we might as well speak [English] more often / I mean … language
is used for communication / I feel being able to communicate is
already [a] very significant [achievement] / and after all being in
Hong Kong / unless you … really want to emigrate elsewhere /
or live in a foreign country / otherwise speaking *Hong Kong
English* in Hong Kong / actually most people will understand /
honestly [based on my experience] listening to so many *professors*
speak / without a doubt [you know] it is the *local professors* who
are easiest to understand / and so … if I have a choice / I will
choose *Hong Kong English* / I feel that [speaking a] different accent
doesn't mean that [it] is wrong // (CBF8, turn 718)

CBF9, too, chose 'HK English' accent and justified her choice with the
following remark in the questionnaire: 'I think he [Donald Tsang] speaks
good English, we are not possible to speak like native speakers since we
only learn and speak in HK environment' (20).

In contrast, the rest of the seven participants chose 'NS-based standard' as their preferred accent. Five of them gave their justifications as
follows (original in Cantonese; my translation; original English expressions in italics):

63. *because I consider it as the highest level of oral English* // (CBF1,
    original in English; turn 740)
64. *Yeah* … me too I feel that [native speaker accent] is easier to under-
    stand [more pleasant to listen to][3] // (CBM5, turn 742)
65. [That is] because me too I feel that *native* [speaker accent] is easier
    to understand [more pleasant to listen to][3] // (CBF2, turn 746)
66. [A NS-based accent sounds] very *professional* // (CBF4, turn 747)
67. I feel that [native accent] is the *accent* which most people under-
    stand / for instance [if you are] thinking of sitting for *TOEFL* /
    sitting for public exams / [the] *listening* [part will] definitely be
    in *native accent* / [if] everyone is required to listen [to this
    accent] it must be the most widely understood [accent] //
    (CBF3, turn 748)

Apart from positive attributes associated with a NS-based accent ('*highest level of oral English*', 'easier to understand'/'more pleasant to listen
to', and '[sounds] very *professional*'), F3's remark in (67) is also highly
pertinent: to the extent that the kinds of accent used for assessing NNSs'
level of listening skills in international public exams are all NS-based,
it follows that NS-based accents have wider currency compared with
non-native accents. I think this point, made by a NNS learner, has at least

two important implications for further research in ELF. First, it provides evidence from NNSs' perspective that the discussion about possible changes in the local ELT curriculum – such as the kinds of accent represented – ought to take into account the real washback effects of assessment (*cf.* Elder & Davies, 2006). Second, the popular perception among NNSs that non-native accents are more difficult to understand vis-à-vis NS-based accents is due at least in part to the fact that non-native accents are underrepresented in teaching materials, in addition to being stigmatized in teachers' 'remedial' feedback to students in class (*cf.* Luk, 1998).

Participants' concern about potential intelligibility problems raised by non-native accents is clearly reflected in their responses to Q.2 regarding their preferred speaker identity. CBF8, who chose the accent of proficient speakers of 'HK English' to be her role model (see 62), made it clear that the bottom line for this preferred accent was that it should not impede communication or cause intelligibility problems to others (original in Cantonese; my translation; original English expressions in italics):

68. Actually for me [English is] really [used] for *communication* / after all .. I am a Hongkonger this .. is an identity / I .. don't have to deliberately imitate a foreigner / it is not that I *pronounce* that sound wrongly / actually I feel that … [when] speaking English [I] have … very strong Hong Kong accent / [but] there is no problem / because this is in fact my identity / fixed from the day when I was born / unless [my accent] affects my *communication* / otherwise I feel that … [there is] no need to imitate [native accent] / of course when I learned [English, my English] already carried a heavy foreign accent that is a different story / but then I am in fact a locally born and bred Hongkonger / [going through] very traditional Hong Kong education / so I feel eh .. I .. *even* though [I] speak English with heavy Hong Kong accent / or very heavy *China English* [accent] / if I was born in mainland [China] / [the fact that my English carried] mainland accent is no problem at all // (CBF8, turn 750)

Interestingly, CBF8's stance was shared by CBF9, who similarly indicated a preference for the accent of proficient 'HK English' speakers in her response to Q.1. To CBF9, to be able to communicate with people 'beyond Hong Kong' effectively, it would be advisable for Hong Kong people to speak English with a 'generally accepted accent':

69. Me too I choose B / my feeling is if eh .. we want to go beyond Hong Kong .. then we need to speak [English with a] *general accept accent* // (CBF9, turn 756)

The concern that non-native accents may lead to intelligibility problems is evidenced by CBF6's remarks in (70) and (71):

70. Yes. I feel that is because .. if [one] speaks a more standard accent .. it is true that everyone will be able to […] that is to understand more clearly. // (CBF6, turns 752)
71. Most important also / of course you need to make others understand you .. as for the question of accent / unavoidably the pronunciation of certain words will be affected .. making it difficult [for others] to follow // (CBF6, turns 754)

The concern as evidenced in the remarks of CBF8 (62, 68) and CBF9 (69) suggests that, for them, there exists a tension between NNS identity and intelligibility: NNS identity is perceived as a desirable goal in its own right, so long as intelligibility is assured. This seems to suggest that to some Chinese NNSs at least, intelligibility should receive a higher priority compared with the expression of NNS identity. More research is needed to ascertain the extent to which this higher-order concern for intelligibility is shared by NNSs from other L1 backgrounds.

Discussion

Perhaps the most striking finding is the percentage of participants who prefer a NS-based accent in this study is comparable to that in Timmis's (2002) study (*cf.* Hu, 2004; Jenkins, 2005, 2007; Kirkpatrick & Xu, 2002; Luk, 1998). While in Timmis's survey, over two-thirds of 400 international students (67%) indicated a preference for a NS accent (except learners from South Africa, Pakistan and India), in this study 90 out of 107 Chinese participants (over 84.1%) wish to speak English with a native accent. This was especially true for working adults (17 out of 18). Very similar patterns of response were obtained for Q.2 on preferred speaker identity: 84 out of 107 participants (78.5%) said that if possible they would like to sound like a NS of English rather than a (HK or mainland) Chinese speaker of English.

A second finding concerns the motivations behind NNSs' preference for a NS accent. As shown in Table 5.2, this exploratory study has generated a number of hypotheses about the different positive attributes of a NS-based accent. The positive attributes are semantically manifold, covering a wide range from general (e.g. 'natural', 'good', 'sounds more English', 'perfect', 'accurate', 'correct', 'proper', 'the standard', 'the prototype') to aesthetic (e.g. 'beautiful', 'pleasant', 'sweeter', 'pure', 'elegant'), and from pragmatic ('more easily understood', 'more comfortable') to ownership and authority ('originated from England/America', 'their mother tongue').

Together they present a rather different picture from NNSs' resistance to the hegemony of English found in earlier studies (see, e.g. Canagarajah, 1999). To what extent could this be regarded as evidence of English-L2 users' reflex submission (Seidlhofer, 2005, cited in Jenkins, 2006a: 172) to the hegemony of NS-based pedagogic models? Could their aspiration of NS accent be a function of their proficiency level and/or socioeconomic background? The participants in this survey are either working adults or university students pursuing an undergraduate or postgraduate degree. Many of them approximate Alptekin's (2002) characterization of success-ful bilingual users of English, or Jenkins's (2006a) 'expert speakers of English', whose perceptions of and needs for English are likely to be very different from those of underprivileged and unmotivated low-achievers who feel obliged to study English against their will (*cf.* Prodromou, 2006). In any case, there is clearly room for further research in this area.

Quite a few participants are specific about their preferred accent: British ('BBC': 9), American ('CNN': 6), Australian (2) and Canadian (1). It is inter-esting that of these 18 participants, 10 of them (55.6%) had lived/studied overseas for some time (less than 1 year: five; 1–3 years: one; 3–5 years: two; more than 5 years: one). With one exception (CLM10, see 16), the accent of the English-speaking country where these 'returnees' had lived matches with their preferred accent (i.e. those who prefer British, American, Australian, Canadian accent had lived in Britain, USA, Australia and Canada, respectively). HSF9, for example, explains her personal prefer-ence thus: '[my preferred accent is an] Aussie accent. I don't like Hong Kong accent and I went to Australia for exchange. I like their accent' (16, 33). Similarly, HSF5 identified with the Aussie accent apparently because she had lived there for five years (15). In an increasingly globalized world, cross-border visits and short- and medium-term exchange programmes are commonplace. One finding in this study suggests that such visits and programmes are likely to have some impact on the NNS visitors' attitude toward the national English variety of the host country. This finding, if proved to be valid in further research, seems to be at odds with criticisms of NS-based models of English being 'imposed' on such NNSs. Here again there is clearly room for further research to enlighten the debate.

A further interesting finding concerns some learners' motivations for aspiring to speak English with an American accent. Two participants mentioned the power and global influence of USA explicitly as the reason for identifying with an American accent (HEM9, 14), and for recommending that deviations from NS pronunciation should be corrected to conform to American English (HSM3, 47). HSM3's remark is reminiscent of those made by a few Hong Kong Chinese learners of English some decades earlier. Back in the 1930s, Robert Simpson, the first Professor of English at the University of Hong Kong, reportedly asked his Chinese students in an exam question why they were so anxious to learn English. To that question more than one responded: because 'Americans use it' (Simpson, 1933, cited in Bolton, 2003: 197, 223). Over 70 years later, after outdoing its arch-rival the (now defunct) Soviet Union, the United States has emerged as the only superpower in the post-Cold War era. The linguistic correlate of its political influence worldwide – the global hegemony of the 'killer language' English – has been the focus of much criticism (e.g. Canagarajah, 1999; Phillipson, 1992; Skutnabb-Kangas, 2000). The NNSs' desire to appropriate English for personal econocultural benefits is variously interpreted as a sign of such learners falling victim to the hegemony of English in the postcolonial era, in that they have internalized the beliefs and values of the former colonizers possibly without realizing it. Such an analysis has been criticized for under-estimating the postcolonial subjects' ability to judge what is in their best interest and, in the case of parents, the best interests of their children's multilingual development (see, e.g. Bisong, 1995; Li, 2003). Whichever stance one takes in this debate, there is some indication in my data that some NNSs are perfectly aware of the global hegemony of English, but rather than being inspired to resist it (Canagarajah, 1999), this is precisely the reason why they want to appropriate it for their own benefit.

The above discussion clearly has implications for the participants' perception of ownership of the English language. The positive attributes in Table 5.3 suggest that, contrary to what is generally believed by WE and EIL/ELF scholars, most participants in this study do not seem to regard English as 'their' own (nativized) language (*cf.* Widdowson, 1994). Apart from the reference to 'native speaker' and various NS accents, in a few participants' commentary on their preferred accent (see 1 and 5), the use of the pronouns 'their' and 'they' indicate that they do not consider themselves owners of the English language.

Preference of a localized variety of English: Motivations and concerns

Of the 107 participants, relatively few (17, or less than 16%) prefer the accent of a highly proficient local bilingual speaker of English as their role model ('HK English': 12; 'China English': 5; see 18–30). Their justifications may be summarized as follows:

- The accent of the role models of 'HK English' or 'China English' is good or fluent enough.
- The local(ized) accent is more intelligible to local bilingual Chinese.

- Effective communication is primary and more important than my English accent.
- The local(ized) accent is more attainable.
- I use English mainly with local NNSs.
- NS accents sound 'pretentious'.
- The local(ized) accent sounds more natural and is closer to my culture.

One mainland participant, CSSF10, justified her unconditional support of 'China English' unapologetically thus: 'I am a mainland student and I live in Beijing. So my English will [be] close to the "China English". And I don't think it's bad' (29, 40; see also Appendix 2).

In contrast to positive remarks in support of the legitimacy of local(ized) accents, several other participants expressed dislike of such accents on aesthetic grounds (31–34; see also 55). At least two participants related their dislike to perceptions of shame (CSSF1, 48) and social stigma or discrimination (WF12, 34). It will be interesting to find out to what extent such perceptions of stigmatization of non-native accents have community-wide validity (see also 49–51; *cf.* Luk, 1998). It should be noted that, despite the participants' attention being drawn to two role models in each case – highly educated bilingual speakers of HKE and China English respectively – when referring to either local(ized) accent many participants' point of reference appears to have been a basilectal 'learner variety' rather than an acrolectal 'educated bilingual-speaker variety'.

NS-based or local(ized) accent? Tension between intelligibility and identity

In addition to subjective perceptions of local(ized) accents, there is some indication that for some Chinese NNSs of English, non-native accents have low prestige because of potential intelligibility problems (see 52–54). A concern with intelligibility is also the main reason why HBF7 (51) recommends that heavily accented pronunciation such as [pərɒdʌkʊtə] ('product') should be improved and corrected, though her view belongs to the minority. While some participants identified with the local(ized) accent, they were concerned about intelligibility problems. Thus CSSF10, who defends her 'China English' accent (29, 40) unapologetically, prefers a native-speaker accent in order to be maximally intelligible when communicating with others. As for her interlocutors' accent, she would not mind their NNS accents at all so long as she could understand them (see also CSSF10's input in Appendix 2). A similar wish for speaking a local(ized) accent while being intelligible is epitomized by

CSF5's response to Q.2: 'I want to be seen as Chinese but can speak fluent English in foreign accent' (36).

Thus for some participants, there seems to be a tension between a preferred local(ized) accent as an 'act of (HK) Chinese identity' and a desire to be intelligible to interlocutors. These two goals appear to be in conflict, however, for approximation to one goal seems to be achieved at the expense of the other. Such a tension between L1-identity and intelligibility is clearly at work with those participants who would prefer a local(ized) ('HK English' or 'China English') accent, but who are nevertheless inclined to target a NS accent as their learning goal (39–42). There is also some evidence of speech accommodation. Thus CBF2 (35) said that when talking to NNSs, speaking English with a non-native accent is more preferable out of respect, while WF19 expresses concern that 'too much [British accented] intonation' makes her 'sound haughty' and appear to 'fawn on foreigners'. In either case, there seems to be pressure for those speaking English with a native-like accent to tone down their nativeness when using English for intraethnic communication with fellow Chinese.

The above findings clearly have implications for ELT curriculum development. Both WE and ELF scholars agree that awareness-raising of linguistic variation in World Englishes is one of the most important teaching strategies to promote communication between NNSs of English with different L1 backgrounds. Prodromou (2006) raises a concern that setting the lexicogrammatical baseline too low, as shown in the tentative lingua franca core features (see Jenkins, 2006a: 170) generated by the VOICE corpus (Seidlhofer, 2004), runs the risk of alienating successful bilingual users of English. His argument seems to be supported by at least two L2-user surveys: Timmis (2002) and this study. ELF researchers' point that LFC features are not meant to be dogmas imposed on non-native learners and teachers of English as a new set of norms is well taken (Jenkins, 2006b; Seidlhofer, 2006). It remains to be seen, however, in what ways insights derived from ELF research at all linguistic levels will inform local teachers' classroom teaching.

Comparison with experimental research on intelligibility and research on NNS teachers' attitudes toward intelligibility and identity

For over two decades, intelligibility has been a major concern to scholars of World Englishes and more recently, ELF researchers focusing on NNS–NNS interactions. However, as Pickering (2006: 220) has pointed out, there is as yet no universally accepted definition of intelligibility, probably because Smith and Nelson's (1985) classic, tripartite distinction between 'intelligibility', 'comprehensibility' and 'interpretability' – various abilities attributed to the NNS listener – are difficult to operationalize. Pickering's review shows that intelligibility problems in a broad sense are most likely due to some combination of speaker and listener factors.

There have been a few experimental studies (e.g. Bent & Bradlow, 2003; Major *et al.*, 2002) showing that English-L2 listeners tend to find the speech of English-L2 'talkers' with the same L1 background more intelligible and comprehensible compared with the speech of English-L1 talkers or English-L2 talkers from other L1 backgrounds. On the basis of sentence intelligibility scores of 21 Chinese-L1, 10 Korean-L1 and 21 English-L1 participants listening to sample speech in English recorded from two Chinese-L1, two Korean-L1, and one English-L1 talkers, Bent and Bradlow (2003) found that for both Chinese and Korean English-L2 listeners, the speech of high-proficiency talkers with the same or different native language background was nearly as intelligible as the speech of English-L1 talkers. Thus in addition to a 'matched interlanguage speech intelligibility benefit', they claim to have found evidence for a 'mismatched interlanguage speech intelligibility benefit', on the proviso that the proficiency level of the English-L2 talker is high. However, given that their speech material took the form of decontextualized sentences (controlled for vocabulary; see Appendix, Bent & Bradlow, 2003: 1608–1609), it remains unclear to what extent either of these benefits obtains in real-world ELF interactions.

Neither benefit was in evidence in another larger-scale study conducted by Major *et al.* (2002). Modeling their listening material on the Listening Comprehension Trial Test, a version of the TOEFL test, Major *et al.* (2002) asked two NSs of four languages – Chinese, Japanese, Spanish and Standard American English – respectively to read aloud excerpts of speech texts (up to two minutes each) in the form of academic lectures. In each of these native language pairs, the talkers were balanced in gender; the topics of the lecture materials were controlled, and the non-native talkers were selected following a rigorous procedure for screening speakers with a moderate degree of accentedness. The recordings were administered to four groups of 100 listeners – all university students and potential TOEFL test takers – with the same native languages in Beijing, Tokyo, Bogotá and Arizona, respectively. After analyzing the listeners' comprehension test scores using ANOVA, Major *et al.* (2002) found that the results do not support the hypothesis that a shared native language between English-L2 talkers and listeners would make the talker's verbal input more intelligible (*cf.* 'matched interlanguage speech intelligibility benefit', Bent & Bradlow,

2003). On the contrary, the Chinese listeners performed significantly better on the lectures delivered by Standard American English talkers than by the Chinese talkers. Nor was such a benefit apparent in the performance of Japanese listeners, who did not do significantly better on lectures delivered by the Japanese talkers. One methodological merit of Major *et al.*'s (2002) study is that the possible bias of the listener's attitude toward the non-native talker's accented English was minimized.

Just as the objective findings of Bent and Bradlow (2003) and Major *et al.* (2002) point to rather different conclusions with regard to the research question 'Do listeners perform significantly better on a test of listening comprehension in English when the speaker shares the listeners' native language?' (Major *et al.*, 2002: 178), so the findings in both of these studies seem to be supported to some extent by the subjective data elicited from 107 NNSs in Hong Kong and mainland China. Thus while CBF8, who asserts that '[speaking in a] different accent doesn't mean that [it] is wrong', claims that 'it is the *local professors* who are easiest to understand' (62; see also turn 718, Appendix 2), CBF7 said she found lectures delivered by non-Chinese professors more difficult to follow (two nationalities mentioned but withheld, see turn 724, Appendix 2). In terms of support for the 'matched interlanguage speech intelligibility benefit' hypothesis (Bent & Bradlow, 2003), the findings in this study are thus inconclusive. What this study shows, however, is that NNSs' subjective views are researchable, and that they have good potential for triangulating findings obtained from more objective experimental studies of intelligibility.

The findings in this study are also consistent with those in more qualitative research on NNS teachers' attitudes toward the relationship between NNS accent and identity. Jenkins (2005, *cf.* 2007) found that the assumption behind the empirically grounded lingua franca core (LFC) features – that they would help learners in the expanding circle project a NNS (as opposed to a NS) identity – is not supported by her data obtained through in-depth, semi-structured interviews with eight female NNS teachers of English from six different countries. These NNS teachers had a high level of English proficiency and were at different stages of their professional development in ELT: from pre-service to very experienced. All were informed about the rationale behind ELF to some extent. The majority of the 12 questions focus on 'their attitudes to and identification with NNS and NS English accents, their perceptions of others' attitudes and identification, and their beliefs about teaching these accents' (Jenkins, 2005: 536). There is no mention of the informants' degree of accentedness. One of the key questions concerns how they would feel if their accent gave others the impression of them being a NS. The results are ambivalent; in general the reasons why a NS accent was perceived as desirable are related to a high level of language learning achievement and better career prospects; however, these positive feelings did not preclude some participants (e.g. the Italian participant E, p. 538) from wishing to project a NNS speaker identity through their accent. For some participations (e.g. Participants A and G, pp. 539–540), this pride in their NNS accent seemed to be associated with negative, sometimes traumatic, experiences when interacting with NSs at a formative stage of the learning process.

As for the eight participants' readiness to teach characteristic features of their own NNS accent to learners with the same L1 background as theirs, the majority of them kept referring to such features as 'errors'. Jenkins (2005: 540) attributes this attitude to three possible factors: the absence of published material for teaching ELF, learners' preference of a NS accent, and parents' reservation about their children learning ELF. The participants' perceptions of their own colleagues' receptiveness to ELF are no more encouraging. Some believed that personal experiences such as overseas travel and measures of codification might make their colleagues more sympathetic to ELF as a legitimate learning goal in its own right. Jenkins (2005: 541) sounds a pessimistic note toward the end of the 'Discussion' section: 'most had some doubts because they saw lack of confidence in NNS accents as an irresolvable issue', before arriving at the following tentative conclusion (*cf.* Jenkins, 2007):

> The most important point is that it cannot be taken for granted that teachers (let alone all speakers) from the expanding circle wish unequivocally to use their accented English to express their L1 identity or membership in an international (ELF) community. Past experiences, both classroom and social, factors in their present situation, and their assessment of their future chances of success may combine to affect their attitudes to English at the deeper level. In some as yet unclear way, these factors may cause them to identify with NSs, or to put it another way, to want a NS English identity as expressed in a native-like accent. Such an accent according to this study's participants is 'good', 'perfect', 'correct', 'proficient', 'competent', 'fluent', 'real', and 'original English', whereas a NNS accent is 'not good', 'wrong', 'incorrect', 'not real', 'fake', 'deficient' and 'strong'. (Jenkins, 2005: 541)

Many of Jenkins's (2005) findings are borne out in this study, in particular NNSs' preference of a NS accent (Table 5.2), and similar positive attributes associated with a NS accent (Table 5.3). In addition, this study shows that a NNS's preference of a NS accent may possibly be a result of having spent some time (e.g. one semester) in the English-speaking country (see 6–17). At the same time, this study also confirms that a smaller number of NNSs found nothing wrong with a local(ized) accent (i.e. 'HK English' or 'China English' accent, see 18–30), suggesting that the intimate relationship between English-L2 accent and speaker identity is a real concern for some participants. Interestingly, however, when asked about their preferred identity when using English with Chinese or non-Chinese speakers (see Q.2 in Appendix 1), seven of the eight participants who identify with a 'HK English' or 'China English' accent in Q.1 indicate that they would like to sound native-like in order to minimize intelligibility problems (see 39–42). This apparent contradiction is reminiscent of the ambivalent attitudes of the eight NNS teacher interviewees toward the relationship between accentedness and identity in Jenkins's (2005) study. In both studies, such ambivalence is arguably indicative of a tension between a wish to project a NNS identity through a NNS accent on one hand, and a concern for intelligibility in ELF communication (probably both NNS–NNS and NNS–NS) on the other. It further suggests that for at least some NNSs, the twin goals of projecting a NNS speaker identity and assuring intelligibility in ELF communication are not mutually exclusive, making it difficult for either to be achieved without the other being adversely affected (for implications on teacher training, see Snow *et al.*, 2006).

Conclusion

Based on a combination of quantitative and qualitative data using a semi-structured questionnaire (Appendix 1) administered to 12 focus groups, this study shows that 78–84% (average 81%) of the 107 Chinese university-educated participants surveyed prefer to speak English with a NS-based accent, while 16–22% (average 19%) of them indicate a readiness to speak English with a local(ized) accent out of a concern for their (Hong Kong or mainland) Chinese identity. The majority's preference may be glossed as follows:

> If I learn a language of wider communication such as English, I might as well learn a NS-based standard variety in order to ensure intelligibility and, by the same token, minimize communication problems when interacting with others, including NSs.

As for the latter group, there appears to be a dilemma between the twin-goals of projecting a NNS identity using a local(ized) accent and assuring intelligibility in ELF communication, since the enactment of Chinese identity through a local(ized) English accent is seen by some participants as a source of intelligibility problems. This may be attributed to three related factors: (1) the dominance of NS-based pedagogic models in the

English curriculum, resulting in local(ized) linguistic features being systematically treated as errors and thus associated with low prestige; (2) a concern for intelligibility problems owing to a lack of familiarity with linguistic features in other varieties of English; and (3) a lack of awareness of the legitimacy of non-native varieties of English.

Further, while the majority of participants indicate that their interlocutors' non-native pronunciation need not be corrected, they are almost unanimous that if such deviations (e.g. pronouncing the word 'product' as [pərɒdʌkʊtə]) occur in an English lesson, the teacher should make an effort to point out the 'errors' and demonstrate the NS-based pronunciation to the learners. This point, if confirmed in larger-scale studies, has significant implications for the use of ELF insights in curriculum development. For example, it has been suggested that the simplification of consonant clusters using additional vowels has been shown to have minimal impact on intelligibility in NNS–NNS communication, and so it should be included in the lingua franca core (Jenkins, 2003). The findings in this study show that such a phonological feature is generally perceived as an error if it occurs in the classroom, and that there is general consensus that some corrective feedback along the lines of a NS-based standard is needed. While ELF features such as those in Jenkins's lingua franca core in phonology and Seidlhofer's 'lexico-grammatical sins' are never intended to be implemented dogmatically in the local ELT classroom, and given that local teachers know best how and to what extent insights obtained in ELF research may be used with regard to their context-specific teaching and learning goals (see Jenkins, 2006b; Seidlhofer, 2006), the findings in this study suggest that the pedagogic option of withholding the teaching of NS-based phonological features in favour of the teaching of the local(ized) accent should be considered with care, for such an important decision might turn out to be unpopular and possibly meet with learner resistance in class (*cf.* Li, 2006).

In terms of directions for further research, World Englishes and ELF to date tend to be focused on corpus-driven analysis of NNS–NNS interactions or carefully controlled experimental studies of intelligibility. There has been little research on NNSs' attitudes toward such complex issues. This exploratory study shows that NNSs, including NNS teachers (Jenkins, 2005, 2007), are perfectly capable of articulating their concerns about such complex and inter-related issues as speaker identity, intelligibility and ownership of the English language. Given that NNSs are supposed to be the primary beneficiaries of empowerment through ELF research, it is high time that we go beyond collecting strictly 'performance data' and 'experimental data' to include NNSs' own views and voices on a range of delicate and contentious issues in ELF communication. This study was conceived as a modest attempt toward this end.

Toward the end of her review article, Jenkins (2006a: 174) appeals for more teacher action in order to raise learners' awareness of other varieties of English than a NS-based pedagogic model as a means to 'encourage learners' confidence in their own English varieties, and in turn reduce the linguistic capital that many learners still believe native-like English to possess'. Her prognosis, however, leaves little room for optimism, and this seems to be largely confirmed by the findings in this study. In the short run at least, researchers and TESOL practitioners who are sympathetic to the cause of pluricentric English norms will continue to be fighting an uphill battle with regard to the goal of changing learners' attitudes toward non-native varieties of English.

Acknowledgements

The work described in this chapter was fully supported by a grant from the Research Grants Council of the Hong Kong Special Administrative Region, China (project no. CityU 1461/05H).

Notes

1. It is not entirely clear whether Hong Kong belongs to the outer circle or the expanding circle. Whereas Kachru (2005: 90) characterizes the varieties of English in Hong Kong, Taiwan and Korea as 'fast-expanding foreign languages', McArthur (2001: 8–9) considers Hong Kong as one of 'the ESL territories'. Bolton (2003: 77 f) likewise places Hong Kong English in the outer circle. Hong Kong's 'circle identity' is theoretically significant for it has direct implications for determining whether 'Hong Kong English' should be regarded as 'norm-developing' or 'norm-dependent'.
2. Participants are represented by a code consisting of four parts: for student participants, the first letter indicates the university ('C': CityU; 'H': HKU), the next letter(s) their discipline of study ('B': Business; 'E': English; 'L': Law; 'S': natural science; 'SS': social science), the last letter gender ('F' vs. 'M'), and finally a group-specific participant number. Working adults are identified by the letter 'W', followed by gender and participant number.
3. The Cantonese expression hou^{35} teng^{55} (好聽), a compound adjective with the literal meaning 'good-listen', may be interpreted as either 'easier to understand' or 'more pleasant to listen to'. Both interpretations are compatible with the point made by CBM5 and CBF2 in turns 742 and 746, respectively.

References

Alptekin, C. (2002) Towards intercultural communicative competence in ELT. *ELT Journal* 56 (1), 57–64.

Bent, T. and Bradlow, A. (2003) The interlanguage speech intelligibility benefit. *Journal of The Acoustical Society of America* 114, 1600–1610.
Bisong, J. (1995) Language choice and cultural imperialism: A Nigerian perspective. *ELT Journal* 49 (2), 122–132.
Bolton, K. (2003) *Chinese Englishes. A Sociolinguistic History*. Cambridge: Cambridge University Press.
Canagarajah, S. (1999) *Resisting Linguistic Imperialism in English Teaching*. Oxford: Oxford University Press.
Cook, V. (1999) Going beyond the native speaker in language teaching. *TESOL Quarterly* 33 (2), 185–209.
Elder, C. and Davies, A. (2006) Assessing English as a lingua franca. *Annual Review of Applied Linguistics* 26, 282–301.
Hu, X.H. (2004) Why China English should stand alongside British, American, and the other 'world Englishes'. *English Today* 20 (2), 26–33.
Hung, T.T.N. (2000) Towards a phonology of Hong Kong English. *World Englishes* 19 (3), 337–356.
Jenkins, J. (2000) *Phonology of English as an International Language*. Oxford: Oxford University Press.
Jenkins, J. (2003) *World Englishes. A Resource Book for Students*. London and New York: Routledge.
Jenkins, J. (2005) Implementing an international approach to English pronunciation: The role of teacher attitudes and identity. *TESOL Quarterly* 39 (3), 157–181.
Jenkins, J. (2006a) Current perspectives on teaching World Englishes and English as a lingua franca. *TESOL Quarterly* 40 (1), 157–181.
Jenkins, J. (2006b) Global intelligibility and local diversity: Possibility or paradox? In R. Rubdy and M. Saraceni (eds) *English in the World. Global Rules, Global Roles* (pp. 32–39). London and New York: Continuum.
Jenkins, J. (2007) *English as a Lingua Franca: Attitude and Identity*. Oxford: Oxford University Press.
Kachru, B. B. (2005) *Asian Englishes. Beyond the Canon*. Hong Kong: Hong Kong University Press.
Kirkpatrick, A. (2006) Which model of English: Native-speaker, Nativised or lingua franca? In M. Saraceni and R. Rubdy (eds) *English in the World. Global Rules, Global Roles* (pp. 71–83). London and New York: Continuum.
Kirkpatrick, A. (2007) *World Englishes. Implications for International Communication and English Language Teaching*. Cambridge: Cambridge University Press.
Kirkpatrick, A. and Xu, Z.C. (2002) Chinese pragmatic norms and China English. *World Englishes* 21 (2), 268–280.
Li, D.C.S. (2003) Between English and Esperanto: What does it take to be a world language? *International Journal of the Sociology of Language* 164, 33–63.
Li, D.C.S. (2006) Problematizing empowerment: On the merits and demerits of non-standard models of English in the EIL curriculum. *Southeast Asia: A Multidisciplinary Journal* 6 (1), 112–131.
Luk, J. (1998) Hong Kong students' awareness of and reactions to accent differences. *Multilingua* 17 (1), 93–106.
Major, R., Fitzmaurice, S., Bunta, F. and Balasubramanian, C. (2002) The effects of nonnative accents on listening comprehension: Implications for ESL assessment. *TESOL Quarterly* 36, 173–190.
McArthur, T. (2001) World English and world Englishes: Trends, tensions, varieties, and standards. *Language Teaching* 34, 1–20.

McKay, S.L. (2002) *Teaching English as an International Language*. Oxford: Oxford University Press.

Phillipson, R. (1992) *Linguistic Imperialism*. Oxford: Oxford University Press.

Pickering, L. (2006) Current research on intelligibility in English as a lingua franca. *Annual Review of Applied Linguistics* 26, 219–233.

Prodromou, L. (2006) Defining the 'successful bilingual speaker' of English. In M. Saraceni and R. Rubdy (eds) *English in the World. Global Rules, Global Roles* (pp. 51–70). London and New York: Continuum.

Rubdy, R. and Saraceni, M. (eds) (2006) *English in the World. Global Rules, Global Roles*. London and New York: Continuum.

Seidlhofer, B. (2001) Closing a conceptual gap: The case for a description of English as a lingua franca. *International Journal of Applied Linguistics* 11 (2), 133–158.

Seidlhofer, B. (2004) Research perspectives on teaching English as a lingua franca. *Annual Review of Applied Linguistics* 24, 209–239.

Seidlhofer, B. (2006) English as a lingua franca in the expanding circle: What it isn't. In M. Saraceni and R. Rubdy (eds) *English in the World. Global Rules, Global Roles* (pp. 40–50). London and New York: Continuum.

Skutnabb-Kangas, T. (2000) *Linguistic Genocide in Education – or Worldwide Diversity and Human Rights*. Mahwah, NJ and London: Lawrence Erlbaum.

Smith, L. and Nelson, C. (1985) International intelligibility of English: Directions and resources. *World Englishes* 4, 333–342.

Snow, M.A., Kamhi-Stein, L. and Brinton, D.M. (2006) Teacher training for English as a lingua franca. *Annual Review of Applied Linguistics* 26, 261–281.

Timmis, I. (2002) Native-speaker norms and international English: A classroom view. *ELT Journal* 56 (2), 240–249.

Widdowson, H.G. (1994) The ownership of English. *TESOL Quarterly* 28 (2), 377–389.

Appendix 1

'One day with only English': Questionnaire survey [recto]

Participants' preferred model of English for teaching and learning, and social interaction

Please circle: I am a   CityU student   HKU student   working adult
Group (field/discipline): _____ Name: _____

1. If possible, I would like to speak English like … (please circle and briefly explain):

Speakers of 'HK English'	Speakers of 'China English'	Native speakers
e.g. Anson Chan, Donald Tsang	e.g. Bo Xilai, Li Zhaoxing	e.g. native speakers with BBC / CNN/ aussie accent

Reason for my preference: _____

2. My preferred identity when speaking English with Chinese/non-Chinese (tick one):
   (a) I want to sound like a (HK) Chinese speaker of English, not a native speaker of English – so long as others can understand me
   (b) I want to sound like a native speaker of English
   (c) other (please specify)
3. My attitude toward non-native English accents when listening to others speak (tick one):
   (Consider some typical learner pronunciation patterns: "I think this product is nice.")
   (a) It's fine when others speak English with a non-native accent – so long as I can understand it.
   (b) The non-native accent should be corrected (which accent should be the norm?).
   (c) other (please specify)
4. Brief explanation for my responses to questions (2) and (3):

_____

_____

Please return this questionnaire after completion.
Thank you.

Note: Some background information to the above questions may be found overleaf.

'One day with only English': Questionnaire survey [verso]

Background:
The following are a few questions for NNSs (Jenkins, 2003: 37):

1. Have you ever given thought to retaining your L1 identity in English?
2. Is it important to you to retain your L1 identity in English?
3. Are you more concerned to be intelligible to native speakers of English or to non-native speakers of English, or do you not distinguish between the two groups of listener?
4. Do you believe it is appropriate to retain your L1 accent in your English or that you should attempt to sound 'native-like'?
5. Do you believe it is possible to retain your L1 accent in English and still be intelligible to native-speakers?/to non-native speakers?

Appendix 2

Focus group data of NNSs' preferred accent

(Nine students of business studies; one student of social sciences [F10]; all post-secondary level; aged 18–22; seven Hong Kong Chinese, three mainland Chinese; nine female and one male; moderators: author [DL] and female research assistant [AC])

Notes

1. Situation: Participants just finished filling out a survey questionnaire (see Appendix 1); their views were being elicited by moderators. Owing to space limitation, only elicited responses to Questions 1–2 are excerpted.
2. Language choice: With Hong Kong participants the conversations took place in Cantonese; mainland Chinese participants felt more comfortable expressing themselves in Putonghua (marked '{PTH}' below). There were a few instances of code-switching to English (marked in italics). The excerpt was translated into English by the author.
3. Participants' identity: Personal names mentioned in the discussion are replaced by a code marking gender and participant number (e.g. F8: 'female speaker no. 8'; M5: 'male speaker no.5').
4. In turn 724, F7 claimed that the accents of professors from certain ethnic backgrounds were difficult to understand. This claim is potentially contentious and so the nationalities were withheld.
5. Prosodic notation (as found in the excerpt below):
   - .. pauses of less than 0.5 second
   - ... pauses of about 1 second
   - // sentence final intonation
   - / continuing intonation
   - ? rising intonation or question
   - HAHAHA laughter

Turn no.	Participant	*Excerpt of focus group with Business majors (CityU of HK). Original in Chinese; author's translation into English; original English expressions in italics.*
717	DL {PTH}	Right / most classmates have filled out [the questionnaire] / I'd like to ask.. the first question / eh.. anyone choosing *'Hong Kong English'? speakers of Hong Kong English*, anyone? Two / ah.. *China English* / one.. *OK* / *native speakers or native-like* / oh there are more [choosing native speakers or native-like] comparatively / could [you] explain a little? *Hong Kong English* /

(Continued)

718	F8	Because actually.. actually [I] choose *Hong Kong English* because for Hongkongers to speak like foreigners it is already quite difficult / and also the accent [you have] when learning a [foreign] language / some [speech] sounds are really difficult to acquire / Instead of … I mean spending time correcting our own accent / we might as well speak [English] more often / I mean … language is used for communication / I feel being able to communicate is already [a] very significant [achievement] / and after all being in Hong Kong / unless you … really want to emigrate elsewhere / or live in a foreign country / otherwise speaking *Hong Kong English* in Hong Kong / actually most people will understand / honestly [based on my experience] listening to so many *professors* speak / without a doubt [you know] it is the *local professors* who are easiest to understand / and so… if I have a choice / I will choose *Hong Kong English* / I feel that [speaking a] different accent doesn't mean that [it] is wrong //
719	DL	On this point I want to ask other Hong Kong classmates / F8 said eh … local teachers / that is Hong Kong people / [when] they speak English they are easier to understand / do you feel the same? //
720	F7	[That] depends really /
721	DL	Depends /
722	F7	Some people [their accents are] so bad that you can't make head or tail of what they are saying /
723	DL	Really /
724	F7	Yes / because … whether [a person's English] is easy to follow really depends on accent / why so? Because for example [among] our *professors* there are {*nationality mentioned but withheld*} / their English is really difficult to follow / {*nationality mentioned but withheld*} [professors] too their English is also very difficult to follow / so in fact [if] you let me listen to British or American [professors] / I feel there is no problem / and compared with {*nationality mentioned but withheld*} [professors] / {*nationality mentioned but withheld*} [professors] / or the accents of [professors of] still other strange places / local [professors] are really easier to follow //

(Continued)

725	DL	What about other classmates / [do you think] local teachers' English is easier to understand? / Have you got this impression? //
726	F3	For the moment I don't / my *professors'* accents are all very easy to understand //
727	DL	What about *F4*? /
728	F4	I don't see any problem here //
729	DL	So it depends on which types of teachers / yours are not the same as theirs //
730	F7	Because in my [department] there are many *professors* from different parts of the world //
731	DL	OK / [could you explain why you choose] *China English* //
732	F10 {PTH}	Eh .. because I live in Beijing / so our English is generally characterized by a Beijing flavor or accent / eh the people around [us] all speak in this way / that is we find it more convenient to communicate in this way .. that is [we can] all understand [each other's English] / and I don't see anything improper about this //
733	DL {PTH}	OK .. here it [= questionnaire] says *if possible* [F10: right] that is if possible / you are actually very eager to imitate them [their accent] .. /
734	F10 {PTH}	[No] that is not imitation / because [all] around [us everyone] speaks in the same way / so it is more comfortable [for us] to communicate [in English with a Beijing accent] //
735	DL {PTH}	But if you yourself are communicating with Chinese [I mean] foreigners ..
736	F10 {PTH}	They too can understand //
737	DL {PTH}	[How about] you yourself? Because you also use this accent when talking to them right? //
738	F10 {PTH}	Yes //
739	DL {PTH}	Right / so [those of you who choose] *native speaker* what is your view? That is *if possible* .. right / *if possible* / why [do you choose] *native speaker*? //
740	F1	*because I consider it as the highest level of oral English* //

(Continued)

741	DL	*The highest level of oral English* [F1: *yeah*] *right. M5 ... you feel the same?* //
742	M5	*Yeah ... me too I feel that* [native speaker accent] *is easier to understand* [more pleasant to listen to]
743	DL	What about the others? /
744	F2	But didn't you say *if possible*?
745	Dl	Yes / I don't mean to blame you [ALL: HAHAHA] I just want to know why //
746	F2	[That is] because me too I feel that *native* [speaker accent] is easier to understand [more pleasant to listen to]
747	F4	[It sounds] very *professional* //
748	F3	I feel that [native accent] is the *accent* which most people understand / for instance [if you are] thinking of sitting for *TOEFL* / sitting for public exams / [the] *listening* [part will] definitely be in *native accent* / [if] everyone is required to listen [to this accent] it must be the most widely understood [accent] //
749	DL	So your viewpoint [main concern] is being able to express one's meaning and being understood / *Number two* eh .. *my preferred identity when speaking English with Chinese* / Anyone choose A? [...] Why do you choose A? //
750	F8	Actually for me [English is] really [used] for *communication* / after all.. I am a Hongkonger this .. is an identity / I .. don't have to deliberately imitate a foreigner / it is not that I *pronounce* that sound wrongly / actually I feel that ... [when] speaking English [I] have ... very strong Hong Kong accent / [but] there is no problem / because this is in fact my identity / fixed from the day when I was born / unless [my accent] affects my *communication* / otherwise I feel that ... [there is] no need to imitate [native accent] / of course when I learned [English, my English] already carried a heavy foreign accent that is a different story / but then I am in fact a locally born and bred Hongkonger / [going through] very traditional Hong Kong education / so I feel eh.. I.. *even* though [I] speak English with heavy Hong Kong accent / or very heavy *China English* [accent] / if I was born in mainland [China] / [the fact that my English carried] mainland accent is no problem at all //

(Continued)

751	DL	Others who choose B / like .. F6 what do you think?
752	F6 {PTH}	Yes. I feel that is because.. if [one] speaks a more standard accent .. it is true that everyone will be able to .. [DL: to understand] that is to understand more clearly.
753	DL	So again your consideration is whether others can understand .. right //
754	F6	Most important also / of course you need to make others understand you .. as for the question of accent / unavoidably the pronunciation of certain words will be affected .. making it difficult [for others] to follow //
755	DL	OK .. I see / eh .. F9 what is your view?
756	F9	Me too I choose B / my feeling is if eh .. we want to go beyond Hong Kong .. then we need to speak [English with a] *general accept accent* //
757	DL	Do you share this feeling? / Anything else [you would like] to add / what about question 3 / those who choose A please raise your hand / {PTH} quite a lot .. What about B? / Why do you feel .. it should be *corrected*? // ...

Chapter 6

Attitudes Towards English as an International Language: The Pervasiveness of Native Models Among L2 Users and Teachers

ENRIC LLURDA

Introduction

In 1973, a group of people were held hostage for six days during a bank robbery in Stockholm. After their rescue, they experienced emotional attachment to their captors and even tried to help and defend them at the trial. Psychiatrist Nils Bejerot coined the term *Stockholm Syndrome* to describe a victim's psychological identification with their captor. Puzzling as this phenomenon may be, it has been explained as a humane defensive mechanism of a person who somehow needs to form an emotional attachment to the nearest powerful figure, and it has later been applied to other cases of person-to-person abuse, such as battered spouses, abused children, members of religious cults, or concentration camp survivors.

My point in this chapter is that non-native speaking English teachers (henceforth, NNESTs) do somehow experience a phenomenon that can be loosely related to that experienced by the victims of the 1973 Stockholm robbery (with all the evident distances between NNESTs and the victims of physically and emotionally abuse) in a world that still values native speakers as the norm providers and the natural choice in language teacher selection.

In this chapter, I will attempt to show how NNESTs have accepted formulations, proposals, and attitudes that relegate them to mere spectators and at times executioners of native speaker (NS) norms. I will provide a short review of research on NNESTs and attitudes to English as an

International Language (henceforth, EIL) in order to support my claim, and I will conclude by suggesting three lines of action that may be helpful in overcoming the current situation.

What Research Tells Us About NNESTs

Speakers of a language are often classified into two great groups, native speakers and non-native speakers. This separation has been used as much in theoretical linguistics (Chomsky, 1965) as in applied linguistics (Davies, 1991, 2003), but such a classification of speakers of a language into natives and non-natives clearly resembles the common division between 'us' and 'the others' present in those communities which try to establish a strong allegiance among its 'true members' (i.e. 'us'), thus preventing 'the others' from fully participating in the community activities. Classifying several speakers of a language as 'the others' (i.e. non-native speakers) may be regarded as a case of discrimination, materialized in the form of 'native-speakerism', which Holliday (2005) describes as a specific variant of the social phenomenon of 'culturism'. Despite several attempts in recent times to discredit or at least minimize the separation between native and non-native speakers of a language (Davies, 1991, 2003; Paikeday, 1985; Rampton, 1990), the concept of non-nativeness continues to be used as a way of labelling a group of speakers, which in the case of the English language, is certainly much larger than the group of so-called native speakers (Graddol, 2006). Liu (1999), Brutt-Griffler and Samimy (2001), and Inbar-Lourie (2005) presented evidence against a clear-cut division between native and non-native speakers. However, there has not been any consensus yet in finding a term that substitutes 'non-native speaker', which despite its many inconveniences is still widely used, for lack of a better alternative.

In this context, and mainly due to the established perception of a clear division between native and non-native speakers among linguists, and more importantly among laypeople, a group of applied linguists led by Braine (1999, 2005) began to actively advocate for the rights of non-native teachers in ELT, and took a clear action towards promoting research focused on this particular group of teachers, which to that moment had almost exclusively been pursued by Péter Medgyes and his associates (Medgyes, 1992, 1994; Reves & Medgyes, 1994). Since then, a growing number of studies have been conducted with the global aim of better understanding the nature of language teachers and what they can specifi-cally contribute to the language teaching profession. I will here review only a few, with the hope of introducing the reader to some of the main topics of research in the area.

I will start with Liu (1999), who conducted a series of email interviews with seven teachers for a period of eight months. One of the insights he obtained from the interviews was that there was no consensus regarding the meaning and implications of the terms NS and non-native speaker (NNS), as three participants 'expressed difficulty in affiliating themselves with either category' (Liu, 1999: 163). One of Liu's main arguments was the need to think of NNS professionals as being seen along 'a multidimensional and multilayered continuum' (Liu, 1999: 163). One year later, Árva and Medgyes (2000) compared the performances of NS and NNS ELT teachers, and their results highlighted the different contributions made by each of the two groups. This study, together with Cots and Diaz's (2005) are to date the only two attempts to conduct research on NNESTs by actually looking at their performance within the classroom. Cots and Diaz (2005) centered their analysis around the comparison of the discourse construction of social relationships by NESTs and NNESTs, as well as their differing ways of using teacher talk as a way of fostering participant inscription, an approach that would certainly require further studies in the same direction.

Students' perceptions about NESTs and NNESTs were studied by Lasagabaster and Sierra (2002, 2005) and by Benke and Medgyes (2005). Lasagabaster and Sierra (2002, 2005) conducted two complementary studies on university students' perceptions of NESTs and NNESTs in an EFL context. They used both closed and open questionnaires to elicit responses, and their conclusions were that students tend to prefer NESTs over NNESTs but that they are aware of some advantages of NNESTs, and therefore a majority of students would like to have a combination of both, NESTs and NNESTs. Lasagabaster and Sierra (2005) also asked students to differentiate their preferences according to level of education (primary, secondary and tertiary) and results showed that students had 'an increasing tendency in favour of the NST as the educational level is higher' (Lasagabaster & Sierra, 2005: 226). Benke and Medgyes' (2005) study involved 422 Hungarian learners of English. The instrument was a questionnaire consisting of five-point Likert scale questions with statements about NSs and NNSs based on Medgyes' (1994) list of characteristics of NS and NNS teachers. The authors concluded that students, on the whole, considered NNS teachers more demanding and traditional in the classroom than their NS colleagues, who were regarded as more outgoing, casual, and talkative.

A new perspective was offered by Nemtchinova (2005), who elicited host teachers' opinions regarding non-native student teachers doing their practice teaching in an MA TESOL program. NNESTs were generally perceived as well prepared and able to build good relationships with their students. However, several host teachers perceived a lack in self-confidence by NNESTs, generally visible through their excessively tough self-evaluations.

Bayyurt (2006) focused on cultural aspects in the teaching of EIL by NNESTs, and dealt with the perceptions of non-native EFL teachers towards culture, as well as whether and how culture should be included in the foreign language curriculum. Bayyurt's conclusion was that 'a successful non-native speaker model of a foreign language might help learners to overcome linguistic as well as cultural barriers in their language learning process' (Bayyurt, 2006: 244).

Finally, Llurda (2005) conducted a survey among TESOL program supervisors in North-American universities, in which participants were asked to give their views on the performance of non-native MA TESOL students in their practice teaching, in comparison to their native counter-parts. Non-native students appeared to be rather well considered, although a small group of them stood out as clearly lacking language proficiency. In a follow-up to that study (Llurda, unpublished manuscript), 14 super-visors were interviewed and most of them agreed on the lack of self-confidence experienced by many NNSs. The reasons given for this lack of self-confidence ranged from their own language skills to the environment, especially in ESL settings, which were regarded as being more demanding on NNS teachers than EFL settings.

The Connection Between NNESTs and EIL

In Llurda (2004a), I discussed the strong connections and interdependence existing between the teaching of EIL and NNESTs, as it was argued that NNESTs are naturally suited to promote EIL, and only the choice of EIL as the target paradigm can really empower NNESTs and set them in the right context for conducting their teaching task without having first to prove their competence, and so discard all possible doubts and criticisms by students, program administrators, and fellow teachers. As Jenkins (2007) pointed out, my approach at that time suggested a vision of EIL as though it consisted of a single uniform variety that could be described and taught in a prescriptive way. My current position refuses any prescriptivist approach to EIL and acknowledges the wide diversity among users. So, my point is that placing diversity embodied by EIL at the centre stage is clearly going to give NNSs a great deal of authority to teach the language. One may argue that NNSs have always had the right to claim ownership of the language (Widdowson, 1994), but repeated and diverse evidence shows that even now many people take the native speaker as the best teacher of a language. And certainly, as long as a native variety of English is used as a model, there will be NESTs who may look down on any NNEST. If, as Cook (2007) notes, none of the goals of ELT is to become a NS, it all falls on the teaching skills and capacities of the corresponding teacher, which will necessarily be a NNEST of that particular 'nativeless variety'. In that situation, NSs and NNSs will be on the same ground, with one extra advantage for NNSs, which is their multilingual experiences. NSs may of course share this condition and be multilingual themselves, but they will need to have some L2 learning and using experience (Ellis, 2006).

A similar argument is presented by Modiano (2005), in relation to cultural aspects associated with language learning. Modiano focuses on the Swedish context and criticizes the excessively British orientation in Swedish EFL materials. He further argues for a perspective that incorporates notions of interculturality, transculturalism and biculturalism, for which NNSs can take full responsibility. In many European countries, teachers of English are trained through their participation in programs that incorporate language training, linguistics, literature and cultural studies. However, as shown in Llurda (2004b), those programs often rely excessively on a monolingual and monocultural vision of the English speaking world, giving little heed to cultural and linguistic diversity. NNSs can do a lot to move the language beyond the exclusive domain of NSs' ownership. In fact, the implementation of an approach that focuses on English as an International Language depends on teachers' exposure to the different forms in which English may appear in international contexts, and their total support to the acceptance and use of EIL in English language classrooms. Unfortunately, that is not a frequent condition among NNESTs, as it will be shown along the next two sections. So, we must be cautious not to simply call all NNESTs fit to incorporate an EIL vision in the classroom just because their condition of non-native speakers makes them an optimal choice. We need therefore to consider what attitudes towards EIL are held by learners and teachers of English.

Attitudes of Learners Towards EIL

Studies looking at the attitudes of learners of English towards different varieties of the language have yielded a set of diverse results, depending on the particularities of the local settings. However, a common feature among learners of English from such distant contexts as Hong Kong (Luk, 1998), Italy (Pulcini, 1997), Denmark (Ladegaard & Sachdev, 2006), or

Austria (Dalton-Puffer *et al.*, 1997) was that they all showed a preference for RP accented British English over their local accents.

Kachru (1981) argued that negative attitudes towards foreign accented English by NSs may not be due to language factors but to stereotyped mental systems, and Trifonovitch (1981) further explained that many competent NNSs identify themselves with NSs rather than with other NNSs, adopting a rather strict and derogatory attitude towards fellow NNSs. The power of stereotypes was observed in many other studies, like Delamere (1996), who studied attitudes by American NSs toward different non-native varieties through the use of the matched-guise technique, which involved a two-time reading of the same text by the same person with the only difference that one of the readings had some grammatical errors. It was observed that grammar errors affected evaluations of readers in different ways depending on their accent, either French, Malay, Farsi, Arabic or Spanish. Llurda (2000) also illustrated the power of accent stereotypes on personality evaluations, and Lippi-Green (1997) provided a thorough discussion of accent discrimination and attitudes related to different English accents.

In their study involving Austrian students of English, Dalton-Puffer *et al.* (1997) found that students showed a preference for native varieties over their own accented variety. They explained these results by means of the constant encouragement on learners to imitate native norms. Additionally, participants with extended periods abroad appeared to be more willing to interact with accented speakers, thus suggesting a detachment of the native variety bias associated to increased contact with the native variety and increased competence in the language. The same results were found in a more recent study involving Catalan teachers of English (Llurda, 2008).

Attitudes towards different varieties of English have sometimes been associated with higher or lower degrees of intelligibility of those varieties. However, as Kachi (2004) notes:

> Even though the intelligibility of nonnative speech is lower than that of native speech, it is not very low in itself, in comparison with perceived comprehensibility. That is, listeners seem to be able to understand nonnative speech better than they say they can, while nonnative listeners tend to claim that they understand native English better than they actually do. (Kachi, 2004: 61)

Attitudes towards a language are dependent on several factors, among which the learner's mother tongue (Baker, 1992; Lasagabaster, 2003) and attendance to language classes (Huguet & Llurda, 2001). In the Catalan city of Lleida, Llurda *et al.* (2006) contrasted the attitudes towards the minority language (Catalan, which is strongly protected by the Catalan educational authorities), the majority language (Spanish, which is the language most massively used in the media and mainstream leisure activities), and a third very powerful but rather external language (English, taught to more than 90% of primary and secondary school students, but with very little presence in students' everyday life and social relations). The study used a Likert-scale questionnaire based on Baker's (1992). Overall attitudes towards languages were divided into three categories: favorable, neutral and unfavorable. For all three languages, unfavorable attitudes were minimal (around 2% for Catalan and Spanish, and nearly 8% for English). However, more important differences appeared when favorable attitudes were taken into account. Spanish was the language that received the widest support, with 68% of students showing favorable attitudes towards it, followed by Catalan (43%), and English trailed at the very end of the ranking (16%). Thus, even though attitudes towards English were not negative, they were not positive either. The high proportion of neutral attitudes (76%) showed a certain degree of indifference towards it. Students probably hear too often that one needs to learn English in modern society in order to succeed in their professional lives, but it looks as though they really do not care much for that language.

Another interesting insight arising from the same study was provided by the analysis of the effect of students' L1 (Catalan, Spanish, others) on their attitudes to the three different languages. Attitudes towards Spanish were rather positive for L1 speakers of Spanish and L1 speakers of other languages other than Spanish, Catalan or English. These two groups also held rather low attitudes towards Catalan. In contrast, L1 speakers of Catalan showed rather low attitudes towards Spanish, and very high attitudes towards Catalan. Attitudes towards English were the lowest in all groups except for L1 speakers of other languages, who ranked English between Spanish (the most positively rated) and Catalan. In sum, attitudes towards English were rather low for all students, with the particular remark that students of immigrant origin (whose L1 was neither Catalan or Spanish, nor English) rated English a little more favorably than students born and raised in Catalonia. Llurda *et al.* (2006) attributed these results to the low presence of English in Catalonia, and more particularly so in a mid-size city like Lleida. This is a rather relevant statement for the purposes of our present discussion, in which we will look at how English is presented in schools in the Expanding Circle (Kachru, 1983), either as an international language or as a native (i.e. British or American) language.

A very similar questionnaire was used by Huguet and Lapresta (2006), who analyzed attitudes towards five languages (Catalan, Spanish, Aragonese, French and English) in the Spanish community of Aragon. Although only Spanish is recognized as the official language in that community, in some parts of its territory the population are bilingual (Catalan/Spanish or Aragonese/Spanish). The study took into account a set of independent variables: area of residence (monolingual Spanish, bilingual Catalan/Spanish, bilingual Aragonese/Spanish); age of students (1st vs 4th ESO); social professional status (high, medium, low); and home language. Differences regarding attitudes towards English only appeared when the social professional status was considered, as 'high status' showed more positive attitudes than 'medium status' and 'low status'. No differences appeared between 'medium' and 'low'. Interestingly, this factor only influenced attitudes towards English, as no other language was affected by it.

Attitudes of NNESTs Towards EIL

Graddol (2006) convincingly argues that the traditional model of EFL teaching based on 19th century premises has failed in many aspects, and only a new approach based on English as a Lingua Franca can contribute to the improvement of English language learning worldwide. But given the preference for native varieties of English encountered among a great deal of learners of the language discussed in the previous section, one might wonder whether non-native teachers of English would fall for the same attitudes as other non-native speakers, or would rather embrace the new paradigm and change of attitude entailed in the international dimension of English.

The current trend in applied linguistics plus the extra beneficial status that NNESTs could gain from this new paradigm might suggest the existence of a complete support to EIL and lingua franca models (Seidlhofer, 2004). However, as Jenkins (2007) pervasively demonstrates, language teachers in general, and NNESTs in particular, hold attitudes towards EIL that are far from being enthusiastic. Tsui and Bunton (2000) analyzed over a thousand electronic messages sent by both NS and NNS English teachers in Hong Kong to conclude that those teachers looked for external sources of reliable information and their model for teaching was exonormative, as they never considered the possibility of turning to Hong Kong English as a possible model. In Sifakis' (2004) terms, they were norm-bound, and they looked for the norm in external, rather than domestic, sources. The majority of NNESTs 'either explicitly or implicitly accepted the NS as a source of authority' (Tsui & Bunton, 2000: 294), and they often had to 'cite codified sources and other sources as supporting evidence before putting forward their own views', and they as well had to 'preface their own personal opinions with hedges and qualifications, and to solicit views from fellow teachers as a signal that they did not consider their own words final' (Tsui & Bunton, 2000: 301). NESTs, instead, often relied on their own judgment, and 'they quite often overtly identified themselves on the network as native speakers as if to stress that this is the source of their authority' (Tsui & Bunton, 2000: 298).

Llurda and Huguet (2003) and Llurda (2008) attempted to discover NNESTs self-perceptions regarding aspects of language proficiency, language teaching methodology, and socio-political aspects related to the NS/NNS debate in the context of EIL. Those two articles analyzed the responses of 101 EFL teachers in Catalonia to a questionnaire dealing with their perceived language proficiency, language teaching ideology, and socio-political concerns regarding EIL and the role of non-native teachers in language teaching. In Llurda and Huguet (2003), some clear differences appeared between primary and secondary teachers, whereas Llurda (2008) observed different patterns between teachers who had spent long periods in English-speaking countries and those who hadn't. Combining the results of both studies, we find that primary school teachers tend to be more insecure regarding their level of proficiency in English, at the same time as they are more enthusiastic about endorsing the native speaker as the ideal teacher, and they are more willing to consider native varieties as the target variety in language classes. Similarly, teachers who had never visited or who had only spent up to three months in an English-speaking country, were more supportive of native norms and models. In any case, differences in self-perceptions seem to be somehow related to aspects of professional self-confidence, which I think is a powerful factor in defining non-native teachers' personalities and teaching practices.

On a more anecdotal level, I have heard some NNESTs praising other non-native speakers whose English accent sounded very close to native. When asking those teachers why sounding 'native' was such a good thing, provided those speakers would never become British citizens with a British identity, they often answered using expressions such as how 'beautiful' or how 'better' a British accent is. Sifakis and Sougari (2005) point in the same direction, as Greek teachers in their study identified NSs as 'the rightful owners of English' (Sifakis & Sougari, 2005: 481). Besides, they also found that primary education teachers were more prone on giving feedback on pronunciation than secondary teachers, a pattern that is very coherent with primary teachers' stronger dependency on native speaker norms found in Llurda and Huguet (2003).

In Llurda (2004b), I attempted to provide a rational explanation of why English teachers in Spain were so strongly governed by 'native models', and I traced it to the influence exerted from university English departments while training those students. My claim was that those university departments do typically take a native speaker orientation (be it British or American) by making them the undisputed model and object of study. The results reported in Llurda and Huguet (2003), Llurda (2008), and Sifakis and Sougari (2005), while not directly dwelling into the reasons for NNESTs perceptions, do actually minimize the training factor, as it is self-confidence which appears to be more responsible of the ultimate perception of oneself with regard to the native speaking community.

Teachers' position with regard to EIL is also expressed through their overall attitudes towards the teaching of culture in the English classroom, and their choices regarding what particular cultural information is selected for the classroom. Many English teachers do not feel comfortable with the inclusion of cultural aspects in their language lessons, and are even more reluctant to incorporate any cultural contents that are not related to the UK and the United States. Suggesting a way to incorporate a more international cultural component in EIL classrooms, Dogancay-Aktuna (2006: 291) argues for 'greater discussion of crosscultural variation in learning and teaching' as part of a 'comprehensive paradigm shift' in the TESOL curricula, and Sifakis recommends interspersing 'material that is culturally informed (...) in sensible doses', as well as 'using learners' metacognitive knowledge and raising their awareness on EIL-related matters' (Sifakis & Sougari, 2003: 66–67), whereas Bayyurt (2006) affirms there is still a lot of work ahead before NNESTs do naturally incorporate the concept of EIL in their classes.

The Need to Overcome NNESTs' Subordination to NS Models

And here we reach the closing section of this chapter, which incorporates its most relevant argument, namely that NNESTs suffer from a severe self-confidence problem, which at times is translated as fear of students catching them 'in fault', or at times it is simply expressed through an excess of fervor in defending the values of the NS, which may eventually lead to instances of self-hatred (Macaulay, 1975). Let us first visualize a situation in which both NSs and NNSs have the right to claim ownership over a particular good, namely the English language (Widdowson, 1994), but only one can get the real benefit of this property, especially in terms of getting well-paid jobs and enjoying professional status and prestige within their community. As stated above, the only way this situation can ever change is by NNESTs finally embracing a non-centered vision of the language, which they can really claim their own. However, many NNESTs do still remain attached to the old values and hierarchies establishing the NS as a model and a symbol of perfection in language use, reducing NNSs to perennial language *learners* and depriving them of recognition as legitimate language *users* (Cook, 2002, 2005). If non-native speakers of a language are regarded as *permanent learners*, they are denied any voice in determining their use of the language and they are naturally often invited to imitate NS models, which become the ultimate target of the learning process.

NNS teachers have typically spent many years learning the language and pursuing that unassailable NS model, often developing a kind of secret admiration for the person they will never be. On realising the impossibility of that goal, NNESTs have an important choice ahead, they can either turn to an EIL-based conception of the language, or they may stick to the old values. It is up to them to decide what side to go. If they stick to the old values, they will find themselves constantly looking for NESTs to assert their authority and give them a slight sign of appreciation. For many teachers of English in the world, being a NNEST has been an unavoidable fate they had to live with, the negative side of which they have tried very hard to minimize. Admiring the others' native condition and secretly hating their own non-nativeness is a sure bet for suffering from lack of self-confidence.

Only by acknowledging this inferiority complex can we account for the story provided by Medgyes (1994: 40) in which a group of Hungarian teachers attending a lecture given by a native speaker respectfully remain silent after the talk until a senior teacher says that 'non-native speakers had better not contaminate the air still resonant with the voice of a real native speaker'. Thus, NNESTs find themselves immersed in a schizofrenic situation (Medgyes, 1983), by means of which they find themselves hating what they are and loving what they can never be. This can actually explain why several NNESTs who have made an entire life career out of teaching English would answer that they would never hire a NNEST (that is, one of their kind) to be their personal teacher were they able to choose between a NEST and a NNEST (Llurda, 2008).

Fortunately, teachers do appear to show a reversal in this attitude when their self-confidence increases. Thus, an important question needs to be raised: How may a teacher's self-confidence be increased? I propose that the following three lines of action will help NNESTs increase their self-confidence and their appreciation of their own status as language teaching professionals:

(1) Teachers need to have a great number of opportunities to develop their language skills, and they need to be exposed to the target language long enough as to feel comfortable when speaking it. Teacher training must include a strong language component, and must as well develop teaching skills. Too often, there has been a tendency to believe that no special skills are required in teaching, and this has negatively affected both NESTs and NNESTS. For instance, many ELT jobs have been filled by monolingual NESTs with no particular training, or NNESTs with a degree in language teaching but insufficient language skills and no opportunities for using them. It is about time that all teachers (both NNESTs and NESTs) are given credit for the complexity of their profession, and that teaching is regarded as a serious business which requires intensive training and strict quality control.

(2) A high level of critical awareness regarding what it means to teach a language needs to be developed so as to avoid repetition of customary practices inherited from past experiences as language learners and established as the dominant commonsensical practices. In that sense, reading and discussion of books which critically discuss the implications of teaching English as an international language (e.g. Holliday, 2005; Jenkins, 2007) is a necessary condition for developing a critical sense of the complexities inherent in the teaching of such a global language as English. New approaches to teacher training need to be tried. For instance, following Ellis' (2006) claim that language teachers' content knowledge must include experience in learning and using an L2, it seems rather necessary for teacher training programs, and especially those mainly addressed to NSs, to incorporate foreign language learning modules. Also, as Sifakis (2007) shows, a transformative approach to teacher training that goes beyond a 'mere description of the established theories' can result in teachers' increased awareness of EIL characteristics and may enable them to 'open up to change by realizing and transforming their worldviews and perspectives about ESOL teaching' (Sifakis, 2007: 370).

(3) Engage NNESTs in discussions regarding EIL, and their own role in promoting a vision in which it is acceptable and desirable to use different non-native varieties of the language. European learners, for instance, tend to think of England as the place to go in order to learn the language, and Standard British English as the model to follow and imitate. This generalized perception is shared by many teachers of the

language, despite the fact that they have often experienced the paradox of interacting with some native British English speakers who may speak a fairly unintelligible variety of the language. Only by actively engaging teachers in discussions regarding the role of EIL and the renationalization of the language (McKay, 2003) can the idea that English is not restricted to one single country become a new paradigm in ELT and have an effective presence in the model of language taught in English language classrooms around the world.

Following these lines of action might hopefully liberate NNESTs from the burdening paradox of feeling downgraded for not being native speakers of the language, while at the same time they 'happily' set themselves as the guardians of purity of language use among other NNESTs who don't comply with native speaker norms.

If a teacher can (1) personally experience the diversity of English language usage, (2) reflect critically on language learning and teaching and (3) perceive the current turn in society towards multilingualism and the international acceptance of English as a language for international communication, rather than as a culturally loaded national language, they will successfully overcome the paradox of being denied the right to own the language and still love it. They will become rightful and powerful free users and teachers of English as an International Language.

Acknowledgements

I am very grateful to Lurdes Armengol, Josep M. Cots, Farzad Sharifian, and two anonymous reviewers for their insights and comments on an earlier draft of this chapter. All errors and shortcomings are exclusively my own.

References

Árva, V. and Medgyes, P. (2000) Native and non-native teachers in the classroom. *System* 28, 355–372.
Baker, C. (1992) *Attitudes and Language*. Clevedon: Multilingual Matters.
Bayyurt, Y. (2006) Non-native English language teachers' perspective on culture in English as a Foreign Language classrooms. *Teacher Development* 10 (2), 233–247.
Benke, E. and Medgyes, P. (2005) Differences in teaching behaviour between native and non-native speaker teachers: As seen by the learners. In E. Llurda (ed.) *Non-Native Language Teachers. Perceptions, Challenges, and Contributions to the Profession* (pp. 195–215). New York: Springer.
Braine, G. (ed.) (1999) *Non-Native Educators in English Language Teaching*. Mahwah, NJ: Lawrence Erlbaum Associates.

Braine, G. (ed.) (2005) *Teaching English to the World*. Mahwah, NJ: Lawrence Erlbaum.

Brutt-Griffler, J. and Samimy, K.K. (2001) Transcending the nativeness paradigm. *World Englishes* 20, 99–106.

Chomsky, N. (1965) *Aspects of the Theory of Syntax*. Cambridge, MA: MIT Press.

Cook, V. (2002) Background to the L2 user. In V. Cook (ed.) *Portraits of the L2 User* (pp. 1–28). Clevedon: Multilingual Matters.

Cook, V. (2005) Basing teaching on the L2 user. In E. Llurda (ed.) *Non-Native Language Teachers. Perceptions, Challenges, and Contributions to the Profession* (pp. 47–61). New York: Springer.

Cook, V. (2007) The goals of ELT: Reproducing native-speakers or promoting multicompetence among second language users? In J. Cummins and C. Davison (eds) *International Handbook of English Language Teaching* (pp. 237–248). New York: Springer.

Cots, J.M. and Díaz, J.M. (2005) Constructing social relationships and linguistic knowledge through non-native-speaking teacher talk. In E. Llurda (ed.) *Non-Native Language Teachers. Perceptions, Challenges, and Contributions to the Profession* (pp. 85–105). New York: Springer.

Dalton-Puffer, C., Kaltenboeck, G. and Smit, U. (1997) Learner attitudes and L2 pronunciation in Austria. *World Englishes* 16 (1), 115–128.

Davies, A. (1991) *The Native Speaker in Applied Linguistics*. Edinburgh: Edinburgh University Press.

Davies, A. (2003) *The Native Speaker: Myth and Reality*. Clevedon: Multilingual Matters.

Delamere, T. (1996) The importance of IL errors with respect to stereotyping by native speakers in their judgements of SL learners' performance. *System* 24 (3), 279–297.

Dogancay-Aktuna, S. (2006) Expanding the socio-cultural knowledge base of TESOL teacher education. *Language, Culture and Curriculum* 19 (3), 278–295.

Ellis, E. (2006) Language learning experience as a contributor to ESOL teacher cognition. *TESL-EJ* 10 (1), A-3.

Graddol, D. (2006) *English Next*. London: British Council.

Holliday, A. (2005) *The Struggle to Teach English as an International Language*. Oxford: Oxford University Press.

Huguet, A. and Lapresta, C. (2006) Las actitudes lingüísticas en Aragón. Una visión desde la escuela. *Estudios de sociolingüística* 7 (2), 265–288.

Huguet, A. and Llurda, E. (2001) Language attitudes of school children in two Catalan/Spanish bilingual communities. *International Journal of Bilingual Education and Bilingualism* 4 (4), 267–282.

Inbar-Lourie, O. (2005) Mind the gap: Self and perceived native speaker identities of EFL teachers. In E. Llurda (ed.) *Non-Native Language Teachers. Perceptions, Challenges, and Contributions to the Profession* (pp. 265–281). New York: Springer.

Jenkins, J. (2007) *English as a Lingua Franca: Attitude and Identity*. Oxford: Oxford University Press.

Kachi, R. (2004) Factors predicting native and nonnative listeners' evaluative reactions to Japanese English. Unpublished doctoral dissertation, Ohio State University.

Kachru, B.B. (1981) The pragmatics of non-native varieties of English. In L.E. Smith (ed.) *English for Cross-Cultural Communication*. London: Macmillan.

Kachru, B. (1983) *The Indianization of English: The English Language in India*. Oxford: Oxford University Press.

Ladegaard, H.J. and Sachdev, I. (2006) 'I like the Americans ... But I certainly don't aim for an American accent': Language attitudes, vitality and foreign language learning in Denmark. *Journal of Multilingual and Multicultural Development* 27 (2), 91–108.

Lasagabaster, D. (2003) Attitudes towards English in the Basque autonomous community. *World Englishes* 22 (4), 585–597.

Lasagabaster, D. and Sierra, J.M. (2002) University students' perceptions of native and non-native speaker teachers of English. *Language Awareness* 11, 132–142.

Lasagabaster, D. and Sierra, J.M. (2005) What do students think about the pros and cons of having a native speaker teacher? In E. Llurda (ed.) *Non-Native Language Teachers. Perceptions, Challenges, and Contributions to the Profession* (pp. 217–241). New York: Springer.

Lippi-Green, R. (1997) *English with an Accent*. New York: Routledge.

Liu, J. (1999) From their own perspectives: The impact of non-native ESL professionals on their students. In G. Braine (ed.) *Non-Native Educators in English Language Teaching* (pp. 159–176). Mahwah, NJ: Lawrence Erlbaum Associates.

Llurda, E. (2000) Effects of intelligibility, and speaking rate on judgements of non-native speakers' personalities. *IRAL – International Review of Applied Linguistics* 38, 289–299.

Llurda, E. (2004a) Non-native-speaker teachers and English as an International Language. *International Journal of Applied Linguistics* 14 (3), 314–323.

Llurda, E. (2004b) 'Native/non-native speaker' discourses in foreign language university departments in Spain. In B. Dendrinos and B. Mitsikopoulou (eds) *Policies for Linguistic Pluralism and the Teaching of Languages in Europe* (pp. 237–243). Athens, Greece: University of Athens Press.

Llurda, E. (2005) Non-native TESOL students as seen by practicum supervisors. In E. Llurda (ed.) *Non-Native Language Teachers. Perceptions, Challenges, and Contributions to the Profession* (pp. 131–154). New York: Springer.

Llurda, E. (2008) The effects of stays abroad on self-perceptions of non-native EFL teachers. In S. Dogancay-Aktuna and J. Hardman (eds) *Global English Language Teacher Education* (pp. 99–111). Alexandria, VA: TESOL.

Llurda, E. (unpublished manuscript) Practicum supervisors' insights regarding non-native teachers in training.

Llurda, E. and Huguet, A. (2003) Self-awareness in NNS EFL primary and secondary school teachers. *Language Awareness* 13, 220–235.

Llurda, E., Lasagabaster, D. and Cots, J.M. (2006) From bilingualism to multilingualism in schools in Catalonia: A study of language attitudes among immigrant and non-immigrant secondary school students. Paper presented at the *Sociolinguistics Symposium 16*. University of Limerick, 5–8 July 2006.

Luk, J. (1998) Hong Kong students' awareness of and reactions to accent differences. *Multilingua* 17 (1), 93–106.

Macaulay, R.K.S. (1975) Negative prestige, linguistic insecurity, and linguistic self-hatred. *Lingua* 36 (2–3), 147–161.

McKay, S. (2003) Toward an appropriate EIL (English as an International Language) pedagogy: Re-examining common assumptions. *International Journal of Applied Linguistics* 13 (1), 1–22.

Medgyes, P. (1983) The schizophrenic teacher. *ELT Journal* 37 (1), 2–6.
Medgyes, P. (1992) Native or non-native: Who's worth more? *ELT Journal*, 46 (4). Reprinted in T. Hedge and N. Whitney (eds) (1996) *Power, Pedagogy & Practice* (pp. 31–42). Oxford: Oxford University Press.
Medgyes, P. (1994) *The Non-Native Teacher*. London: Macmillan Publishers (1999, 2nd edn). Ismaning: Max Hueber Verlag.
Modiano, M. (2005) Cultural studies, foreign language teaching and learning practices, and the NNS practitioner. In E. Llurda (ed.) *Non-Native Language Teachers. Perceptions, Challenges, and Contributions to the Profession* (pp. 25–43). New York: Springer.
Nemtchinova, E. (2005) Host teachers' evaluations of nonnative-English-speaking teacher trainees – A perspective from the classroom. *TESOL Quarterly* 39 (2), 235–262.
Paikeday, T.M. (1985) *The Native Speaker is Dead!* Toronto: Paikeday Publishing Inc.
Pulcini, V. (1997) Attitudes toward the spread of English in Italy. *World Englishes* 16 (1), 77–85.
Rampton, M.B.H. (1990) Displacing the 'native speaker': Expertise, affiliation, and inheritance. *ELT Journal* 44 (2), 97–101.
Reves, T. and Medgyes, P. (1994) The non-native English speaking EFL/ESL teacher's self-image: An international survey. *System* 22 (3), 353–367.
Seidlhofer, B. (2004) Research perspectives on teaching English as a lingua franca. *Annual Review of Applied Linguistics* 24, 209–239.
Sifakis, N.C. (2004) Teaching *EIL* – Teaching *International* or *Intercultural* English? What teachers should know. *System* 32, 237–250.
Sifakis, N. (2007) The education of teachers of English as a lingua franca: A transformative perspective. *International Journal of Applied Linguistics* 17 (3), 355–375.
Sifakis, N. and Sougari, A.M. (2003) Facing the globalisation challenge in the realm of English language teaching. *Language and Education* 17 (1), 59–71.
Sifakis, N.C. and Sougari, A. (2005) Pronunciation issues and EIL pedagogy in the periphery: A survey of Greek state school teachers' beliefs. *TESOL Quarterly* 39 (3), 467–488.
Trifonovitch, G. (1981) English as an international language: An attitudinal approach. In L. Smith (ed.) *English for Cross Cultural Communication*. London: Macmillan.
Tsui, A.B.M. and Bunton, D. (2000) The discourse and attitudes of English language teachers in Hong Kong. *World Englishes* 19 (3), 287–303.
Widdowson, H.G. (1994) The ownership of English. *TESOL Quarterly* 28, 377–389.

Chapter 7

'I Thought I was an Easterner; it Turns Out I am a Westerner!': EIL Migrant Teacher Identities

BOJANA PETRIĆ

Introduction

> Embassy of the Russian Federation. Budapest, 2000. I am applying for a visa for a trip to Samara, where I am invited to teach a course for university lecturers of English.
> **Consular official:** What is the purpose of your visit?
> **BP:** Teaching.
> **Consular official:** What will you be teaching?
> **BP:** English.
> **Consular official:** A Serb going to teach Russians English?!

The spread of English and its status as a global language have led, among other changes, to increased mobility of English language educators. While traditionally ELT jobs outside of one's country were reserved for native speaking professionals, more recently, English teachers of various nationalities have begun to cross borders and find employment in English and non-English speaking countries alike. Although precise data on this trend are unavailable, it is likely that this type of migrant teacher is characteristic of English more than other languages.

As the exchange above illustrates, there is something counterintuitive about migrant English teachers in non-English speaking countries other than their own. They are native speakers of neither English nor their students' language, which may lead to the conclusion that they lack the advantages attributed to both types of teachers (for a discussion of these advantages, see, e.g. Benke & Medgyes, 2005; Braine, 1999; Llurda, 2004;

Medgyes, 1999; Seidlhofer, 1996). Yet, their presence in the profession suggests otherwise. Studying the case of migrant English teachers in third countries may therefore provide a fruitful way to explore the nature of teaching expertise and the interplay of different types of cultural content in English classrooms.

This chapter presents an initial exploration of the case of English teachers from non-English speaking countries teaching English in another non-English speaking country, here referred to as migrant teachers of English. Using in-depth interviews, I investigate how such teachers construct their identities in their classrooms and what role, if any, their students' and their own linguistic and cultural backgrounds play in their teaching of English.

Method

This study is based on interviews with four English language teachers from non-English speaking countries living and working in Hungary. I conducted semi-structured interviews, lasting about an hour each, covering the following themes: the participants' educational and teaching backgrounds; their perspectives on their position as non-Hungarian non-native English teachers in Hungary, particularly in comparison to their colleagues from English speaking countries, on the one hand, and Hungarian teachers of English, on the other; and the role of the students' and their own language and culture in their teaching.

The interviews were transcribed and analyzed by repeated reading and coding. The participants' responses were first grouped thematically according to the areas outlined above, which was followed by identifying relevant points, common patterns and points of divergence in the participants' opinions and experiences. Finally, the participants' opinions were sought on my interpretation of the interview data.

Participants and the context

The four teachers of English in this study – who I will refer to as Jadwiga, Svetla, Elena and Ana – obtained an English teaching degree and started teaching in their home countries prior to moving to Hungary, where they continued active professional development. None are economic migrants as all moved to Hungary to join their partners or husbands. They come from four Slavic countries (Poland, Bulgaria, Russia and Macedonia), which used to be part of the former socialist world and are now experiencing transition, as is the host country itself.

As for the differences, Jadwiga and Svetla moved to Hungary from Poland and Bulgaria, respectively, in the early 1980s and are now in their late 40s, while Elena and Ana, who come from Macedonia and Russia, respectively, moved in the late 1990s and are now in their early 30s. There is a difference in the length of acculturation to the host country but also in the sociopolitical situation in Hungary after the fall of the Iron Curtain. When Jadwiga and Svetla arrived, Hungary was part of the Eastern bloc, where migration of professional labor was relatively rare and largely restricted to its confines. As Jadwiga says, she was the only Pole in the south of the country at the time. Foreigners enjoyed a certain prestige, and both Jadwiga and Svetla stress the positive responses they received as foreigners. This was partly related to their origin: as Jadwiga says, 'Poland had a positive image due to political and cultural reasons'. Before 1989, the ELT sector was, for the most part, state owned, and both Jadwiga and Svetla found employment in state institutions; Jadwiga in the English department at a university and Svetla in a secondary school, where they still teach.

When Elena and Ana moved to Hungary, the political map of the region had changed considerably. The fall of the Iron Curtain and the shift towards the market economy were accompanied by an influx of foreigners and a dramatic change in the status of English. In education, the magnitude of this change can be illustrated by the rise in the numbers of children attending English classes: in 1989 less than 3% of primary school pupils had access to English instruction, while in 1997 this rose to 40% (Medgyes & Miklósy, 2000). Initially, the demand for English teachers was so enormous that even unqualified backpackers from English-speaking countries could easily find a teaching job in the booming ELT sector; however, by the late 1990s the shortage of teachers had decreased, especially in cities, due to an increase in the numbers of teachers graduating from the new teacher training colleges. Although the changes after 1989 created more opportunities for English teachers, job security, in fact, decreased: as Elena says, 'it's easy to get a few classes here and there but hard to get a permanent teaching job'. Both Elena and Ana have taught in several privately owned institutions. Currently, Elena teaches at an English-medium foreign-affiliated business school, while Ana teaches at a private language school offering courses to individuals and companies.

The Participants' Language Repertoires and Affiliation

Before discussing the teachers' self-presentation practices in the classroom, it is important to overview their language repertoires and attitudes towards the languages they use in everyday life. For this analysis, it is useful to apply Rampton's (1990) concepts of language inheritance, expertise and affiliation. All four participants inherited only one language, the one I refer to as L1 for convenience. The use of L1 is restricted to home for Svetla and Jadwiga (Svetla: 'I tend to speak Bulgarian when I am tired, at the end of the day, as a kind of relaxation'), while Elena states she does not use Macedonian in Hungary at all. Only Ana has Russian-speaking friends in the country.

As for expertise, all four emphasize their life-long commitment to studying English, best illustrated by Ana, who says: 'I've studied English all my life'. In terms of their use of English, the two pairs of teachers differ considerably: for Jadwiga and Svetla, English is the language of the classroom and 'professional things' (Jadwiga), while in all other situations, they use Hungarian, except for home, where L1 is also used. Yet, they both stress their inadequate expertise in Hungarian, especially for writing and speaking in public. In Elena's and Ana's lives, English plays a much more prominent role: they use it at work, for socializing and in the wider environment. Both lived in an English-speaking country for four years, Elena as a child and Ana as a teenager, and can pass as native speakers of English (Piller, 2002). Thus the nature of their expertise may be different from Jadwiga's and Svetla's, since they learnt English both in classroom and naturalistic settings. When asked whether they consider themselves as native speakers, Ana describes herself as 'closer to the native speaker due to the way I speak without a Russian accent' and 'professionally native', while Elena labels herself 'quasi-native' (which echoes Medgyes' (1999) 'pseudonatives'), saying:

> I am sort of ambivalent about it. It comes as naturally to me as Macedonian does, so in that way I guess, but it's hard to justify it with just four years. (Elena)

In contacts with the larger environment, both use some Hungarian (they rate their proficiency as intermediate) as well as English. In casual contacts, Ana sometimes finds it easier to respond to the unavoidable 'where are you from?' question by presenting herself as a person from an English-speaking country. Elena even says that she lives in 'a bubble full of people who are speaking English' and that 'there are days when [she] forget[s] she is in Hungary'.

In terms of affiliation, Svetla, Elena and Ana show attachment to both English and their L1s, although data for this aspect are somewhat sketchy. Elena talks about the two languages coming equally 'naturally' to her; Svetla juxtaposes her desire to learn English (Norton, 1997) to the practical need to learn Hungarian (Svetla: 'English I always wanted to learn. Hungarian was a "must" for me'), while Ana's attachment to English is related to her professional, teacherly self ('professionally native'). However, Jadwiga's case shows that expertise and professional dealing with English do not necessarily imply social identification with it:

> In English I am not myself (...) I am myself in Polish and in Hungarian. (Jadwiga)

> What I would think of as good English communicates such attitudes and values which are absolutely not part of my identity, who I am. (Jadwiga)

When comparing her two L2s, English and Hungarian, Jadwiga stresses that her expertise in English makes her 'feel more secure' when using it; however, despite lower expertise in Hungarian, it is the language she affiliates with:

> I feel Hungarian much better, certain Hungarian expressions, Hungarian mentality beyond, behind the language, all that is expressive, attitudinal, interpersonal is much closer – absolutely – in Hungarian, not English. (Jadwiga)

As will be seen, patterns of affiliation are closely related to the ways teachers represent themselves in their classrooms.

Self-representation in the Classroom

The growing literature on language and identity (e.g. Block, 2007; De Fina *et al.*, 2006; Norton, 2000), and language teaching and identity in particular (Duff & Uchida, 1997) rests on the common assumption that individuals have multiple identities, reflecting their belonging to different social groups. Of direct relevance to the discussion of migrant teacher identities is the thesis that identities are not fixed but negotiated in interactions with others, in which individuals highlight different aspects of their identities depending on the situation. This study looks at only one aspect of teachers' classroom identities: that related to the fact that they are foreigners teaching English in a third country. Discussing the situation of non-native teachers of English teaching in their own countries, Medgyes (1999: 37) pointed to such teachers' 'double-barrelled nature', that is, the fact that '[b]y birth we represent our native language and culture, but by profession we are obliged to represent a foreign language with its cultural load'. Teachers are thus confronted with a dilemma about the identity they should project in the classroom. In the case of non-native English teachers in third countries, such dilemmas become more complex with the wider range of identification and self-representation options. How migrant

English teachers present themselves in terms of their national background may reflect various factors, including their views of their role as teachers, linguistic and cultural affiliations, perceptions of students' expectations and of wider social issues, some of which may be conflicting.

The teachers in this study markedly differ in self-representation practices concerning their national background. Jadwiga and Svetla are quite open about their origins:

> They know that I am Polish and I also say that I am happy that I am Polish. (Jadwiga)

> I usually introduce myself and tell them about my origin, my nationality. (Svetla)

They also feel accepted by their students as foreign teachers of English:

> I think [students] appreciate that I am honest, that I am not pretending to be somebody who I am not. (Jadwiga)

> [Students] always show interest in my personality and my nationality; I think it's memorable for them. (Svetla)

In contrast, Elena and Ana are uneasy about telling their students where they are from. Elena's statement aptly illustrates her concerns about her professional image:

> When I say that I am Macedonian, I immediately have to justify it. *But I grew up in London!* (Elena)

Ana does not reveal her national origin to her students and consciously tries to minimize its role when teaching:

> I try not to define myself too much. I try to stay in the background, and if my Russianness comes out in any way, I try to subdue it. (Ana)

The stark contrast between Jadwiga's and Svetla's matter-of-fact, even proud manner of relating their origin to their students and Elena's and Ana's unease and reluctance to address the topic is a result of a variety of factors, of which I will discuss only two: native-speakerism (Holliday, 2005) and the teacher's awareness of her country's image in the host country, which may have a bearing on her relationship with her students through mechanisms of national stereotyping. Discussion of more general factors that may explain the difference between the two pairs of teachers, such as changes in global migration patterns leading to the emergence of new types of migrants living in 'transnational social spaces' (see, e.g. Block, 2007), are – while important – outside of the scope of this chapter.

Native-Speakerism

Native-speakerism, the ideology behind the privileged status of native speakers as language teachers, particularly affects teachers working in the private sector, where the myth of the superiority of the native speaker is used as bait for paying students. Ana's case illustrates this well since her school 'places emphasis on native speaking teachers'. Although she easily got a job there as a 'near native', the school discourages her from telling students where she is from. Consequently, Ana is 'professionally native'. She is aware that students 'come for the exotic experience of meeting the native speaker' and recognises that part of her task is to deliver that experience: 'I don't want them to walk away thinking that I am Russian and not a native speaker', which is why she 'avoid[s] [students'] questions' about her background. Elena also experienced native-speakerism. She describes her unsuccessful applications for jobs where native speakers were sought: 'they saw my name and would chuck out the CV without reading it'. She eventually found employment in an international chain of language schools by using passing practices, that is, her impeccable British accent: 'I phoned them first and didn't send the CV'. When the job interviewers realized that she was a Macedonian national, 'they surprisingly said *Ok, you are a native speaker according to us*'. She was then asked what she would do if a student told her s/he preferred a native speaker for a teacher. Her initial response about the years spent in the UK was interrupted by the interviewer, who said 'No, you tell them you ARE a native speaker' (Elena). Both Ana and Elena are highly critical of the native speaker bias in the teaching profession, listing numerous examples of unqualified native speaking 'teacher amateurs' (Ana). Their cases also show, however, that native-speakerism is beginning to show cracks as the definition of the native speaker is becoming increasingly unclear. While language schools justify their preference for native speakers by students' demand for them, both Ana and Elena report that students who knew their backgrounds did not mind because 'to them, the most important thing is that they can learn' (Ana). In fact, their students, just like Svetla's and Jadwiga's, were curious and showed interest in them:

> I think for them it's refreshing if a foreigner comes along. They come into the classroom and there is somebody different, they think I have a funny name and I look different. (Elena)

Growing numbers of migrant teachers, often hard to place and label, will likely contribute to further destabilization of the native teacher concept.

Teachers' Awareness of Their Country's Image in the Host Country

The teacher's awareness of the relations between her own and her students' country is another powerful factor impacting on her self-representation in the classroom. As shown earlier, Jadwiga was aware of the positive image Poland had in Hungary in the 1980s. Today, both countries are members of the European Union, both belonging to Central Europe, which places Jadwiga and her students in a shared cultural and sociopolitical framework, with which she strongly identifies:

> I am sure that students can tell, apart from my proficiency in English, that I am not a person from the West, that I am Central European. It's in my gestures, in my reactions. (Jadwiga)

Ana's case illustrates the opposite situation. She is aware that 'many [Hungarians] still feel resentful towards the Russians and associate Russia with the Soviet Union', which was seen as the oppressor during the Cold War. Explaining why she does 'not think of [her]self as Russian as a teacher', she makes references to political events, such as the 1956 Hungarian uprising against the Soviets and the recent visit of Russia's President Putin, the first visit of a Russian president to Hungary after 1989, and states: 'I try not to get into that'. She prefers not to reveal her national origin so as 'not to get into the politics and ideology' and 'to avoid conflict', because 'talking about the details of one's nationality may not have positive effects'.

Instead, she considers that her role is 'to be neutral, only a medium of the language and nothing else', because 'as a teacher, you perform'. In constructing her classroom self, she highlights those experiences and aspects of her identity which have the potential to support her teaching of English and imparting related cultural knowledge. She draws on her experience of living in the United States, which enables her to provide the students with 'authentic information' on details of everyday life, such as the meaning of 'the brown bag for booze'. The lived experience of the language also helps her teach grammar. She compares the abstractness of grammar knowledge learnt from books to the ability to feel when to use the present perfect. Being able to act as a source of 'authentic information' about both language and culture, she feels 'like a Westerner when with students although [she is] from the East'. She also feels that she is 'different in [students'] mind[s]' than her Hungarian colleagues, because 'they perceive [her] as a foreigner'.

There is, however, a limit to performing as a professional native. Ana admits that if students are interested in issues such as elections, she needs to find sources of relevant information.

In some cases, however, her Russianness becomes a visible part of her classroom self:

> I have a group of students in a X company where I teach, it's a group of adults, probably in their 50s, and they have had the full experience of the Soviet regime, and they know a lot about Russia and Russian words, so if we talk in class, we often talk about politics and culture. (Ana)

Although earlier Ana stated that she avoided 'getting into the politics and ideology', with this particular group she does exactly that. This can be explained by her perception of the students' experiences of and attitudes towards what her national origin may represent as positive, which allows her to use the common cultural framework based on experiences from the formerly shared ideological and cultural system. In the case of this group, then, her Russianness is part of her classroom self, and, as will be seen in the next section, has a role to play in her teaching of English.

In sum, in constructing classroom identities, migrant teachers highlight those aspects of their selves and experiences they believe are useful for teaching and will be accepted and appreciated by their students. In so doing, they may prefer not to disclose their national origin due to the pressures of native-speakerism in their institutions, in which case it is partly an economic strategy, and if they perceive the relationship between their own and the host country as potentially harmful to their image. Importantly, these factors may affect the same teacher negatively in one teaching situation but not in another, even within the same institution.

Teachers' L1 and Cultural Background in Teaching English

Migrant teachers' L1 and cultural background, being different from both English and their students', may be thought of as irrelevant in teaching English, especially if teachers are reluctant to reveal their national origin. However, the participants' accounts suggest that their L1 backgrounds do play a role, although in different ways: Jadwiga and Svetla tend to use it as a teaching tool, while Elena and Ana draw on it as a background resource.

Migrant teachers may refer to their L1 and culture as a teaching tool to help students develop an awareness of different linguistic and cultural frameworks. Jadwiga explains that her use of Polish examples in the classroom 'helps [students] understand the link between culture and language'. In the following example, she both foregrounds her national identity and uses it to address a teaching point: 'Sometimes I say *As a Pole, I feel this way about that issue* or *We in Poland say . . .*' (Jadwiga). At the same time, she also provides students with a model of an expert user of English with a cultural identity unrelated to English. Similarly, Svetla notes that she does not only refer to the culture related to English-speaking countries but also includes elements specific to the Hungarian and Bulgarian social realities and lifestyles. 'I actually compare three cultures', she states, since that 'contributes to language learning and personal development'. For example, in a lesson on housing, she uses examples of houses in the UK and the United States provided in the textbook but also describes houses typical in Bulgaria and elicits descriptions of Hungarian houses. In this way, what is taught is 'more memorable' because 'students like these real things'.

Direct use of the teacher's L1 is also noted when it helps illustrate a teaching point:

> I would even use bits of the [Polish] language (. . .) There is a big contrast phonetically, and when I switch [from English to Polish], my voice sounds softer, higher, perhaps more like a child. (Jadwiga)

The contrast is also in terms of the register: the switch from 'someone speaking English professionally, with terminology and so on' to 'something very private' where she 'reveal[s] some kind of more vulnerable part of [her]self' is immediately noticeable to the students and provides a memorable illustration of the linguistic features taught.

Elena and Ana tend to use their L1s and L1-related cultural references in teaching English indirectly, drawing on them conceptually; however, the process remains internal and invisible to the students. Elena describes the role of her L1 in terms of having access to a different linguistic system, which gives her 'another framework to work by' in that it makes her 'aware that different languages might have different ways of achieving the same thing'. She sees a direct benefit of such awareness for teaching English:

> It makes me more aware that when explaining constructions I'd need to give a bit more attention to certain aspects, saying that this particular tense would be more appropriate for situations where such and such things happen. (Elena)

Having an L1 other than English helps Elena not to take features of English for granted, as logical or natural, in the way a monolingual speaker may do, that is, it makes her multicompetent (Cook, 1992). She refers to the benefit of knowing another language in general terms: 'it's the language itself, whether it's Macedonian or another, it doesn't matter'. In contrast, Ana sees the knowledge of Russian, specifically, as a tool that helps her understand the students' language, due to some similarities in grammatical features and common roots of words. She thus uses Russian to decipher students' errors or communicative intentions in English. In addition, with students who know she is Russian, she 'would tell them about the [Russian] language' if 'they are genuinely interested'. She illustrates this with an episode from a lesson in which the students were reading a passage from Oscar Wilde's *The Importance of Being Earnest* in which the characters were served cucumber sandwiches. The discussion that followed moved from the significance of the detail about cucumber sandwiches to numerous Hungarian varieties of pickled cucumbers, which students were eager to explain. One type, *kovászos* cucumber, made only in the summer, was particularly difficult for students to explain until Ana suddenly realized the similarity of the Hungarian word *kovász* to the Russian *kvass*, a fermented summer drink, made in a similar way. This led them to discuss similar words in the two languages.

In addition to linguistic resources, teachers may draw on cultural frameworks related to their L1 background:

> The main reason why I think the Russianness plays an important role is that … because … er … since the Soviet times the two countries sort of shared the same sort of political regime, the same sort of values. There are still remains of the common ideological framework, the way people think. (Ana)

This common framework enables her 'to understand some things that a Westerner would find strange' in Hungary and also 'to recognise what would be strange to Hungarians' in English speaking countries. This is not dissimilar to Jadwiga's reference to the common Central European framework. The main difference, as shown in the previous section, is that, in Ana's case, references to the common framework may be indirect, except with groups of students such as the one discussed above.

Students' L1 and Culture in Teaching English

Despite different levels of proficiency in their students' L1, all four teachers report using the Hungarian language and references to Hungary in their EIL classrooms to some extent, primarily to create rapport with their students. Jadwiga's use of Hungarian words and examples is motivated by her desire 'to get closer to the students' and 'to reduce distance', even though she is aware that her Hungarian is only 'domestic'. Hungarian 'creates a common ground' between Jadwiga and her students due to its ability to invoke a sense of 'our reality' (reflecting her reference to the Central European identity), 'something more personal', which has 'relevance to [students'] lives'. The advantages of using Hungarian outweigh the potential loss of face for her, as the students 'somehow tolerate [her] mistakes'.

Ana also uses Hungarian to create rapport but based on a different foundation:

> I sometimes drop a Hungarian word. It's fun if I say something wrong or mispronounce the word. (Ana)

She makes a bridge to the students by drawing on their shared experience of learning a language, which involves making mistakes. Having this kind of empathy with students is often quoted as one of the advantages of non-native teachers since they, too, were once learners of the language they teach (Braine, 1999; Medgyes, 1999; Seidlhofer, 1996). Ana's example shows that her current efforts to learn Hungarian may even more readily provide the experience necessary to relate to the students' process of learning English. In addition, by presenting herself as a learner of her students' language, she reverses the teacher-student relationship and gives her students – albeit temporarily – the opportunity to be experts in the classroom.

Another rationale for the use of Hungarian mentioned by the teachers refers to more effective teaching, particularly ensuring comprehension (Svetla: 'when it's important for everybody to grasp the exact meaning') and using a shortcut in explanations (Elena: 'If I know the word, I'd nod and say *Yes, you've got it*'). Even without direct reference to Hungarian, teachers' cultural knowledge gained by living in Hungary may help them predict students' learning difficulties. Ana gives an example of the confusion among her students caused by the word *pie chart*, which she immediately understood, having noticed that Hungarian pies are square, not round. In this respect, the ways migrant teachers and Hungarian teachers of English use Hungarian do not seem to differ considerably, except, obviously, in their proficiency levels in Hungarian.

The teachers also see advantages to not being proficient in Hungarian:

> Students can't rely on me switching to Hungarian, which forces them to speak English in all circumstances. (Ana)

Elena similarly tries 'to downplay [her] knowledge of Hungarian deliberately in order to make them use English'. The teachers have developed techniques based on their present or past lack of knowledge of Hungarian. Ana inquires about the Hungarian culture and words, which involves students in genuine communication and increases their motivation to use English. Svetla tells her students anecdotes from her early days in Hungary to show them how pragmatic mistakes may sound awkward to native speakers. She tells of an anecdote about an informal visit during which she used a Hungarian expression for declining an offer with an English word order. Such vignettes are amusing to students, but they also enable them to see their own language in a detached way:

> The students never think of this, and when I say it, they say *Oh, yes! Now that you are saying this, yes, it is like that [in Hungarian]!* (Svetla)

Only one incidence of negative experiences related to the lack of proficiency in the host language was mentioned. Svetla recounts her early days of teaching English, when 'translation was a very important part of teaching' in Hungary. Her inadequacy to deal with the task and the need to rely on the help of her Hungarian colleagues to check students' homework involving translation made her 'feel vulnerable' because of her students' potential reactions ('You don't speak Hungarian well, so what do you do?'). However, her teacher education based on Lozanov's suggestopedia method and early teaching practice in Bulgaria, which instilled in her the belief that avoiding L1 in the classroom is 'the only way to teach English', gave her the confidence to deal with the situation:

> I always explained to the students that my purpose was to teach them English and I felt quite confident in what I was doing in English. As far as Hungarian was concerned, I was not a teacher of Hungarian, so they had to bear with it. In particular, I was trying to explain the advantages of using the target language in the classroom. But honestly, it was rooted in my education and my early practice. (Svetla)

In justifying her approach, Svetla was also responding to expectations to apply a different teaching method. This illustrates the potential difficulties migrant teachers may face due to differences in teacher education and methodologies between their own and the host country. Unlike the native teacher, whose teaching expertise is rarely questioned as it is assumed to be a 'natural' part of being a native speaker, the migrant teacher may need to find a balance between her teaching credo and the expectations in the host country if the ELT cultures differ.

As can be seen, teachers see advantages in both using Hungarian (regardless of their proficiency level) and avoiding its use in the classroom. Migrant teachers may move between the native speaker model, with its

emphasis on avoidance of L1, supported by dominant teaching methodologies, and the model of the teacher who shares the same L1 as her students.
In the former case, they use their foreignness as a basis for developing
students' interest in genuine communication in English, whereas in the
latter they rely on the power of the students' L1 to create rapport. However,
as shown, this is not a matter of completely free choice but is partly the
result of various external factors.

Conclusions

This case study of migrant English teachers' self-presentation practices
has shown that a variety of factors – personal and interpersonal, institutional and socio-political – impact on the ways these teachers construct
their classroom identities. While important for any teacher (see Duff &
Uchida, 1997), effective self-representation, that is, foregrounding those
aspects of one's identity and experiences that are both acceptable to
students and pedagogically useful, seems to be an essential element of
migrant teachers' expertise due to many possible ways their foreignness
can be perceived in the host country.

The study also points to areas for further research into the case of
migrant English teachers, whose numbers are likely to rise in the globalized world of increased mobility. As shown, there are constraints on
migrant teachers' self-presentation options: while in this study the most
salient seem to be native-speakerism and strained socio-political relations
between the teachers and the host country coupled with national stereotyping, other factors, including race, class and gender play a more prominent role in other cases (as discussed in Braine, 1999; see also Holliday, this
volume). The effects of such factors, and teachers' and students' responses
to them, are some of the issues worth exploring further.

Despite these obstacles, migrant teachers are well-positioned to teach
EIL. They draw on the various cultural experiences and types of knowledge gained by living in more than one country. Interactions between
them and their students often occur in English as it is the only common L2.
Their classrooms may easily become a multicultural learning space.
As shown earlier, students taught by the teachers in this study gained
cultural knowledge beyond what is commonly associated with English –
such as Bulgarian houses, Polish sound patterns, Macedonian names, or
words of their language having the same root as Russian words – through
the medium of English and in communication with a competent English
user of a different national background. These examples show that migrant
teachers' classrooms may already be offering a practical response to the

call to disassociate teaching English as an International Language from teaching the culture (and especially Culture) of English speaking countries only (e.g. Llurda, 2004; see also Llurda, this volume). Studying their classrooms may therefore contribute to the development of EIL pedagogy. It would be particularly interesting to explore interactions in migrant teachers' classrooms, the use of different types of cultural references, and teachers' and students' perceptions of them.

Finally, investigating migrant teachers in a variety of sociopolitical contexts also provides a possibility for a fresh perspective on the native/ non-native debate. As shown in this study, migrant teachers do not easily fit the descriptions of either, yet they share some features with both. Thus, focusing on this specific group of teachers may productively destabilize the prototypical categories and point to a more fine-grained way to approach issues of expertise and excellence in the language teaching profession.

Acknowledgements

I am indebted to the four teachers for their time, stories, comments and interest in this study. I also wish to thank Amy Jo Minett, Louisa Buckingham and Ingrid Piller for their generous help in providing me with books and articles unavailable in Hungary at the time of writing this chapter.

References

Block, D. (2007) *Second Language Identities*. London: Continuum.
Benke, E. and Medgyes, P. (2005) Differences in teaching behaviour between native and non-native speaker teachers: As seen by the learners. In E. Llurda (ed.) *Non-Native Language Teachers: Perceptions, Challenges, and Contributions to the Profession* (pp. 195–215). New York: Springer.
Braine, G. (ed.) (1999) *Non-Native Educators in English Language Teaching*. Mahwah, NJ: Lawrence Erlbaum.
Cook, V. (1992) Evidence for multicompetence. *Language Learning* 42 (4), 557–591.
De Fina, A., Schiffrin, D. and Bamberg, M. (eds) (2006) *Discourse and Identity*. Cambridge: Cambridge University Press.
Duff, P.A. and Uchida, Y. (1997) The negotiation of teachers' sociocultural identities and practices in postsecondary EFL classrooms. *TESOL Quarterly* 31 (3), 451–486.
Holliday, A. (2005) *The Struggle to Teach English as an International Language*. Oxford: Oxford University Press.
Llurda, E. (2004) Non-native-speaker teachers and English as an International Language. *International Journal of Applied Linguistics* 14 (3), 314–323.
Medgyes, P. (1999) *The Non-Native Teacher* (2nd edn). Ismaning: Hueber Verlag.

Medgyes, P. and Miklósy, K. (2000) The language situation in Hungary. *Current Issues in Language Planning* 1 (2), 148–242.

Norton, B. (1997) Language, identity and the ownership of English. *TESOL Quarterly* 31 (3), 409–429.

Norton, B. (2000) *Identity and Language Learning: Gender, Ethnicity and Educational Change*. Harlow: Pearson Education.

Piller, I. (2002) Passing for a native speaker: Identity and success in second language learning. *Journal of Sociolinguistics* 6 (2), 179–206.

Rampton, M.B.H. (1990) Displacing the 'native speaker': Expertise, affiliation, and inheritance. *ELT Journal* 44 (2), 338–343.

Seidlhofer, B. (1996) 'It is an undulating feeling …': The importance of being a non-native teacher of English. *Views* 5 (1–2), 63–80.

Part 3

EIL, Teacher Education and Language Testing: Gaps and Challenges

Chapter 8

Global Warning? West-based TESOL, Class-Blindness and the Challenge for Critical Pedagogies

VAIDEHI RAMANATHAN and BRIAN MORGAN

Introduction

Dialogic in form, this chapter addresses the importance of not losing sight of some localized tensions when debating issues around 'global'/ world English. Specifically, this chapter calls attention to: (1) issues of class and the complex ways in which class inequities align with globalization; (2) issues relating to the outsourcing of jobs and their implications for West-based TESOL programs; and (3) issues relating to critical pedagogies for novice teachers.

The purpose of this dialogue is to shed light on several foundational inadequacies and critical possibilities for the Teaching English to Speakers of Other Languages (TESOL) profession – hence, the 'global warning' and 'West-based' qualification in this chapter's title. Perhaps ironically, our collaborative effort here coincides with the publication of a book chapter in which the commonsense notion of a 'global' or 'international' English is seriously undermined (e.g. Pennycook, 2007). Of course, such controversy does not emerge out of a research vacuum. Rather, it is a reflection and continuation of a determined critique of West-based TESOL (WBT) and the relevance of its dominant discourses and technologies for non-Western settings.

Over the past decade or so, TESOL has been the subject of critical probing into several related fronts: for example, its colonial legacy (Pennycook, 1998; Phillipson, 1992), its positioning in various postcolonial communities (Canagarajah, 1999; Mazrui, 2004; Ramanathan, 2005), and its often predatory effects vis-à-vis the world's other languages (Skutnabb-Kangas & Phillipson, 1995). Some have raised concerns over the transference of Communicative Language Teaching into non-Western spaces (Holliday, 1994, 2002; Hu, 2002), while others have formalized principles and practices for a 'decolonized' approach to TESOL (Kumaravadivelu, 2006) more sensitive to local knowledge (Canagarajah, 2002). Similar problems have been identified in respect to TESOL's lack of attention to community and institutional power relations (Benesch, 2001; Morgan, 2002) as well as the moral dilemmas of language teaching (Johnston, 2002), not least of all how the field perceives and addresses the learning needs of ethno-linguistic minorities (Hornberger, 2003; McCarty, 2002; Wiley, 2004).

Missing however from these valuable perspectives is an articulated sense of what English's 'global'/'international' status means for practitioners (teachers, teacher-educators, policy makers, administrators, researchers) in West-based TESOL. For decades now, strains of WBT have tended to be Anglophone in nature, assimilationist in orientation and dominated by ESL needs. EFL contexts have tended to remain in our peripheral vision (with a general attitude being: it is interesting to know about English in other lands, but it really does not impact us, does it?!), and now finds itself playing catch up. MA-TESOL programs in the West are waking up to the fact that they need to educate themselves about English-language needs in worlds that have remained distant and marginal. As the ensuing dialogue uncovers, many of these realities concern issues around the world's other languages (the OL – or Other Languages – of our acronym) and the importance of class to our professional understanding.

Based as both of us authors are in West-based TESOL, with one of us being a 'native' speaker and researcher and the other a postcolonial, (and traditionally regarded as a) 'non-native' scholar, we draw on the above discourses and our individual and conjoined research trajectories in ESL and teacher-education to speak to three issues around 'global' English: (1) the persistence and relevance of class in the 'post-socialist condition' (Fraser, 1997), and how it aligns with local and global developments in EIL; (2) ways in which the outsourcing of jobs to call centers in places like India force us to pay heed to how we are educating potential MA-TESOLers in the West; and (3) critical pedagogies for novice teachers. Our current discourses around 'global'/international English seem to lose sight of crucial areas of tension and unease that we need to pay heed to and build into our TESOL programs.

VR: So, we begin with the first of our points, namely the issue of class and class-blindness in TESOL. While our field has over the years heightened our awareness of the importance of addressing English teaching to sociopolitical issues, especially those relating to issues of sexuality (Moita-Lopes, 2006;

Nelson, 2006), ethnicity (May, 2001), race (Kubota & Lin, 2006) and caste (Canagarajah, 1997; Ramanathan, 2005), it has tended to avoid addressing class. My own work over the last eight or nine years with English and vernacular-medium teachers in Gujarat has made me acutely aware of the extent to which English teaching is both a class-based endeavor while also one that is seen to ostensibly have the power of splintering class-based enclaves. Several vernacular-medium teachers in Ahmedabad – the city in which my long-term endeavor is based – have conflicted views about it: its connections to globalization, its neo-colonial echoes, its unequal positioning vis-à-vis Gujarati and Hindi (the state's other two official languages) and ways in which class issues are encoded and entrenched in all of these issues. As a field, though, especially West-based TESOL, we seem to be uncomfortable acknowledging poverty in our communities and ways in which it intersects with concerns about devalued pedagogies and unequal access, as well as related satellites of other languages to say nothing of religious, ethnic, and racial identities. Is it because class issues get tied to Marxist concerns, and that many of us see ourselves as having moved into post-Marxist terrains? Or is it because West-based TESOL is by and large a middle-class endeavor oriented primarily towards middle-class learners? With the exception of a few scholars, namely you (Morgan, 1998) and others such as Auerbach (1996), Menard-Warwick (2004) and Vandrick (1995, 2001), there are very few in our field seriously concerned with community, class-based issues and language teaching. Why this reluctance, I wonder?

BM: There would seem to be several plausible and interrelated reasons why TESOLers feel uncomfortable confronting class issues. Class will always be tied to Marxism and Marxism tied – or *chained*, in the collective (un)consciousness of North Americans – to the social engineering disasters of the former Soviet Union. Why such associations seem 'truthful' can be theorized in several complementary ways: by Gramsci's notion of hegemony, or Foucault's notions of discourse and power/knowledge, or in part how public consent is 'manufactured' via control of mass media and education in liberal democratic states, as Chomsky argues in his propaganda model. For over 70 years, the equation of 'class = Marx = the USSR, Bolshevism and the Gulag' served as a familiar – albeit crude – rhetorical weapon in the service of those aligned against trade unionism, socialized medicine, old age pensions, progressive taxation and the like. The Fall of the Wall appears to vindicate this pejorative chain of meaning to the point where it is very much the 'common sense' threshold on what we can imagine – what is *comprehensible* in public discourse – in terms of defining human rights and the conditions of freedom: Freedom to consume, to vote and to express our individuality? Or, freedom from want (food, shelter, clothing, health care and education)? Of related note: Canada was recently criticized by the United Nations for its poor human rights record, specifically its failure to address poverty issues, many of which have become worse in spite of the country's growing affluence and productivity during the past decade (Calderhead, 2006). In short, Canadian governments – and let's not absolve the people that vote for them – fail to treat social and economic rights as fundamental or inseparable from civil, political or ethnolinguistic rights.

This Canadian 'paradox' – public indifference to increasing disparities in wealth – is also indicative of what Nancy Fraser (1997) terms the 'post-socialist condition', our current predicament in which a 'politics of recognition' has eclipsed a 'politics of redistribution' in the global and local marketplace of ideas. Still, despite the apparent triumph of recognition politics, Fraser is correct in pointing out that contemporary demands for identity rights often overlap with and subsume economic claims. Thus, class displaced is not class denied. The challenge, for both activists and educators, is negotiating these new norms for comprehension and compassion.

Fraser's *postsocialist condition* is quite illuminating and complements a Foucauldian and Gramscian perspective as to why things are happening the way they are. In the field of politics, it is doubtful that there is an identifiable locus of power, hidden cabal or identifiable puppet master, consciously and surreptitiously pulling our collective strings. Both politicians and citizens alike feel 'uncomfortable' talking about or addressing economic exploitation. Power resides in that tension-filled space – that creation of discomfort and self-silencing by the subject-in-discourse (cf. Foucault). TESOLers, like everyone else, want to be taken seriously, to be perceived as 'worthy of speech' (Norton, 2000). I think most of us enter the profession with an ethic of care, a genuine desire to help others and make a difference. And that desire to help can be easily redirected towards activities that are deemed 'worthy' and most likely to be supported by the 'majority' (perhaps this is where North American, middle-class values come into play). We may be doing good things, as in our advocacy for minority cultures and languages, but our success in these endeavors may be due, in part, to the possibility that they are less threatening and disruptive of entrenched, class-based privilege and power.

VR: So class issues in the West, then, are deeply rooted in collective histories, with obvious reminders to the USSR and Bolshevism, and individual constraints as well, with the discomfort of speaking about it openly stemming from conditions around openly acknowledging one's privileged class positionings. Unfortunate, because it keeps us – teachers, administrators, researchers – from openly discussing how so much of teaching and learning is embedded in very material actualities: lack of textbooks, finding money to pay bus fares to get to school, having a place at home to do homework, paying for exam paper, having a set of clean clothes to wear. The picture, of course, gets far more complicated when we see how this lack of access coincides with other languages in three-quarters of the world, issues that need more prominence in WBT. Recent debates about outsourcing and 'call center training' both in India and the West raise interesting issues around this nexus of TE (Teaching English) and OL (Other Languages). Look for instance at the advice that this particular West-based website called CVTips offers about why call center training is important, especially for Indians speaking English.

Not everyone who wants to get into a call center can get into it. Why? Because of many factors:

- *Bad accent* – Indian languages are heavily accentuated and these put demands on the English language. For example, a Telegu person's English and a Bengali person's English can have a hell and heaven difference, even if both attended English-medium schools in their childhood.
- *Tendency to translate verbatim* – most of the Indian languages are highly metaphorical, constantly comparing nature, animals and feeling with something; the sounds, occupations, feelings are always emphasized with comparisons – when these are translated verbatim, they make some massive howlers; similarly, translating verbatim English phrases can totally send the communication on a different tangent.
- *Limited vocabulary* – people here speak English for two reasons – one when they travel and they do not know the local language and two when they study; unless they are high-class hobnobs people who do not speak English at home or at the workplace. This is why their vocabulary stays limited to the field they usually move in – and most people are lost when they are out of their field …
- *Phone etiquette* – people in India are pretty abrupt on the phone. They need to learn the small talk of polite conversation that is needed to keep the customer buoyant and satisfied.

CVTips.com (n.d.)

So what are we, as West-based TESOL professionals to make of this? One the one hand, I find this rhetoric deeply offensive: 'Indian languages are highly accented' (are not all languages?), or are 'highly metaphorical, constantly comparing nature, animals and feeling with something' (was not aware of this) or that we lack phone manners (I did not know that West-based phone manners are the norm), but on the other hand, the globalizing surges (liberalizing of markets, the country opening its shores to foreign investment after decades of colonialism, availability of jobs) are opening doors and spaces that were hitherto not possible. It reminds me of the segment in our 2005 article about current globalizing surges being simultaneously homogenizing and heterogenizing (Morgan & Ramanathan, 2005).

BM: In the case of call center criteria, there does seem to be a global homogenizing affect taking place – and I agree; it *is* offensive for several related reasons. First, a specific language, English, which is socially and economically inaccessible for most, comes to displace other regional and local languages of commerce and opportunity. But it's also a case of the *kind* of English or restricted code that is adopted by call centers that's offensive. The call center website does not ask for lingua franca competencies in which communicative responsibility is *shared* between interlocutors – conversational *partners* who might feel the need to employ 'face-saving' pragmatic strategies to smooth over intercultural gaps (House, 2002). Rather the onus and liability is placed solely on the call center employees to micromanage conversation, unilaterally, towards narrow corporate ends. The website, for example, talks about 'communication skills – in which people [can be] trained to *transmit more in less time and words*' (my emphasis). Self-confidence, similarly, is defined primarily in terms of deflecting accountability. The self-assured call center employee becomes the verbal front line against customer 'aggression' and 'bullying'. And again, these are portrayed as 'trainable' communication skills.

In spite of what the website claims, I'm skeptical about the extent to which these call center skills *are* 'teachable'. As you note, not everyone will have acquired, nor can ever afford, the prerequisite foundations for teachability – social access to 'native speakers' and exposure to their phonological and pragmatic norms, access to center-based cultural goods, opportunities for travel abroad and/or schooling in English-dominant societies and the idiomatic familiarity this contact provides. For all intents and purposes, call center want ads could simply read, 'Only "high class hobnobs" need apply'!

VR: Relating this back to our previous point about class and TESOL: it is precisely in this interesting way that call centers get positioned centrally in the TESOL-class crux. In India, English and its speakers are conceived in terms of 'human capital' – 'natural resources' to be utilized and exploited in a highly competitive global economy. One reason why India has become a hub for outsourcing jobs is because of its large English-speaking population coupled with cheap labor. Indeed, the outsourcing surges especially around call centers, has boomed to a point where you now have entire undergraduate degrees (with developed curricular materials and syllabi) on 'Outsourcing Management'. Certainly issues of learning, teaching, and education – including deeply entrenched language policies – are going through a sea change.

BM: Looking at the website, it's interesting to see the underlying assumptions about language and language learning – many of which facilitate outsourcing and management – that come to the fore: most strikingly, information as measurable commodity, amenable to scientific management (*cf*. Taylorism), hence increased throughput and exchange value (i.e. the transmission of 'more in less time and words'). It's also interesting for me to see how closely this 'transmission' assumption reflects what linguists have termed conduit or telementational metaphors of language (see van Lier, 2004: chap. 2). As well, your comment on the normalization of 'West-based phone manners' reminds me of Deborah Cameron's (2002) insightful chapter on globalization and the teaching of communication skills. There's the problem of particularistic discourse norms becoming internationalized. Many EIL speakers may indeed find it incongruous or offensive when exposed to the kinds of instrumental speech moves ('Fries with your burger?') and manufactured rapport ('Have a nice day') characteristic of North American service-sector transactions, especially if 'creatively' transposed across speech situations to which they may not apply. But Cameron's other key point is perhaps cause for greater concern – specifically the extent to which *other* languages and their speakers feel compelled to adopt these and similar 'value-adding' or 'consensus-building' norms as their own, and as the new semiotic standard by which global citizenship is acknowledged. This is where the nexus of TE and OL perhaps extends beyond conventional notions of linguistic imperialism in the context of language enumeration and/or endangerment discourses. To what extent does the persistence of a specific lexicogrammar and phonology system count as language 'maintenance' when its underlying symbolic and functional uniqueness has been colonized or technologized in the service of globalized 'efficiencies'?

VR: What gets filtered out of these various West-based narratives – language rights, language maintenance, English and neocolonialism, English and globalization – are grounded, class-related notions of inequities and ways in which English is completely sutured in them. Going back to that egregious, but interesting website, there is an entire subtext there that needs articulation: local, social inequities tied to mediums of instruction; English-medium students sliding into these jobs with ease, while poorer vernacular-medium students find their vernacular backgrounds and languages devalued. Then there are the ungodly hours call center workers have to work in with many of them starting shifts at midnight or very early morning to match the time differences in the West). Also, many call center workers have to take accent-reduction classes so as to sound more comprehensible to the Western ear (colonialism coming in through the back door?), and they assume different Western names for the same purpose (e.g. 'Nandini Nair' from Bristow Road, Cochin, Kerala becomes 'Kathy Johnson' from Ohio). Conversations I've had with call center callers, especially Keralite and Tamilian ones, who have had their schooling in the Malayalam or Tamil-medium – speak openly of how the pragmatic pulls around their jobs tend to override personal ambiguities about assuming Western names (often explained as: 'this is my job; I have to do it'). These are class-based perspectives that we need to make room for in WBT.

BM: Yes, and TESOL is primarily a West-based institution generating a knowledge base that reflects and resists the historical class-based struggles you speak of. So, another reason why TESOLers might have problems with 'class' issues relates to the practice of theory, or the lack thereof. Obviously, we academic theorists in TESOL, for the most part, come from privileged backgrounds, so our class-consciousness is skewed and sometimes even patronizing, given the profession's muted attention to the precarious working conditions of most ESL teachers in the settings that I'm familiar with. Equally obvious, as academics we are heavily invested in the presumed use-value of our activities – specifically, that our ways of studying and theorizing about the world are somehow consequential to its unfolding.

But a less obvious point also worth considering is that social theory in TESOL is relatively new and underdeveloped in relation to linguistic and psycholinguistic ways of thinking and framing the world. Outside a small group of critical TESOL theorists/researchers such as yourself, Canagarajah, Lin, Pennycook and others, there may be a tendency in TESOL to conceptualize class in somewhat 'structural' or 'grammatical' schema that are not adequate to the task. Inequalities present themselves in different ways throughout the world and at different times, so a static, uniform conception of class is likely to predispose its possessors not to recognize its embeddedness in 'non-classlike' phenomena like race, ethnicity, religion, gender, geography and so on. What's preferable is a sense of *articulation*, in Stuart Hall's use of the term, which I remember studying in some detail in my undergraduate anthropology degree – for example, how pre-capitalist and feudalistic systems persist alongside modern, capitalist modes of production, not as anomalies, but precisely because of the complex ties and forms of dependency that arise between seemingly incongruent forms of socioeconomic organization.

VR: This point about articulation – especially as it also relates to the languaging in documents such as those on the web about call center training – is crucial. It is a way of understanding how English gets taken up in countries like India, how the language and its speakers get positioned vis-à-vis their complex milieus (their home and community languages, their work spaces, the onslaught of media, pressures to catch up or problems with local language polices around mediums of instruction). A nuanced, localized articulation is a key way of addressing class, since doing so would allow us to see it as assuming particular forms as it constantly interacts with and informs a host of historical, political, institutional and policy-related tropes. Given how easily accessible information is on the web, the language in sites such as the one we've been discussing can and does put communities, and certainly those teaching and learning in local, vernacular languages, on the defensive. So, on the one hand, we have globalizing discourses that are supposed to render all spaces democratic, while on the other the very same discourses generate resistances to them. This means that our West-based discourses in TESOL need to pay heed to how our articulations of what we do or claim to do have far-reaching consequences in other parts of the world. So what I am trying to get at is that we need to think about making serious changes in local curricular and pedagogic contexts. How might we proceed?

BM: I think one of the best ways to proceed, as a teacher-educator, is to foster a sense of what you describe as 'meta-awareness' in TESOL programs (Ramanathan, 2002). Simply put, teachers need to attain a sense of attachment to what is a fairly abstract notion – that language policies shape classroom practices and practices, in turn, shape policies. It's not something to be ignored or left to administrators and outside 'experts' to sort out. They are a key component of the 'serious changes' that occur, especially at the local level. I think David Corson's (1999) work has been significant in this respect.

At York, I teach a course called 'Socio-Political Issues in Second Language Teaching' as part of our undergraduate, TESOL certificate program. From day one, I try to get students to see this 'articulated' perspective, especially in the Canadian context, where most of our graduates end up teaching. We look at how ELT curricula and the teaching of grammar, pronunciation and vocabulary are shaped by *extra-linguistic* factors (i.e. mainstream politics, economics, collective identities and ideologies) and not always – or often! – in a coherent fashion. I bring in chapters and articles that specifically problematize the presumed benefits of a global language and reveal its disruptive effects on local languages and opportunities (Tollefson, 2002). I also try to formulate study questions that encourage critical perspectives on language policies – to reveal their often ad hoc nature or consequences; for example, policies that claim to help integrate newcomers, in effect, can serve to further marginalize them (see Cooke, 2001). Through readings and assignments, I also try to get student-teachers to recognize the ambiguities inherent – and often intentional – around policies and curricula and to see themselves as 'change-agents', even when confronted with over-bearing demands to 'teach by the book' or 'to the test'. To be honest, some students are not happy to be implicated in policy or social change. They sometimes respond by saying 'I just want to teach the language' reflecting a still common belief that a language can be taught separate from its social context and uses.

VR: This idea of language being separate from social milieus and of student-teachers feeling a tension between accounting for their participation in teaching contexts and the more 'pragmatic', use-oriented obsession with 'teaching just language' is a very sticky issue. Like you, I too orient my course readings around sociopolitical types of issues. But I've also realized that readings are not enough; student-teachers actually need to go through a process of awakening to local policy and ideological issues on their own, and toward this sometimes have them engaged in a term-long pair-project. In a second language writing seminar, for instance, I have them, in pairs or groups of three, download a list of two and four colleges in the state. They are then to pick three to four colleges from the list, get as much policy-related information as they can from the institutional websites (textbooks currently used, placement exams, syllabi, sequence of courses, attendance). After this, they are to contact (by e-mail) two to three instructors teaching in these colleges to see if they can either interview them on the phone or get their responses to a survey of questions. These are questions that we jointly coconstruct in class (about the student population, students' prior writing experiences, about the instructor, about policies in the institution, what instructors would like changed, on-the-ground tensions in which instructors wrestle with pedagogic materials, institutional policies, and examination constraints. At the end of the term we write up abstracts to submit to the local CA-TESOL conference.

A project like this not only introduces student-teachers to local colleges where many end up seeking employment, but also gets them to move into spaces where, by listening and hearing other instructors in other colleges speak/write about their pedagogic practices and tensions and by connecting these to both language policies and debates in the field, they are able to begin to conceptualize their own positionings vis-à-vis so many aspects of their social world and professional development. It also gently leads them into voicing not only their own tensions but how their voicing of them – their languaging – in turn impact the spaces they are part of. This is where critical practice comes in, doesn't it?

BM: I think so. For me, what you're doing is essential for critical pedagogy in our field – linking concepts/ideas to concrete practices and settings, particularly those in which theoretically informed graduates must begin to become practically informed professionals whose transformative voices, as a result, are more likely to be heard by colleagues and supervisors. I've tried to develop something of parallel concreteness in the sociopolitics course at York. Building on a course component first developed by my colleague Nick Elson, I spend a lot of time on something we call an 'issues analysis project' (Morgan, forthcoming). It's the last assignment of the year and follows a research essay and short response paper. It's a group project and based on course themes and ideological perspectives on ELT raised in the readings. Each group identifies a gap or weakness in the profession and designs a practical 'intervention' to address it. This intervention can be in the form of an advocacy letter to a politician or administrator (e.g. for stable adult ESL funding). It can be a draft of a policy statement (e.g. proposal to the TESOL organization to address age discrimination in hiring practices), a consultant's report (e.g. the comparative utility of Information Technologies in ESL), a thematic unit of curricula (e.g. challenging homophobia and heteronormativity; a history of racism and anti-racism in Canada) or a pre-service and/or in-service workshop (e.g. utilizing popular culture in ESL; encouraging family L2 literacies). A written section that provides a rationale for the project accompanies each intervention. I evaluate each project on its practical organization, its interweaving of applied linguistic and sociopolitical concerns, and its references to current literature. On the last class of the course, each group presents its project to the class for discussion and critique.

So, this is what I imagine critical ESL pedagogy to be – a notion of *praxis*, theory and practice mutually informing and grounded in specific places with contingent problems/opportunities emerging from cultural and institutional histories. Still, the issues analysis project is not easy to do. I have to bring a lot of examples of previous projects into class, and we have to spend a lot of time discussing and thinking through how each project might best be actualized, or what might be achievable given the practical constraints of each intervention format. Some students find the transposition of critical theory into 'mundane' practices difficult and, in this respect, find the grand rhetorical flourishes of theory somewhat intimidating. We also have a lot of international students in our program (about a third to half each year), and it's interesting to see how they respond to the sociopolitics course in general and the challenges of the issues project in particular. From their responses – and they're not too different from things said by many domestic students – I can see that the whole idea of a critical EFL or EIL pedagogy comes across as something unusual, maybe even undoable or inappropriate for international settings. What are your thoughts on this?

VR: I think there are very interesting ways of encouraging international TESOLers to engage with sociopolitical issues around language teaching. In the assignment that I described, many of the international students design projects around procuring language policy-related information from institutions in their home countries. In contexts where college-level writing courses are not part of undergraduate degrees – as in India, for instance – student-teachers focus on addressing where and how writing/ composition gets positioned vis-à-vis other subjects, the K-12 contexts in which it is taught, ways in which instruction in it overlaps with or is different from writing instruction in home languages. While the idea of how to use English and the discourses around it to address issues of community change may, at first glance, seem improbable for international students (since many of these students are getting MA-TESOL degrees to learn to teach 'the English language' in their home countries), getting them to see that community engagement in English is not that different from community engagement in their own home languages is crucial. Also, creating contexts where they are able to articulate how civic and community engagements in their home spaces occur helps all of us in the class to move the discussion beyond dichotomies around whether or not it is appropriate to raise sociopolitical concerns to spaces where we recognize that it goes in different contexts and takes different forms in diverse geographical spaces. Moving the discussion to this plane opens up the possibility of also addressing contextual dynamics that might disallow or constrain open discussion of sociopolitical issues in classrooms or in research. What are the contexts of hesitation and what are some moral dilemmas in open engagement of them (Johnston, 2002)? Certainly in the Gujarat context – where much of my work in the last many years has been based – raising political issues in the classroom might be most incendiary, especially in parts of downtown Ahmedabad which has seen most painful

Hindu-Muslim violence. But institutions and teachers find alternative contexts by which to connect students' educational experiences to those in the community (through volunteer programs, or through projects that emphasize Gandhian notions of non-formal education (Ramanathan, 2006) through classes in 'moral science' (a secular, civics and ethics-based class). Critical practices and critical pedagogies, then, are not necessarily a Western prerogative.

BM: I agree that critical pedagogies are not necessarily a Western prerogative. Yet I would also argue that the obviousness or apparent truthfulness of this point *is* a Western prerogative. And this point might allow us to retrace our steps as we wind our discussion down. One of our main themes has been to explore the possible relevance and conceptualization of class in the 'postsocialist condition' (Fraser, 1997), a condition of emerging global preeminence, and one in which Marxian analyses, in particular, have been discredited. Increasingly, in this new global marketplace of ideas, one can witness the logical connections made by which redistributive, class-based initiatives are depicted as 'Euro-centric' and 'immoral'. And a key question becomes whose interests are being served when the meaning of 'critical' is pluralized (i.e. moralized, spiritualized, indigenized) to the point of dilution, or alternatively, it is reduced to semiotic play in the case of culture jamming whereby the reinforcing images of consumerism are subverted (Strangelove, 2005)? In both cases, the notion of critical has been safely domesticated. So, in our roles as ELT policy makers and as language teacher educators, we'll need to think carefully about what is or is not critical. Similarly, we'll need to ask ourselves the extent to which we must jettison Western-originating ideals and idealize non-Western and/or indigenous ones.

VR: You are right. There's a fine set of in-between spaces there that we need to carefully text into existence; there are dangers in over-romanticizing the vernaculars, just as there are dangers in not being critical enough about English. The globalizing currents that are tweaking language policies at institutional, state and national levels to accommodate to EIL suddenly casts into light spaces between TE and OL, spaces that are sometimes tension-filled and that get cast as binarisms. We need to think carefully about how we can cultivate contexts where we speak openly about how assuming particular positions does not mean the cancellation of other points of view, but a lamination of our own. Arguing in support of critical practices in other parts of the world does not, for instance, cancel out the 'critical' in West-based TESOL; attempting to understand language policy issues around English and local languages in other parts of the world does not run counter to the 'teaching English' tenet of West-based TESOL. Expanding TESOL's horizons to bring in perspectives hitherto relegated to other research domains ('Other languages' tends to get appropriated by those doing 'heritage languages', for instance, when it is encoded in the acronym of our discipline) complexifies our understandings of our discipline's 'truths' and, as you point out, makes us wrestle with the 'critical' by pushing us to uncover some of processes by which our understandings of both 'truths' and 'critical' become normalized.

BM: The 'in-between spaces' and competing notions of the critical that you summarize above suggest exciting possibilities for future research and teacher education in TESOL and EIL. Imagine if we were having this dialogue, say, 15 to 20 years ago. We might have been debating the role of error correction and the explicit teaching of grammar rules in second language acquisition (cf. Krashen), or the relevance of contrastive minimal pair (segmental) activities in an L2 pronunciation syllabus. Of course, such debates are still necessary, but our frames of reference for them have changed substantially – away from an exclusive preoccupation with cognitive and linguistic factors to encompass more ideological and ethnographic dimensions, for example, how issues of national, regional, or ethnic identity – and of the class-based power relations that adhere in specific settings – might influence the production of 'non-standard' varieties of English. Similarly, 20 years ago, debates over the status and expertise of NNS teachers were nonexistent, bottom-up, micro-perspectives in language policy and planning were rare, and concerns over the maintenance of the OL in TESOL were minimal. That the global spread of English might be predatory in respect to the vitality of other languages, or that it might represent a calculated, neo-colonial power play (cf. Phillipson's linguistic imperialism) seemed beyond the commonsensical, apolitical utility and benefits assumed by most in the field.

In sum, globalization and the post-socialist condition present significant challenges to come, especially for new scholars and practitioners in TESOL. For the former, there's much to be done – new questions to pose and new articulations, in Stuart Hall's sense of the word, to formulate. For the latter, there are new openings and new responsibilities shaped in part by the profession's engagement with the local and contingent. Teachers can imagine for themselves roles that are not simply subservient to theorists. As moral agents, transformative intellectuals, cultural workers, perhaps even global citizens, the avenues currently available for creating meaningful and inspiring classrooms seem greater now than at any time, that is, if the required resources and a modest degree of teacher autonomy are made available. We will see – and continue our dialogue from there.

References

Auerbach, E. (1996) *Adult ESL/Literacy from the Community – to the Community: A Guidebook for Participatory Literacy Training*. Mahwah, NJ: Lawrence Erlbaum Associates.
Benesch, S. (2001) *Critical English for Academic Purposes*. Mahwah, NJ: Lawrence Erlbaum Associates.
Calderhead, V. (2006) Canada could do so much better: Economic and social rights are not seen as fundamental human rights. *Toronto Star Newspaper*, 25th May, p. A23.
Cameron, D. (2002) Globalization and the teaching of 'communication' skills. In D. Block and D. Cameron (eds) *Globalization and Language Teaching* (pp. 67–82). London: Routledge.
Canagarajah, S. (1999) *Resisting Linguistic Imperialism in English Teaching*. Oxford: Oxford University Press.
Canagarajah, S. (2002) *Critical Academic Writing and Multilingual Students*. Ann Arbor: University of Michigan Press.
Corson, D. (1999) *Language Policy in Schools*. Mahwah, NJ: Lawrence Erlbaum Associates.
Cooke, D. (2001) Lives on hold: ESL in a restructured society. *TESL Canada Journal* 18 (2), 65–77.
CVTips.com (n.d.) Call center training on WWW at http://www.cvtips.com/call_center_training.html. Accessed 16.1.07.
Fraser, N. (1997) *Justice Interruptus: Critical Reflections on the Postsocialist Condition*. New York: Routledge.
Holliday, A. (1994) *Appropriate Methodology and Social Context*. Cambridge: Cambridge University Press.
Holliday, A. (2002) *Doing and Writing Qualitative Research*. London: Sage Publications Ltd.
Hornberger, N. (2003) *Continua of Biliteracy*. Clevedon: Multilingual Matters.
House, J. (2002) Developing pragmatic competence in English as a lingua franca. In K. Knapp and C. Meierkord (eds) *Lingua Franca Communication* (pp. 245–267). Frankfurt am Main: Peter Lang.
Hu, G. (2002) Potential cultural resistance to pedagogical imports: The case of communicative language teaching in China. *Language, Culture and Curriculum* 15, 93–105.
Johnston, B. (2002) *Values in English Language Teaching*. Mahwah, NJ: Lawrence Erlbaum Associates.
Kubota, R. and Lin, A. (2006) Race and TESOL. *TESOL Quarterly* 40, 3.
Kumaravadivelu, B. (2006) TESOL, globalization, and the Empire: A dangerous liason. In J. Edge (ed.) *Relocating TESOL in the Age of Empire* (pp. 1–32). London: Macmillan Palgrave.
May, S. (2001) *Language and Minority Rights: Ethnicity, Nationalism, and the Politics of Language*. New York: Longman.

Mazrui, A. (2004) *English in Africa: After the Cold War*. Clevedon: Multlingual Matters.

McCarty, T. (2002) Between possibility and constraint: Indigenous language education, planning, and policy in the United States. In J. Tollefson (ed.) *Language Policies in Education: Critical Issues* (pp. 285–307). Mahwah, NJ: Lawrence Erlbaum Associates.

Menard-Warwick, J. (2004) I always had the desire to progress a little: Gendered narratives of immigrant language learners. *Journal of Language, Identity, and Education* 3 (4), 295–311.

Moita-Lopes, L. (2006) Queering literacy teaching: Analyzing gay-themed discourses in a fifth-grade class in Brazil. *Journal of Language Identity, and Education* 5 (1), 31–50.

Morgan, B. (1998) *The ESL Classroom: Teaching, Critical Practice, and Community Development*. Toronto: University of Toronto Press.

Morgan, B. (2002) Critical practice in community-based ESL programs: A Canadian perspective. *Journal of Language, Identity, and Education* 1 (2), 141–162.

Morgan, B. (forthcoming) Fostering transformative practitioners for critical EAP: Possibilities and challenges. *Journal of English for Academic Purposes*.

Morgan, B. and Ramanathan, V. (2005) Critical literacies in language education: Local and global perspectives. *Annual Review of Applied Linguistics* 25, 151–169.

Nelson, C. (2006) Queer inquiry in language education. *Journal of Language, Identity, and Education* 5 (6), 1–9.

Norton, B. (2000) *Identity and Language Learning: Gender, Ethnicity and Educational Change*. New York: Longman.

Pennycook, A. (1998) *English and the Discourses of Colonialism*. London: Routledge.

Pennycook, A. (2007) The myth of English as an international language. In S. Makoni and A. Pennycook (eds) *Disinventing and Reconstituting Languages* (pp. 90–115). Clevedon: Multilingual Matters.

Phillipson, R. (1992) *Linguistic Imperialism*. Oxford: Oxford University Press.

Ramanathan, V. (2002) *The Politics of TESOL Education: Writing, Knowledge, Critical Pedagogy*. New York: Routledge Falmer.

Ramanathan, V. (2005) *The English-Vernacular Divide: Post-Colonial Language Policies and Practice*. Clevedon: Multilingual Matters.

Ramanathan, V. (2006) Gandhi, non-cooperation, and socio-civic education: Harnessing the vernaculars. *Journal of Language, Identity, and Education* 5 (3), 229–250.

Skutnabb-Kangas, T. and Phillipson, R. (1995) *Linguistic Human Rights*. Berlin: Mouton de Gruyter.

Strangelove, M. (2005) *The Empire of Mind: Digital Piracy and the Anti-Capitalist Movement*. Toronto: University of Toronto Press.

Tollefson, J. (ed.) (2002) *Language Policies in Education: Critical Perspectives*. Mahwah, NJ: Erlbaum.

Wiley, T. (2004) Language planning, language policy, and the English-only movement. In E. Finegan and J. Rickford (eds) *Language in the USA: Themes for the Twentifirst Century* (pp. 319–338). Cambridge: Cambridge University Press.

Vandrick, S. (1995) Privileged ESL university students. *TESOL Quarterly* 29, 375–381.

Vandrick, S. (2001) Teachers' cultures, teachers' stories. *Journal of Engaged Pedagogy* 1 (1), 19–39.

van Lier, L. (2004) *The Ecology and Semiotics of Language Learning: A Sociocultural Perspective*. Dordrecht: Kluwer.

Chapter 9

Desirable But Not Necessary? The Place of World Englishes and English as an International Language in English Teacher Preparation Programs in Japan

AYA MATSUDA

Introduction

In 2003, the Ministry of Education, Culture, Sports, Science and Technology (MEXT) of Japan developed an action plan to 'cultivate Japanese with English abilities', which emphasized the importance of English by referring to its function as an international language:

> English has played a central role as the common international language in linking people who have different mother tongues. For children living in the 21st century, it is essential for them to acquire communication abilities in English as a common international language. In addition, English abilities are important in terms of linking our country with the rest of the world, obtaining the world's understanding and trust, enhancing our international presence and further developing our nation. (Ministry of Education, Culture, Sports, Science and Technology [MEXT], 2003: 1)

The status of English as an international language has made it a popular foreign language in the expanding circle where English is not commonly used for intranational communication. Teaching English as an *international* language, however, requires a mindset that is significantly different from the approach traditionally used in English language teaching (ELT) that positions English as the language of UK and/or United States and its people.

In her book titled *Teaching English as an International Language*, McKay (2002: 1) argues that 'the teaching and learning of an international language must be based on an entirely different set of assumptions than the teaching and learning of any other second or foreign language'. In terms of a target model in English classrooms, McKay illustrates how the emergence of World Englishes complicates the notion of *standard* because there are now multiple varieties that could serve as the target model. She also emphasizes the importance of recognizing linguistic and rhetorical variations in EIL (English as an international language) classrooms and challenges the appropriateness of the native speaker model.

The relationship between language and culture is also reexamined in this book. McKay argues that the inner circle alone can no longer provide adequate cultural content in EIL teaching, and thus materials from the source culture (i.e. the learners' culture) and international culture must also be included. Furthermore, the ability to critically analyze the cultural content and reflect on their own culture in relation to that of others is crucial for future users of English as an international language. McKay also problematizes the possible 'West-bias' in popular teaching methods in the field of ELT, and reminds us of the importance of developing and implementing a method that is suitable for a local context.

In my previous work, I also have critiqued the current practices in ELT which tend to privilege the United States and UK, in terms of both linguistic and cultural contents, and argued that such 'traditional' approaches may not adequately prepare future EIL users who will encounter English users from other countries (Matsuda, 2006). In addition to the challenges in the selection of instructional variety and cultural content that McKay (2002) addressed, I discussed how teaching materials and assessment need to be reenvisioned in order to serve the needs of EIL learners better. For instance, assessment should not focus exclusively on how closely the learner approximates the native speaker model but rather how effectively learners use the language vis-à-vis their purpose for learning the language.

In fact, the increased awareness of World Englishes (WE) and EIL has encouraged curriculum developers to create curricula that take into account the linguistic and sociocultural complexity of English today (e.g. Burns, 2005). Some textbooks targeted specifically at EIL learners have also been published (e.g. Shaules *et al.*, 2004; Yoneoka & Arimoto, 2000).

In spite of the increasing attention given to the teaching of EIL, however, we know much less when it comes to the question of how such ideas as

World Englishes and EIL are dealt with in teacher preparation programs. One study that investigated the place of World Englishes in such programs focused specifically on the treatment of institutional varieties of English (IVEs). Vavrus (1991) surveyed 10 'reputable' MA programs in the United States that prepared ESL professionals in order to find out whether prospective teachers were exposed to information about IVEs. Among 10 programs Vavrus surveyed, none of the programs required a course that emphasized non-native varieties of English. Two programs listed such a course as an elective, but even in those cases, the course was difficult to access as it was not offered regularly.

A set of more recent works has been collected by Dogancay-Aktuna and Hardman (2007). In this book, contributors share challenges in creating teacher education programs that are 're-imagined from a perspective that would no longer make narrow assumptions regarding the cultural/ linguistic context of teaching, ESL-centric models of teaching, and the nature of the English language itself' (Dogancay-Aktuna & Hardman, 2007: 8–9). Focusing on different aspects of the world-wide spread of English and its implications for various aspects of teacher education curricula – the structure of English, language and culture, TESL/TEFL method and practicum – the authors collectively illustrate the problems with current practices in teacher preparation, emphasize the need for changes, and even provide some suggestions for possible changes. However, the majority of studies, including all five from the expanding circle, focus on issues other than the teacher education programs themselves. Their central foci are the historical and present context of English and English language teaching in various parts of the world, teachers' attitudes toward English, beliefs and professional identity of teachers, and pedagogical practices in English language classrooms. These are all important in creating a teacher education program, and the findings present critical implications for EIL teacher preparation, but it is still unclear what is actually being done in teacher preparation programs in countries where English is used, learned and taught as an international language.

This lack of understanding of how EIL teachers are being prepared is a problem. The changes in English language teaching urged by various scholars (e.g. Burns, 2005; Kachru, 1984, 1992; Matsuda, 2005, 2006; McKay, 2002) cannot be successfully implemented without changing teachers: teachers must have a good understanding of the historical spread and current use of English in order to implement changes in the curriculum that better reflect the needs of EIL users today (Brown, 1995; Matsuda, 2006). The English language instruction that pre-service teachers receive before entering teacher education programs tends to be

American/British-oriented, meaning teacher education programs play a crucial role in introducing these teachers to the linguistic and functional diversity of English, and how the language may unite or divide the global community. However, without knowing how these teachers are currently prepared, we do not have a sense of how to approach the curricular innovation – whether it is for teaching the English language or teacher education.

The current project attempts to shed light on this under-researched topic, namely how the perspectives of WE and EIL are incorporated into teacher preparation programs that prepare teachers of EIL, using Japan as an example. While the project in its entirety addresses various aspects of teacher preparation programs, including the course requirements and topics related to NNEST (non-native English speaking teachers), this chapter focuses on two questions: (1) how much exposure do pre-service teachers of English have to different varieties of English, World Englishes literature, and 'English speaking cultures' other than British and American, as well as the notion of World Englishes and English as an international language; and (2) what do teacher educators believe regarding the importance of such exposure in their teacher preparation programs?

Methods

In order to capture both the overall trend and variation among approaches that are currently used in teacher preparation in Japan, I chose to use a questionnaire to collect information. The questionnaire was sent via email and regular airmail to all 307 universities that had an accredited teacher preparation program for the first-class certificate in English for the upper secondary level (10–12th grade) as of April 2005.[1] Ninety-five questionnaires were returned, making the return rate 32.6%.[2]

The questionnaire included 16 open-ended items regarding: (1) the course requirements; (2) the program requirements for the English proficiency of pre-service English teachers; (3) the availability of opportunities for the pre-service teachers to be exposed to different varieties of English, English literatures, and cultures as well as the notion of World Englishes and EIL; (4) teacher educators' beliefs regarding the importance of (3); (5) the strengths and weaknesses of non-native-English-speaking teachers (NNESTs), as perceived by the teacher educators; and (6) the availability of opportunities for the pre-service teachers to reflect on their role as NNESTs.[3]

The current chapter reports the findings regarding (3) and (4). For the purpose of comparison, the responses were coded and tallied. For the qualitative interpretation of data, emerging patterns were identified through recursive reading. The original survey and all responses were in Japanese, except for one copy that was translated into English by the author per request of a native-English-speaking respondent who could not read or write in Japanese. All Japanese responses presented in this chapter have been translated into English by the author. English words used in the original responses are shown in italics.

Findings

Exposure to different varieties of English

The first focus of the study was the varieties of English that pre-service teachers are exposed to. Table 9.1 shows which varieties of English were taught in their English language courses. The majority of programs listed American English, British English or both. In other words, the varieties students encounter in classroom settings are predominantly American and British English.

According to the responses, the selection of the instructional variety depends mostly on the English teachers' background and the availability

Table 9.1 In English language courses, which varieties of English (e.g. American, British) are being taught?

Variety	Frequency
American	62
British	46
Australian	15
Canadian	9
Japanese	8
Irish	3
Asian	2
'Various'	2
International	1
Indian	1
'English spoken by Chinese people'	1
Unknown	15

of teaching materials. When asked which varieties of English were taught, respondents wrote:

> Depends on who your teacher is, whether native English speakers (American, Canadian, Australia, New Zealander, Irish, British, etc.) or native Japanese speakers (and where they may have studied English). The largest groups are of course American and British. [original in English]

> Teaching materials are predominantly in American English. But English courses are taught in English, and depending on the teachers' background, students encounter Canadian, British, Australian, and even Japanese English. We have adopted the notion of English as an international language.

> I'd think it's mostly American English. The reason is that all three native English speaking teachers in our program are from the United States.

In fact, at least 23 respondents (24%) explicitly wrote that there is no consensus regarding the choice of the instructional variety:

> The choice depends on each instructor. I think we should avoid a bias toward a particular regional or social dialect of English, but we don't do anything special to diversify. It's OK as long as students are learning 'English'.

> We do not make distinctions between different varieties, but we have native speakers of both American and British English.

> We do not know [which varieties are being taught], but all the native speakers are from North America or England.

> I do not know, because we do not choose the target variety for the entire program. It depends on each instructor's decision.

While American and British Englishes seem to be preferred instructional varieties in most language courses, the majority of the programs responded that they do offer exposure to other varieties, in or out of classes (see Table 9.2). These opportunities were available through the English language and subject area courses that are taught by teachers from inner circle countries other than United States and UK (e.g. Australia, New Zealand) as well as international scholars from the outer and expanding circles. Some universities also place international students from Europe and Asia and Japanese students together in subject area courses, creating opportunities for international communication using both English and Japanese. Students can also interact with international students through

Table 9.2 Do students have opportunities to be exposed to Englishes other than American and British English (e.g. Australian English, Southeast Asian English)?

	Yes	No	Others	No response
Number	53	31	3	8
%	55.7	32.6	3.2	8.4

extracurricular activities or participate in a study abroad program. How often pre-service teachers actually take up such opportunities is unknown, although one respondent wrote: 'Students who are seriously considering becoming an English teacher tend to put themselves in the situation where they can use English to communicate with international students from different parts of the world without our [teacher educators'] prompting.'

When asked whether the exposure to Englishes other than AE and BE were necessary for pre-service teachers, almost 80% of the respondents felt it was either necessary or desirable (see Table 9.3). According to their responses, one reason why teacher educators consider such exposure necessary or desirable is that it empowers Japanese pre-service teachers of English. They believe that, by witnessing the fact that effective communication is possible even when English deviates from American and British norms, students will feel more confident about their own English. For example:

> When they see people use accented English confidently and successfully and listen to their accents, students will realize that Japanese people's English is not so bad. In addition, they will realize how silly it is to think that we, Japanese, must sound like Americans and Britons when speaking in English.

> Through exposure to Englishes other than American and British, students will recognize the diversity and international function of

Table 9.3 Do you believe such opportunities [to be exposed to Englishes other than American and British English] are necessary for English language teachers?

	Necessary	Desirable but not necessary	Unnecessary	Others	No response
Number	51	24	11	1	8
%	53.7	25.2	11.5	1.1	8.4

English. They will also become more accepting of differences in their own English (pronunciation, for instance).

Experiencing diversity will make teachers more accepting of students' errors and expand the list of possible teaching materials. It also motivates students and teachers to learn English if they see that other Asian people *empower* themselves through English.

Another reason that emerged from the responses is that such exposure helps prospective teachers understand the reality of English language today:

I want the future teachers of English to understand the reality of *Englishes*.

Since English is an international language, it is meaningful to experience different varieties of English.

The increasingly diverse backgrounds of assistant language teachers (ALTs), who are recruited from English-speaking countries and assigned to school districts all over Japan by the government-sponsored JET (Japanese Exchange and Teaching) program, also increases the need for the awareness of and sensitivity toward different varieties of English.

In recent years, ALTs from the JET program include those from Malaysia and Singapore, which seems to mean that Japanese teachers are expected to be familiar with their English. That is what I hear from the graduates of our program. From that point of view, the more exposure they have to such varieties of English, the better.

The primary reason for not considering such exposures necessary, respondents write, relates to the question of priority. No one stated that such exposure was harmful or undesirable, but for some teacher educators and programs, it is not the top priority:

Such opportunities are nice, but improved English proficiency (regardless of its regional origin) is more urgent and necessary.

It is better to have such an opportunity than not have, but I don't think it is necessary. You can teach just fine if you know standard English.

A respondent also pointed out the 'irrelevance' of such exposure given current practice in secondary school English classes:

I believe our curriculum should focus on the English of English-speaking countries (United States, UK, Australia) since the target model at the secondary school level is that of native English speakers.

Exposure to World Englishes literatures

The second focus of the study was on pre-service teachers' exposure to English literatures other than American and British. Among 95 programs that participated in this study, such opportunities are available in only 21 programs (22%), which is less than half the number of programs that expose students to different varieties of English (discussed in the previous section) (see Table 9.4).

Furthermore, teacher educators believed that exposure to WE literature is not as important as the exposure to different varieties of English itself (see Table 9.5).

Different reasons were given as to why such exposure is considered necessary or desirable. The most common reason was that it is a contextualized way to introduce the forms and history of World Englishes.

> By introducing a course like this, students will understand the diversity in grammar and expressions in written English.

> At our university, we offer a course called 'Survey of literature in English-speaking world', which includes literature from Canada and Australia. It has been very useful in encouraging students to gain a broad perspective on how English has become an international language and how world languages should be.

Some teacher educators also felt that literature provides crosscultural and intercultural experiences that may not be available otherwise. For instance:

> There are various ethnic groups in the world, and students will better understand their way of thinking through literature written in the English variety of that country or region. I believe that would prevent students from falling into the idea of American/British supremacy.

> I don't think students have many opportunities, expect perhaps for examples used in the courses on intercultural communication or comparative culture. But such experience seems necessary in order to understand a multicultural society.

Table 9.4 Do students have opportunities to be exposed to English literatures other than American and British (e.g. English literature from India or Africa)?

	Yes	*No*	*Others*	*No response*
Number	21	64	1	9
%	22.1	67.3	1.1	9.4

Table 9.5 Do you believe that such exposure (to English literature other than American and British) is necessary for English teachers?

	Necessary	*Desirable but not necessary*	*Unnecessary*	*Others*	*No response*
Number	20	29	33	4	9
%	21.1	30.5	34.7	4.2	9.5

In contrast, there were respondents who did not consider such exposure necessary for different reasons. The most frequently mentioned reason was that it is not required by the MEXT.[4]

> We are offering courses in American and British literature, following the guidelines put forth by the MEXT, and have not expanded our offerings to include literature from other countries. I believe it is important to be familiar with the culture of different countries but not so much with the literature.

> Such literature is rarely included in the secondary school English textbooks. Even if some literary pieces were to be included, I don't think they would be published in such a way that the linguistic characteristics of the particular English variety (vocabulary, grammar, style) would be clearly represented.

Another reason given to explain why such exposure may not be necessary is that, although the knowledge of English literature may be important, its country of origin is not considered crucial:

> I think it is important to be exposed to literature in English, but I don't think it really matters where it comes from. It could be Shakespeare, Harry Potter, Updike, or Commonwealth – doesn't really make a difference.

Aside from the discussion of literature, several teacher educators – both those who believed that WE literature was necessary and those who did not – stressed the importance of exposure to Englishes in various text forms, including but not limited to literature:

> I hesitate to evaluate the importance of texts solely from the point of view of which variety of English it is written in. Regional characteristics found in the language of literature are only one aspect of diversity, and the pedagogical appropriateness of texts should be looked at

holistically and with other genres such as natural science, journalism and documents about human rights.

Written English is, in fact, used as an international lingua franca in a very practical way, and thus it is important to read different kinds of English, including those written by nonnative speakers and texts other than literature.

Exposures to various cultures

The preservice teachers' exposure to cultures other than American and British was also explored in the survey. According to the responses, such exposure exists much more than the exposure to varieties or literatures of other varieties of World Englishes (see Table 9.6).

The high number (64.2%) of affirmative answers may be related to the fact that the MEXT requires at least one-credit of academic work on intercultural understanding, a course whose content often includes examples of different cultural practices. The responses often stated that exposure to different cultures takes place in one or more of the required courses that fulfill the MEXT requirement.

Other opportunities for the exposure mentioned in the survey included required and optional study abroad programs to countries other than the United States and UK, and elective courses in languages other than English, 'non-English cultures', and/or area studies. Some universities also host numerous international students, providing opportunities for intercultural learning in and out of the classroom.

When asked if such exposure was necessary, the number of teacher educators who believed so (47) was much smaller than the number of programs that offered such courses (61). This gap again seems to reflect the influence of MEXT requirements. However, if those who believe it was 'desirable but not necessary' are included, the findings show that the majority of teacher educators do consider that exposure to different cultures is a positive influence on pre-service teachers (see Table 9.7).

Table 9.6 Do students have opportunities to be exposed to cultures other than American and British?

	Yes	*No*	*Others*	*No response*
Number	61	21	3	7
%	64.2	22.1	3.4	7.4

Table 9.7 Do you think such exposure (to cultures other than American and British) is necessary for English teachers?

	Necessary	*Desirable but not necessary*	*Unnecessary*	*Others*	*No response*
Number	47	31	7	3	7
%	49.5	33.2	7.4	3.2	7.4

According to the respondents, one way in which such exposure becomes meaningful is that it helps preservice teachers contextualize the English language and English-speaking culture in the global community. For instance:

> A real cosmopolitan should be familiar with various cultures and accept the differences. In Japan, *globalization* tends to focus on North America and Western Europe, but true *globalization* should aim at interacting with and co-existing with countries all over the world. Teachers should experience diverse cultures and truly understand what it means to globalize or to be a cosmopolitan.

> In our department [of international relations], students are required to take one language in addition to English – they can choose from Chinese, Korean, Hindi, Spanish, Indonesian, and Arabic. We also offer area studies courses that are parallel to our language offerings. It does put a burden on students, but we feel it is necessary. It gives students a chance to look at English objectively, too.

Several teacher educators also pointed out that exposure to different cultures often involves the use of EIL in an authentic context:

> English is no longer the language of the UK and US only. To understand its use as an international lingua franca, it is important for English teachers to actually visit the countries other than the US and UK and experience their local cultures.

> If you look at the news, you will see immediately that people from all over the world are trying to communicate with each other in English. In our program, there are some opportunities to interact with students and tourists from non-English-speaking countries. It would be nice to have more situations where students can use English, rather than Japanese, to communicate with others.

A more practical and immediate need brought up in the survey was that pre-service teachers' future students and colleagues may come from culturally diverse backgrounds. One respondent referred to the diverse backgrounds of ALTs:

> The reality is that ALTs [through the JET program] are now brought in from various countries in the world.

Another respondent pointed out the presence of immigrant workers and their children in schools:

> The number of foreign workers is increasing, and there are 2,000,000 foreigners now living in Japan. Given this, teachers may need to use Portuguese, for example, to teach students. Perhaps we'll need to require languages like Chinese, Korean and Portuguese for prospective teachers.

As was the case in response to the value of exposure to different varieties and literatures of English, no respondent expressed reservation about exposure to various cultures in teacher preparation. However, several – especially those who believe this exposure was desirable but not necessary – expressed the opinion that given the limited time and number of courses students can take, cultural learning should focus on that of traditional 'English speaking countries'.

There were also teacher educators who felt the understanding of Japanese culture should come before exposure to other cultures. The importance of *understanding* and *accepting* different cultures, rather than simply *being exposed to* them, was also mentioned in several responses.

Courses on the linguistic and functional diversity of English

The study also investigated if there was a course where students could gain meta-knowledge of linguistic and functional varieties of English. As Table 9.8 shows, only four of the participating programs currently offer a course specifically devoted to the linguistic and functional diversity of English. However, at least four other programs are discussing the

Table 9.8 Is there a course on linguistic and/or functional varieties of English in your program?

	Yes	*No*	*Others*	*No response*
Number	4	81	0	10
%	4.2	85.3	—	10.5

possibilities of creating such a course, and more than half (44) of other programs offer courses that touch upon such topics as the spread of English, World Englishes, and social and regional dialects of English. These courses come from a variety of subject areas, including English language (e.g. listening, oral communication), literature (e.g. American literatures, World literatures), linguistics (e.g. History of English, sociolinguistics), intercultural communication, and comparative cultures (e.g. English-speaking culture, American and British English and culture, Multiculturalism). In addition, many teaching methods courses touch upon this topic, although the coverage does not seem to go beyond one to two class periods at the most.

I also asked the respondents who have such a course to describe what is covered in a course on linguistic and functional diversity within English. For both institutions that have such a course and those that offer this topic as a part of a course with a broader focus, the most frequently mentioned were the study of 'social and regional dialects' and 'World Englishes' discussed in the context of sociolinguistics or historical changes of the language. Linguistic differences between American and British English are often addressed in English linguistics as well as English language classes. Several respondents also mentioned special topics courses and seminars focusing on linguistic imperialism and/or multilingualism.

Regarding the importance of the awareness of linguistic and functional diversity in English, the overwhelming majority of the respondents felt it was necessary (see Table 9.9). Not many people elaborated on the reasons why such awareness is needed, but one reason that was mentioned repeatedly was that their future interlocutors and colleagues may speak different native and non-native varieties of English, and thus the meta-knowledge about the existence of such diversity would prepare preservice teachers better for such future encounters. Several teacher educators also pointed out that this awareness is crucial because 'they will be teaching in a country, Japan, where you find many different Englishes' and 'the goal of Japanese learners of English needs to be determined taking into consideration of

Table 9.9   Is the awareness of the linguistic and functional varieties of English necessary for pre-service English teachers?

	Necessary	*Yes but a course is not necessary*	*Unnecessary*	*Others*	*No response*
Number	64	10	5	1	15
%	67.4	10.5	5.3	1.1	15.8

the number of different varieties of English that exist in Japan'. At the same time, a few teacher educators emphasized that 'it is knowledge of, and not the competency in, World Englishes that these preservice teachers should have'. Furthermore, in some programs, even the acquisition of knowledge or increased awareness of such diversity is not a top priority because 'one can teach a regular course as long as he/she has knowledge of standard English'.

Courses on the role of English as an international language

Among 95 programs that responded to the survey, 12 offered a course that specifically focused on the role of English as an international language. Not all of these courses, however, are part of the requirement for certification (see Table 9.10). The number of EIL courses is much greater than the number of courses on linguistic and functional diversity (discussed in the previous section), possibly because, as one respondent stated, 'the notion of EIL is much more familiar and better accepted among people in Japan than that of *World Englishes*'. Courses appear with many different titles, including *World Englishes, English as a global language, International English communication, English for international understanding, Internet English, Intercultural communication in English*, and *EIL*. There were also respondents from two different programs who stated that the entire curriculum was based on the perspective of EIL.

As was the case with the previous topics, many programs (39) which do not offer courses that exclusively focus on EIL do have courses that touch upon the topic, including *Teaching methods, Introduction to (English) linguistics, Sociolinguistics, Contrastive linguistics, Introduction to communication theory, Multicultural society* and *Multicultural education*. Five of these programs explicitly stated that the topic is important enough to be addressed in multiple courses.

Regarding the necessity of the understanding of EIL, again, the majority of respondents felt it was necessary. About a third of them, however, believed that a course entirely devoted to the topic was not necessary (see Table 9.11). The most frequently mentioned reason why respondents

Table 9.10 Is there a course focusing on the role of English as an international language?

	Yes	*No*	*Others*	*No response*
Number	12	74	1	8
%	12.6	78.0	1.1	8.4

Table 9.11   Is the awareness of the role of EIL necessary for pre-service English teachers?

	Necessary	*Yes, but a course is not necessary*	*Unnecessary*	*Others*	*No response*
Number	48	22	8	0	17
%	50.5	23.2	8.4	–	17.9

felt such awareness was necessary was that English's role as an international language is directly related to the purpose of ELT today. It not only clarifies the mission of English language teachers, the respondents wrote, but also helps motivate their future students. For example:

> In *Teaching Methods I*, we try to connect the questions of the significance of and motivation for English learning with the reality of EIL, its dominance, marketability, and implications for the language-culture relationship. I believe that such awareness as well as the neutral attitude toward the role of EIL is crucial for English teachers.

> I know there is concern about linguistic imperialism, but it is a fact that English is functioning as the international language ... Through learning English, students [in secondary schools] broaden their perspectives and become interested in current international events. Through using the language, they can interact with and better understand people from different countries of the world (some middle and high schools are already providing such opportunities).

In contrast, those few who stated it was not necessary to address these issues in class believed so because 'pre-service teachers already know that English is an international language'. A teacher educator also wrote that 'there's not much difference in teaching English as an international language and teaching the English of native speakers, and thus it is not necessary to emphasize the fact that it is an international language as long as students know American (or British) English'. This was a perspective shared by at least two other respondents.

Discussion

First, the findings from the current study suggest that there is an interest among teacher educators in Japan in introducing WE/EIL perspectives into their programs, and such attempts are already being made, especially at the individual level. Respondents often demonstrated familiarity with scholarship in this area, using such terms as 'World Englishes' and 'linguistic imperialism' and citing prominent scholars in the field (e.g. Braj Kachru, Robert Phillipson and Alastair Pennycook). Although this may not be a representative group (i.e. programs and teacher educators interested in WE/EIL perspectives are more likely to have responded than others), the presence of WE/EIL topics in these programs contrasts with the findings from Vavrus' (1991) study on MA programs in the United States.

One explanation for this difference between Vavrus' (1991) study and the present investigation may be when the research was conducted. As Brown (1993) pointed out, it takes time for research findings to be disseminated and start making a tangible impact in curriculum development and policy. It may be that the work on World Englishes in the past three decades is finally making a difference in our pedagogical practices, and programs that did not integrate the WE and EIL issues back in the early 1990s are doing so now.

Another possible explanation is that the differences between the two studies reflect differences between the inner circle, where English is used as the dominant language of communication, and the expanding circle, where English use is mostly reserved for international communication. Although their English language teaching has been criticized as being too biased toward American and British English (e.g. Matsuda, 2002), English teachers and teacher educators in the expanding circle are much more exposed to the discourse of English as an international language, which in turn is often used to justify or promote English language teaching in the expanding circle. Furthermore, their personal experience in using EIL, including the sense of frustration as well as the opportunities that accompany the use of EIL, may have made these teacher educators more enthusiastic about the idea of WE and EIL than professionals working in the inner circle.

Although more research is needed in order to understand *how* the perspectives of World Englishes and EIL are being incorporated into these teacher preparation programs, the current study suggests that the effort to promote the understanding of WE and EIL seems to exist in many programs in Japan. This finding, which contrasts with that of Vavrus (1991) mentioned above, makes the research conducted a worthwhile contribution to the studies in this area.

Second, while some teacher educators do believe that such notions as WE and EIL have a legitimate place in their programs, these notions are still considered supplementary. English language, literature and culture from the inner circle, specifically from the United States and UK, are still considered as the 'default' content of the courses, to which other varieties will be added only when there is extra time or extra resources.

However, I would argue that the notion of WE or EIL cannot be conveniently separated from the 'default' curriculum. It is rather a new way of

looking at and defining the English language itself. It calls for the fundamental change from a monolithic view of English, which allows only the
static notion of standard, to a pluralistic view of the language, which
acknowledges the existence of multiple standards that are defined and
implemented differently in different contexts. Thus, the most important –
and perhaps most challenging – transition is to accept the World Englishes
and EIL perspectives as the guiding framework for preparing Japanese
teachers of English, and to position the inner-circle varieties, literatures
and cultures within that framework. The American and British English
and literature may be selected to play a dominant role in ELT in Japan, but
it should be done so only after its appropriateness and relevance to the
objectives of each program are evaluated. This literature should no longer
have the protected and privileged status that it has enjoyed in the past.

One encouraging finding from this study was that there are many
creative ways to incorporate WE/EIL perspectives into a teacher preparation program. The most committed approach would be to create a program
that is *based on* the perspective of WE and EIL, but the responses suggested
other smaller scale initiatives (e.g. course, unit, study abroad, extracurricular activities) that can be adopted at the individual, program and institutional level. If students are equipped with the analytical and reflective
skills to interpret their encounter with these new concepts, they will not
only gain a knowledge base but also be able to use the exposure to these
concepts to (re)shape their perception of English and English speakers.

Future Research

As I stated in the previous section, we need to investigate the teacher
preparation programs in the expanding circle further in order to understand how EIL teachers can and should be prepared. Using a broad overview provided by the current study as a spring board, more in-depth
studies of how teacher preparation programs around the world incorporate the WE/EIL perspectives in their curriculum need to be conducted.

In addition, research on the role of teacher preparation programs in the
construction of teacher beliefs and practices is also needed. In order to
better understand the process of knowledge construction in teacher
education programs, we must address questions such as how the beliefs of
teacher educators regarding the place of WE/EIL perspectives influence
what is introduced in the teacher program, how pre-service teachers
understand, interpret, and negotiate the meaning of such new concepts as
WE and EIL while in the teacher preparation program, and how the new
teachers, once in the classroom, use their understanding of WE and EIL to
shape their teaching.

Conclusion

The current study explored what kind of exposure pre-service teachers in Japan have to the perspectives of World Englishes and (teaching) English as an international language. The responses suggested different ways future EIL teachers are being exposed to the linguistic, literary, and cultural diversity of World Englishes and showed that a number of programs are indeed attempting to increase their students' awareness of the sociolinguistic complexity and intricacy of the English language today. Changes are always difficult to implement, and teacher preparation programs, which must struggle with various requirements and constraints related to the certification, will not be easy to change. However, these programs can be one of the most powerful agents of change in our society, because changes in teacher preparation programs are passed along to children at schools through teachers and then dispersed through the whole society through the attitudes of the students and graduates of those schools. Although the study of teaching English as an international language to date has focused predominantly on EIL classrooms (e.g. the curriculum, teaching materials), research on EIL teacher preparation programs is equally necessary in order to create and implement a coherent and informed EIL curriculum.

Acknowledgements

I would like to thank Paul Kei Matsuda and two anonymous reviewers for their insightful comments on an earlier version of this chapter and Yoonhee Lee for her assistance with the preparation of the manuscript.

Notes

1. For English teachers in Japan, five different types of teaching certificates are currently available (MEXT, n.d.):

Degree Grades to teach	Master's program	Undergraduate (Bachelor's) program	Two-year program
Lower secondary (7–9th grade)	Advanced class certificate	First-class certificate	Second-class certificate
Upper secondary (10–12th)	Advanced class certificate	First-class certificate	n/a

First-class certificates are the most common at both lower and upper secondary level, constituting over 90% and 70% respectively of newly obtained certificates in all subject areas in 2004 (MEXT, 2005).
2. The questionnaires were sent to the coordinator of a teacher preparation program. When the coordinator was not known, it was sent to the department chair or the administrative staff with a request to be forwarded to the faculty member who regularly taught in the teacher preparation program. All returned questionnaires were completed by teacher educators.
3. A copy of the questionnaire is available upon request.
4. Regardless of the certificate type, all pre-service English teachers are required to take 20 credits in the subject area that includes English linguistics, English/ American literature, English communication, and international understanding. The area distribution requirements put forth by the ministry of education are rather loose, requiring only one credit in each of the above sub-areas. This loose definition of the requirements allows each program to establish its own emphasis.

References

Brown, K. (1993) World Englishes in TESOL programs: An infusion model of curricular innovation. *World Englishes* 12 (1), 59–73.
Brown, K. (1995) World Englishes: To teach or not to teach? *World Englishes* 14 (2), 233–245.
Burns, A. (ed.) (2005) *Teaching English from a Global Perspective*. Alexandria, VA: TESOL.
Dogancay-Aktuna, S. and Hardman, J. (eds) (2007) (forthcoming) *Global English Teaching and Teacher Education: Praxis and Possibility*. Alexandria, VA: TESOL.
Kachru, B.B. (1984) World Englishes and the teaching of English to non-native speakers: Contexts, attitudes, and concerns. *TESOL Newsletter* 18 (5), 25–26.
Kachru, B.B. (1992) Teaching World Englishes. In B.B. Kachru (ed.) *The Other Tongue: English Across Cultures* (2nd edn) (pp. 355–365). Urbana, IL: University of Illinois Press.
Matsuda, A. (2002) Representation of users and uses of English in beginning Japanese EFL textbooks. *JALT Journal* 24 (2), 80–98.
Matsuda, A. (2005) Preparing future users of English as an international language. In A. Burns (ed.) *Teaching English from a Global Perspective* (pp. 63–72). Alexandria, VA: TESOL.
Matsuda, A. (2006) Negotiating ELT assumptions in EIL classrooms. In J. Edge (ed.) *(Re)Locating TESOL in an Age of Empire* (pp. 158–170). Basingstoke: Palgrave MacMillan.
McKay, S. (2002) *Teaching English as an International Language: Rethinking Goals and Approaches*. Oxford: Oxford University Press.
Ministry of Education, Culture, Sports, Science and Technology (MEXT) (2003) Regarding the establishment of an action plan to Japanese with English abilities. On WWW at http://www.mext.go.jp/b_menu/houdou/15/03/03033101/001.pdf. Accessed 08.02.08.
Ministry of Education, Culture, Sports, Science and Technology (MEXT) (2005) *Gakko kyoin toukei chousa [School Teacher Statistical Survey]*. Tokyo: National

Printing Bureau. On WWW at http://www.mext.go.jp/b_menu/toukei/001/002/2004/002/006.htm. Accessed 19.07.08.

Ministry of Education, Culture, Sports, Science and Technology (MEXT) (n.d.) Chuugakko/koutou gakkou kyouin (eigo) no menkyo shikaku wo shutoku surukoto no dekiru daigaku [Universities at which secondary school (English) teacher certificate qualification can be obtained]. On WWW at http://www.mext.go.jp/a_menu/shotou/kyoin/daigaku/07051619/014.htm. Accessed 19.07.08.

Shaules, J., Tsujioka, H. and Iida, M. (2004) *Identity*. Oxford: Oxford University Press.

Vavrus, F.S. (1991) When paradigms clash: The role of institutionalized varieties in language teacher education. *World Englishes* 10 (2), 181–195.

Yoneoka, J. and Arimoto, J. (2000) *Englishes of the World*. Tokyo: Sanshusha.

Chapter 10

Imperialism of International Tests: An EIL Perspective

SARAH ZAFAR KHAN

Introduction

This chapter discusses the role of internationally recognized standard-ized high-stakes proficiency tests vis-à-vis the notion of English as an International Language (EIL) (McKay, 2002; Smith, 1976). The title of this chapter is derived from Davidson's (1994) reference to the 'imperialism of major international tests', and the belief that high-stakes tests like TOEFL (Test of English as a Foreign Language) are biased against individuals who may be proficient in using English for international communication but have not been exposed to certain nuances of an inner-circle variety of English (Davies *et al.*, 2003; Jenkins, 2006), which in the case of TOEFL is standard American English. In this chapter, the imperialism of tests like TOEFL is discussed at two levels. At the first level, the focus is on the dominance of standard American variety of English and the items constituting the TOEFL test. At the second level, the prestige and power associated with TOEFL, and its widespread use in higher education institutions in non-English speaking countries like Saudi Arabia is highlighted. The case study discussed in this chapter explores the rationale for the use of the institutional version of TOEFL in a private higher education institution in Saudi Arabia, where English is used as a foreign language. This study investigates the perceptions of teachers and students towards reasons governing the use of TOEFL in their local educational context and towards promoting English as an international language. Findings from the study emphasize the need to reassess admission criteria for higher education and eliminate the bias against test takers that occurs through the use of TOEFL in settings like that in Saudi Arabia.

Background

There is no single way of teaching English, no single way of learning it, no single motive for doing so, no single syllabus or textbook, no single way of assessing proficiency and, indeed, no single variety of English which provides the target of learning. (Graddol, 2006: 82)

Graddol and other academics studying the spread of English, 'world Englishes', 'global English' and 'English as an International Language' would agree that the ownership of English cannot be restricted to a geographically bound location. Kachru's (1989) description of the use of English in the world and the prediction that the number of English language users will reach its maximum (of around 2 billion learners or one-third of the world's population) in the next decade (Graddol, 2006) signal that several 'Englishes' and educational methodologies will be inevitable in the future. In this regard, assessment, which is one aspect of English language education, should focus on a global view of English in order to promote English as an international language.

Hegemony, English as an International Language (EIL) and Linguistic Imperialism

Although the majority of English language speakers in the world are in the 'expanding circle' (Kachru, 1989), hegemony of the 'center' ('inner circle' countries where English is used as the primary language) persists when it comes to English language educational management. The control of English speaking countries is maintained through hegemony rather than mere political imposition. Gramsci's concept of hegemony (in Kalyvas, 2000) states that power and control exerted by a dominant class in society is sustainable if it gains support through 'consent' of the masses. This consent is achieved through ideological manipulation of the weaker group so that the group perceives the ideology of the ruling class as 'natural' and 'common sense'. It is through hegemony that countries located in the 'inner circle' have become providers of professional expertise and norms for teaching English to speakers of other languages.

Smith (1976) was one of the first people to define 'international language' as a means to communicate and interact with people from different nations. Smith (1976, in McKay, 2002) clarifies that 'English as an international language belongs to no single culture' and adds that:

Learners of an international language do not need to internalize the cultural norms of native speakers of that language; the ownership of an international language becomes de-nationalized; and the educational goal of learning it is to enable learners to communicate their ideas and culture to others. (Mckay, 2002: 12)

The assertion made by Smith clarifies that an international language is used to promote intercultural and intracultural communication in linguistically diverse situations. This view does not depend on the 'native speaker' criterion in measuring second/foreign language education. Phillipson (1992) refers to the importance given to native speaking models as the 'native speaker fallacy'. In his seminal work, Phillipson maintains that English linguistic imperialism is one example of *linguicism*, which is defined as 'ideologies, structures, and practices which are used to legitimate, effectuate, and reproduce an unequal division of power and resources (both material and immaterial) between groups which are defined on the basis of language' (Phillipson, 1992: 47). It is argued that 'locally appropriate pedagogy' is essential for teaching English as an international language (McKay, 2002) where the 'local context is the norm' (Holliday, 2005).

In Phillipson's (1992) terms, 'educational imperialism' arises when countries located in the expanding circle follow the professionalism of countries located in the inner circle. This notion of domination has strong roots in the history of colonialism, and one reason given by Phillipson is that many elites in society have strong links with the inner circle because they have been educated in inner circle countries. In other words, they have been influenced by the hegemony of the West. Educational imperialism may refer to all aspects of education including testing which is an important aspect of education. Davidson (1994) mentions the 'prevalent imperialism of major international tests of English' and believes that these tests support and serve the variety of English prevalent in the country where they are produced. Phillipson refers to the promotion of English by British and American governments as the 'new international crusade', and tests like TOEFL are instrumental in this crusade. Moreover, reliance on TOEFL to make high-stakes decisions leads to increased demand for TOEFL preparation material and courses. This 'gold plating' (Graddol, 2006) yields high profits to publishers who disseminate TOEFL preparation material to individuals and institutions. Hence, in addition to promoting American English and cultural norms, TOEFL provides economic gains to the government it represents, to individuals and institutions that prepare students to succeed in TOEFL, and to publishers of TOEFL preparation material who are 'cashing in on this linguistic bonanza' (Templer, 2004).

High-Stakes English Language Tests and Linguistic Imperialism

TOEFL and standard North American English

A strong criticism against high-stakes English tests like TOEFL and IELTS (International English Language Testing System) is that these tests are specific to inner circle varieties of English (Davies *et al.*, 2003; Johnson *et al.*, 2005; Jenkins, 2006). Davies *et al.* compare the norms used in international English language proficiency tests like IELTS and TOEFL and national English language proficiency tests in five countries where English is used as a second or a foreign language. They found several words in the TOEFL sampler that have different referential meanings in British, American and Australian English. They also found words that are culturally specific to North American contexts and do not even exist in other English speaking contexts. Davies *et al.* argue that TOEFL is biased against individuals who may be proficient in using English as an international language but are not familiar with American English. Davies *et al.* (2003: 572) argue that in 'proficiency testing in high stakes contexts, for example, TOEFL …. What is at stake here is whose norms are to be imposed?'. They add that tests like TOEFL are not an accurate reflection of a test taker's proficiency because the items assess candidates on just the North American variety of English which is unfamiliar to many candidates. Nevertheless, the study by Davies *et al.* is based on their preliminary analysis of items on proficiency tests and not on empirical study. Based on this argument, it can be surmised that in foreign language contexts, TOEFL may not be a valid test because English used in these local contexts is more international than American.

Brown (2004) responded to Davies *et al.* (2003) and listed eight categories or 'English(es)' that have an impact on tests. He believes that a test is free from bias if all eight Englishes are the same. These include:

(1) the English(es) of the test takers' local community,
(2) the dominant English of the test taker,
(3) the English(es) of the test content,
(4) the English(es) of the test proctors,
(5) the English(es) of the test scorers/raters,
(6) the English(es) of the decision target community,
(7) the English(es) of the decision target purpose,
(8) the English(es) of the decision makers. (Brown, 2004: 318)

Brown reiterates the recommendation of Davies *et al.* to engage in empirical research to study bias in major internationally recognized high-stakes tests like TOEFL and IELTS and the factors that affect validity of these proficiency tests.

Jenkins (2006) looks at the major international proficiency tests vis-à-vis an EIL perspective on testing and comments that:

> There is nothing 'international' about deferring to the language varieties of a mere two of the world's Englishes, whose members account for a tiny minority of English speakers. Nor is there reason to suppose that the study of British or American English will promote international understanding'. (Jenkins, 2006: 44)

Jenkins suggests that since the purpose of EIL is to facilitate communication amongst English language users in inner, outer and expanding circle countries, the tests should be based on evidence from EIL interaction rather than on one or two varieties of English that do not represent the English used by majority of its speakers.

TOEFL test items

TOEFL is an essential admission requirement for second and foreign language learners who aspire to study in North American universities and need to be familiar with the standard American English. The TOEFL Institutional Testing Program Examinee Handbook (ETS, 2001) issued by ETS (Educational Testing Services) states that each institutional version of TOEFL measures candidates' ability to 'understand North American English' (ETS, 2001: 5). Section 1 on Listening Comprehension 'is designed to measure the ability to understand spoken North American English'; Section 2 on Structure and Written Expression measures standard written English, which again refers to standard American English, and Section 3 on Reading Comprehension 'is designed to measure the ability to understand short passages similar in topic and style to those found in North American universities and colleges' (ETS, 2001: 18).

In his analysis of TOEFL test items, Templer (2004) notes that in addition to the specificity of the variety of English tested in TOEFL, the speech in certain sections does not represent authentic English usage. He maintains that in TOEFL, '"artificial" English may be tested, especially in canned oral comprehension sections ... Clearly TOEFL in a sense imposes an "American" standard on the globe.' In many second and foreign language contexts, TOEFL may not be a valid test because English used in these local contexts is more international than American. Templer indicates the political agenda of TOEFL and warns that if TOEFL continues to hold ground worldwide, then it will inevitably produce a 'TOEFL'd generation of EFL learners', and this would hamper the struggle to move towards an international view of English. Johnson *et al.* (2005) found that teachers and students in their English programme believe that TOEFL is 'full of tricks' and '. . . the variety of English tested was not the variety of English used in day-to-day interactions with native speakers of English'. One of the teachers in the study even told his students that 'TOEFL English is not real English'. By using TOEFL as a placement test, educators and learners depend on tests that may be isolated from their learning culture. Furthermore, for many students in expanding circle countries, TOEFL is the first standardized test that they take in life (Templer, 2004), and it is unfortunate that TOEFL scores are used to determine their admission into higher education institutions.

Local Educational Institutions and Imperialism

Higher education institutions in many countries in the expanding circle where English is the medium of instruction adopt the Test of English as a Foreign Language (TOEFL). TOEFL is used in many colleges and universities in the Middle East and is regarded as 'a valuable tool for students who would like to study abroad in English', and it 'opens more doors than any other academic English test' (ETS, n.d.). Brown (2004) proposes a different reason and believes that high-stakes international tests are used for placement purposes in developing countries simply because they are readily available and have high face validity. However, concerning the content of language tests, Lanteigne (2006) suggests that placement tests should include information about the curriculum that the students will encounter. This echoes Jenkins' (2006) suggestion that English language proficiency tests should be based on understanding how well candidates are able to interact in English with speakers of other varieties of English.

A Case Study from Saudi Arabia

Distinctive features of English used in Saudi Arabia would qualify it as having a foreign language status. English is the medium of instruction in many private higher education institutions where teachers come from several countries in the world, such as Canada, the UK, the United States, Philippines, India, Pakistan, South Africa, Egypt, Jordan and Lebanon. Thus, students are exposed to several varieties of English. Students learn English for higher education, traveling and to communicate with staff in hospitals and international restaurants. Hence, students in Saudi Arabia are exposed to the use of English in international contexts. However, in order to obtain the relevant cut scores on TOEFL required by local colleges and universities, students need proficiency in standard American English. In these educational institutions, TOEFL marginalizes individuals who are not familiar with the nuances of American English but are otherwise proficient in using English for communication. This issue of marginalisation caused by adopting a foreign test in a local context was explored in a preparatory English program in a private college for women in Jeddah, Saudi Arabia. Two main questions that guided the case study were:

(1) What reasons govern the use of TOEFL in a private college for women in Jeddah, Saudi Arabia?
(2) Does TOEFL facilitate teaching and learning of English as an international language?

This study follows the interpretive tradition of research and is situated within the domain of critical applied linguistics (Pennycook, 2001). An instrumental case study (Creswell, 2002) is used to examine the suitability of the institutional version of TOEFL in a women's college in Jeddah, Saudi Arabia, and its impact on students and teachers in the English programme and on the use of English as an international language.

Participants

Twenty-four female students aged 18–21 from the upper two levels in a college preparatory English program participated in this study voluntarily. All the students used Arabic as their first language. Students in these classes had previous experience with the ITP (Institutional) version of TOEFL at the time of placement in the English program and were (at the time of data collection) anticipating sitting the TOEFL again at the end of the semester, which would determine their entrance to college. Students signed a letter accepting their participation in the study.

Five teachers from the English language program responded to my research request and participated voluntarily. One teacher was Saudi, one was British, one was Pakistani and two were Jordanian. Participants were informed about the purpose of the study and were informed that their participation was voluntary. All the teachers had experience of working with students aspiring to obtain the relevant cut scores on the TOEFL test.

Data collection

Data for this research were gathered in two stages. Focus group discussion with students was followed by semi-structured interviews with faculty members.

Data were collected through the following two methods.

Focus group discussion with students

Participants were divided into four groups of six students and were asked to express their views regarding TOEFL, particularly concerning its impact on the use of English as an international language. Focus group discussion was chosen because of time constraints, similarity among the groups, and to minimise any hesitation from participants (Creswell, 2002). Students recalled their experience of taking the TOEFL test and their familiarity with TOEFL preparation books. Structured questions were used to facilitate the discussion and assist students in recalling their experience of taking the TOEFL test. The questions, used as prompts, focused on students' opinion about TOEFL test items, their ability to answer the TOEFL test adequately, and their suggestions concerning assessment preferences. The discussion sessions lasted for 50 minutes, and were audio taped with permission from the participants. Data were transcribed immediately after the session to identify speakers' voices and to record their comments accurately.

Interviews with teachers

Five teachers in the English programme were interviewed on a one-to-one basis once during the study after the focus group discussion with students. Semi-structured interviews were organised that focused on teachers' understanding of the rationale behind the use of TOEFL in the college, their opinion about the various items on TOEFL. Teachers shared their views candidly, and the interviews were audio taped (with permission).

Findings

Data obtained from focus group discussion and interviews were analyzed qualitatively in light of the research questions. Pseudonyms are used for teachers and students who participated in the study. Students and faculty members' responses are reported simultaneously under general themes that emerge from the data and the literature review. Teachers' comments are marked by T in parentheses (T), and students' comments are marked by S in parentheses (S). Some comments have been edited for clarity.

Reasons Governing the Use of TOEFL

All the students participating in the study stated that TOEFL is used as an entrance test for college because it is the norm in all reputable colleges 'to know the level' of students. The following reasons for the use of TOEFL were observed by faculty members.

Americanization in Saudi Arabia

TOEFL is considered by some faculty members as a conduit to Americanization. Amal (T) mentioned direct link between TOEFL and Americanization, and believes that TOEFL is used in the college because it 'is easier ... and it appeals to Americanization in Saudi Arabia'. Commenting on the popularity of TOEFL in Saudi Arabia, Arwa (T) mentioned that TOEFL is popular with individuals and institutions because many Saudi students prefer multiple-choice questions rather than other test types where they have to do many different things. As a result of its popularity, TOEFL preparation courses are easily available, and many American housewives tutor students at home.

Emma (T) believes that in addition to the fact that TOEFL is a recognized English language proficiency test, it has a special position in the college because 'a lot of the top management studied in the States where TOEFL was the standard, so they kind of assume that it should be the standard for everything. I think it has to do with the educational background of the top management in the college'. This reason echoes Phillipson's (1992) concept of 'educational imperialism' where local decision-makers in the educational field maintain strong links to inner circle countries and tend to promote educational ideologies of those countries, hence strengthening the hegemony of inner circle countries.

International acceptance of TOEFL

Faculty members believe that TOEFL is used to display international standards achieved by the college and to assure students and their families that the college stands for quality education. Emma (T) thinks that TOEFL is used by the college as a 'marketing ploy' to impress students and increase recruitment. According to Saba (T) TOEFL is used in the college to 'satisfy them [parents] that it is a standardized test that comes from the West. They feel happy ... and think that if it has to do with English and if it comes from America, it is proper'. This false assumption and over-reliance on Western knowledge products, which in this case is TOEFL, gives prestige to a local institution and is common in many countries in the region.

Luna (T) thinks that TOEFL is just politics ... accreditation, the college's image, competition with other colleges ... having a standardized test is good, whether it is useful or not who cares!' Luna believes that the college will never replace TOEFL with a local entrance test because TOEFL is significant for local and international accreditation. Another reason suggested by Arwa (T) is that TOEFL is used to align college entrance cut off scores with what is acceptable in different parts of the world. Amal (T) added that 'here [in Saudi Arabia] people like the word TOEFL. It symbolizes something international ... something that can be recognized wherever we go'. In the college mentioned in this study, advancement is associated with TOEFL because it is developed in an inner circle country and is accepted internationally.

English as an International Language and TOEFL

The majority of the students mentioned that as an international language, English can be used to communicate with people of different nationalities. None of the students referred to America or other inner circle countries when describing English as an international language. Nevertheless, they were swift to declare that TOEFL is not a suitable test for the college because it requires facility in American English.

American English in TOEFL and difficulties faced by students

Many students mentioned difficulties in answering questions in TOEFL because the cultural content and dialect used in the test leans heavily towards American English. Amani (S) believes that the English represented on the test is 'only American language ... like in the listening [section of TOEFL] they speak in American English and not how everyone speaks'. The view expressed by this student implies an understanding of the use of English as an international language, and the realization that English used in TOEFL does not reflect the English used by global speakers of English. The problem is compounded by the fact that test items, particularly in the section on 'Structure and Written English', focus more on form than on use in global scenarios. Emma (T) thinks that some sentences and questions in the grammar section of TOEFL are 'too pedantic on minor grammatical points. Some questions are just meant to fail the students – let's catch them somehow!'

Another difficulty in the language used in TOEFL is caused by a narrow discourse focus and an element of 'artificiality' in the spoken language (Johnson *et al.*, 2005). Eman (S), a student, mentions that 'when you watch a movie, you notice that there is a big difference between what you listen

[hear] in the movies and what you listen in the TOEFL'. Emma (T) maintains an even more critical view and thinks that the TOEFL test does not represent North American culture in its entirety. She observes that the speech in the listening section on TOEFL represents 'middle-aged, middle class Americans, and I don't see how that represents the average student today ... over there and definitely not over here ... I think it is very middle class white American. Look at the television and you see the language they use. It's very different to language that comes out on the TOEFL'. It therefore seems inappropriate to assess learners on items that do not represent authentic interaction even in the country where it is produced.

Students' and teachers' views indicate their anxiety and frustration with the fact that the linguistic and cultural content of TOEFL is limited to the standard North American dialect of English and is biased against speakers of other varieties.

TOEFL Item Types and Difficulties Faced by Students

With respect to the different parts of the TOEFL test, students' primary concern was that in the 'Listening Comprehension' section, the pronunciation and speed of the spoken discourse are appropriate for use in an English speaking context, like the North American context (ETS, 2001). However, in a foreign language context like in Saudi Arabia, TOEFL alienates test takers who do not have the same kind of exposure to English that international students in inner circle countries have. This causes unnecessary anxiety, which affects students' performance on the test. Another difficulty faced by students was the excessive use of idiomatic expressions specific to North American culture. Heba (S) mentioned that: 'We don't know what these idioms mean, we don't use idioms when we speak and we are not native speakers so we find it difficult.' Saba (T) shares this view and mentions that: 'the idioms are mostly related to the American way of life. For example, 'I'm swamped with work'. Our poor students have never heard of a swamp in Saudi Arabia. It hardly gets muddy and they haven't seen rain much, so it's very unlikely for them to understand such a meaning. It's about everyday happenings, and some of these happenings are not related to the culture'. Reference to specific cultural elements and unfamiliar expression make it even more difficult for the students to grasp the semantic elements in the test.

Another criticism against TOEFL item types emerges from the nature of questions in the grammar section. These items require students to only identify the mistake and not correct it or present a reason for the correct choice. Heba (S) believes that such tasks are isolated from real life learning and English use. She observes that: 'we use English here in Saudi Arabia, but it is not this American [English]. We use English for talking but not for grammar when you must concentrate to find the mistakes'. Several students and teachers also felt that the reading comprehension section in the TOEFL test is loaded with texts that deal with American history and lifestyle. Amani (S) thinks that some passages are good '... but we don't want to know how they live in America. Like in the reading we want to read something interesting ... something about here'. Another criticism of the reading section on TOEFL comes from Emma (T) who notes that 'typically one third of the readings are about the formation of the United States, historical texts about cowboys or Lincoln or something like that which doesn't interest anybody. This cultural indoctrination may be useful for people who are going to live and study there ... but it's certainly not important to speakers of English as a second or foreign language'. Interestingly none of the learners mentioned in the study plan to study in North American universities. It therefore becomes redundant for them to be tested on and learn about specific events in American history and culture.

Imperialism of TOEFL and Gatekeepers to Higher Education

The high-stakes maintained by TOEFL threatens many students like Reda (S), who is 'terrified of it because the TOEFL is very scary ... if something goes wrong you cannot go to the college'. Another reason for anxiety caused by TOEFL originates in students' unfamiliarity with TOEFL format and test setting. Arwa (T) believes that schools in Saudi Arabia test students in class which is a familiar situation for many students, and TOEFL is their first encounter with standardized testing. As a result, students are unable to perform well and are denied higher education opportunities. Luna (T) mentions the terror that TOEFL instils and adds that 'students are dead frightened because they come with no experience of the test at all, wanting to go to college, and this exam [TOEFL] decides where to go'. Pressure from parents and teachers who want students to succeed adds to students' anxiety and may have negative impact on students' performance on the test.

Ownership of English

Concerning the ownership of English, Emma (T) mentioned that as an international language, English is not the 'property' of a single nation, and 'it needs to be internationalized more in the way that it is taught and in the way that it is tested as well'. Considering the local educational context, she appropriately notes that in Saudi Arabia, 'learners interact more with non-native speakers than they do with actual native speakers, and that needs to be reflected in the testing that takes place ... Our girls here need to be able to react with all the people out on the streets and if you look at our professors ... we have very few white middle class Americans here, you know. They need to be able to cope with a whole range'. In order to 'denationalize' English (Smith, 1976), testing needs to be realigned to the goals of a relevant curriculum and should adequately predict the skills and strategies that learners will internalize (Lanteigne, 2006).

Maintaining English as an International Language

Luna (T) believes that in order to maintain English as an international language, TOEFL or any other test should include 'neutral' content that is of general interest and does not privilege a specific culture. She believes that TOEFL can become truly an international test if it has international factors. With respect to TOEFL reading passages, Luna believes that 'it is geared towards one thing that the students have no clue about ... If it is an international test then it should at least have international factors'. Arwa (T) feels that it is imperative to think about the students' needs and their English language requirements in the future. She says that: 'there is imposition of the TOEFL. The TOEFL is not an international test and we are not preparing our students to study abroad. This is a college in Saudi Arabia and we are catering to students from private and government schools'. Hence, local identities and the purpose of testing should be paramount and they should guide the process of testing rather than create obstacles for students who may have facility in a global variety of English which facilitates international communication. Amal (T) suggests that in-house English language placements tests should replace tests like TOEFL. She suggests collaboration with other language teachers to create a test that will have international features so that 'you are really looking at English as an international language and not just one culture'.

Discussion

By over-emphasizing the American way of life and language in the TOEFL test items, American English permeates into the social and educational levels in society and gradually achieves consent of the masses. As a result of this hegemony (Gramsci, in Kalyvas, 2000) in the academic and social lives of the learners in this study, learners and educators have accepted TOEFL as the standard measure of assessment that can be used to make high-stakes decisions. Although students participating in the study are aware of a bias in TOEFL, which is evident from the differences in the 'Englishes' involved in the test (Brown, 2004), most of them are in tacit agreement to use TOEFL as the college entrance test. Nevertheless, they dislike the test because it is inappropriate, long and difficult, and does not reflect the language that they hear in class or on television. Teachers share this view and believe that TOEFL promotes American English, and even though it may be useful in predicting language use in the United States, it is an unsuitable measure for institutions in countries like Saudi Arabia which do not share the cultural and educational context of universities in North America. In this regard, the TOEFL test is biased. All the more so, since the results from this high-stake test are not used to place students in American universities but in a local college in Jeddah, Saudi Arabia.

The popularity of TOEFL across the globe and findings from the case study in this chapter indicate that TOEFL as an entrance test cannot easily be replaced in Saudi Arabia because of numerous socio-political and institutional benefits that ensue from it. These benefits include higher student recruitment due to the trust gained from students and their families who believe that a curriculum that uses TOEFL as a benchmark for language proficiency must be of high educational standard. This domination is rooted in 'educational imperialism' (Phillipson, 1992) and restricts the ownership of language to 'native speakers' or countries located in the 'inner circle.' Furthermore, the economic benefits that the creators of TOEFL enjoy in collaboration with publishers of test preparation material contribute to maintaining the status quo (Templer, 2004). Hence, while on one hand, there is imperialism of the standard American English used excessively in TOEFL (Davies *et al.*, 2003), on the other hand the hegemony of the test continues to colonize the minds of educators who maintain their professional links with countries in inner circle countries and believe that the prestige associated with TOEFL and its international acceptance will assist the college in gaining local and international accreditation.

To promote English as an international language, English language tests should cater to international speakers and societies, and should aim to foster communication amongst linguistically diverse groups of people. By accepting and promoting the use of only high-stakes standardized tests developed in the English speaking West, we as educators tacitly accept that the countries that develop these tests are the custodians of English and the rest of the world their 'clients.' Educators and the elites in Saudi Arabia are powerful agents of change and unless they decide to promote local norms of proficiency testing and change the perception of the stakeholders (including students and their parents), the imperialism of TOEFL will continue to plague teachers and students in non-English speaking contexts.

Conclusion

In Saudi Arabia, and particularly in the local educational context where the study was conducted, students are familiar with the use of English for intercultural communication. However, they are not proficient in the standard American English used in TOEFL. In addition to the North American biased lexicon in the test, there is heavy reliance on cultural topics that are specific to the North American context. Certain terms may not refer to anything that exist in the local contexts of particular foreign language settings, and expecting students to recognise and use such terms is not only redundant but adds an unnecessary burden to their studies. A test that measures students' ability to use English as an international language must lay emphasis on communication tasks rather than on distinguishing and nitpicking 'errors' or deviations from the standard North American English found in the TOEFL. However, testing decisions rest with the senior management of an institution who must be convinced that the focus of proficiency tests has to shift from the North American context to an international context before any change can occur. Importing ideologies and content from English speaking countries in the west will thwart efforts to teach English as an international language. In order to lead to effective pedagogy and to promote English for international communication, assessment practices must also be linked to cultural and contextual realities.

References

Brown, H.D. (2004) *Language Assessment: Principles and Classroom Practices*. White Plains, NY: Longman.

Brown, J.D. (2004) Comment 1: What do we mean by *bias, Englishes, Englishes in testing*, and *English language proficiency? World Englishes* 23 (2), 317–319.

Creswell, J.W. (2002) *Educational Research: Planning, Conducting and Evaluating Quantitative and Qualitative Research*. New Jersey: Merrill Prentice Hall.

Davidson, F. (1994) Comments and replies. *World Englishes* 13 (1), 119–120.

Davies, A., Hamp-Lyons, L. and Kemp, C. (2003) Whose norms? International proficiency tests in English. *World Englishes* 22 (4), 571–584.

ETS (n.d.) The TOEFL® Test – Test of English as a Foreign Language. On WWW at www.ets.org/toefl/. Accessed 8.8.07.

ETS (2001) *TOEFL Institutional Testing Program – Examinee Handbook and Admission Form* (overseas edition). New Jersey: Educational Testing Service.

Graddol, D. (2006) *English Next. Why Global English May Mean the End of 'English as a Foreign Language'*. London: British Council.

Holliday, A. (2005) *The Struggle to Teach English as an International Language*. Oxford: Oxford University Press.

Jenkins, J. (2006) The spread of EIL: A testing time for testers. *ELT Journal* 60 (1), 42–50.

Johnson, K.E., Jordan, S.R. and Poehner, M.E. (2005) The TOEFL trump card: An investigation of test impact in an ESL classroom. *Critical Inquiry in Language Studies: An International Journal* 2 (2), 71–94.

Kachru, B.B. (1989) Teaching World Englishes. *Indian Journal of Applied Linguistics* 15 (1), 85–89.

Kalyvas, A. (2000) Hegemonic sovereignty: Carl Schmitt, Antonio Gramsci and the constituent prince. *Journal of Political Ideologies* 5 (3), 343–376.

Lanteigne, B. (2006) Regionally specific tasks of non-western English language use. *TESL-EJ*. On WWW at http://www-writing.berkeley.edu/TESL-EJ/ej38/a2.html. Accessed 17.11.07.

McKay, S.L. (2002) *Teaching English as an International Language*. Oxford: Oxford University Press.

Pennycook, A. (2001) *Critical Applied Linguistics. A Critical Introduction*. New Jersey: Lawrence Erlbaum.

Phillipson, R. (1992) *Linguistic Imperialism*. Oxford: Oxford University Press.

Smith, L. (1976) English as an international auxiliary language. *RELC Journal* 7 (2), 38–43.

Templer, B. (2004) High-stakes testing at high fees: Notes and queries on the international english proficiency assessment market. *Journal for Critical Education Policy Studies* 2 (1). On WWW at http://www.jceps.com/?pageID=article&articleID=21.

Part 4

The Scope of EIL: Widening, Tightening and Emerging Themes

Chapter 11

Broadening the ELF Paradigm: Spoken English in an International Encounter

PAUL ROBERTS and SURESH CANAGARAJAH

Introduction

With research into English as a lingua franca (ELF) gaining more significance, we suggest in this chapter a broadening of the perspective which has been prominent up to now. Since native speakers also find themselves in communicative situations where English serves as a lingua franca, we seek to investigate the extent to which patterns emerging from 'traditional' ELF research might also account for English used in international encounters where Native Speakers are present.

After briefly reviewing a selection of the empirically-based research in ELF and drawing out the reported salient characteristics of ELF interaction, we introduce our own study, centered on a conversation among five people of different nationalities, one of whom is an Anglo-American. We focus our attention on lexicogrammatical forms, lexical simplicity/complexity, co-operative interaction and topic management (corresponding to areas of study in 'traditional' ELF research). We demonstrate how the native speaker in our data makes use of conversational strategies which are very similar to those used by the other participants in the interaction.

Background

ELF excludes 'native speakers'

In this chapter we focus attention on an instance of spoken English among an international group of users. We hesitate to use the label 'ELF' to describe this instance for reasons which will become clear, but we begin by referring to research carried out under the ELF heading. The empirical data supporting this research has not normally included so-called 'native speakers', except by way of comparison: recordings have been made of English spoken among 'non-native speakers' and the results held up against instances of English spoken between 'native speakers' and 'non-native speakers'. While the former fall within the ELF framework, the latter do not (e.g. Firth, 1996; House, 1999, 2002; Jenkins, 2000; Lesznyák, 2004; Mauranen, 2003; Meierkord, 2000, 2002; Seidlhofer's, 2000–2007 introduction to VOICE). Jenkins (2006: 160) summarizes the situation in a recent paper: 'ELF researchers specifically exclude mother tongue speakers from their data collection. Indeed, in its purest form, ELF is defined as a contact language used only among non-mother tongue speakers'.

The exclusion of 'mother-tongue' speakers from ELF research up to now has allowed for a different, less prejudicial view of the way in which English is used by the majority of its speakers. We would like to build on the principles and methodologies established by this research and to move on to a further level of consideration in the global status of English by asking the question: How is English used as a contact language by all speakers, irrespective of their English language acquisition history? From this area of consideration, ELF has a second, broader level of meaning. For convenience, we will call this ELF2. Our aim here is to examine whether the forms and strategies identified in ELF research have any relevance for ELF2.

This orientation of exploration has already begun on a theoretical level in the World Englishes literature. Scholars such as David Crystal, Henry Widdowson and Marko Modiano have debated what might serve as the common medium for English as a global language, given the acknow-ledgment that different varieties in all communities hold equal status. In considering a potential common contact form of English for global speakers, some alternatives have been posited and projected, but without empirical support. We hope that our study will go some way towards answering what common norms facilitate English as ELF2.

To review briefly the alternatives proposed, Widdowson (1993) and Davies *et al.* (2003) have argued for permitting local varieties for intra-community interactions, and a British/American standard variety for international communication. Their rationale is that the varieties which have the longest pedigree, the 'native-speaker' varieties, enjoy universal acceptance and have the systematization and status required to perform this function. However, empirical evidence from ELF does not support this proposal: multilingual, non-mother-tongue speakers do not necessarily defer to inner circle norms when using English for contact purposes (e.g. Jenkins, 2000; Seidlhofer, 2004).

Others have considered the possibility of an evolving common norm that is neutral for all communities. Crystal (2004: 40) argues: 'it may not be many years before an international standard will be the starting-point, with British, American and other varieties all seen as optional localizations'. Many labels have been given for this common variety, for example Crystal's (1997) 'World Standard Spoken English' and Modiano's (1999): 'International English'. McArthur (2004) wonders whether it is 'World' or 'International' or 'Global' English and whether it matters. Perhaps ELF research provides an empirical basis for this theorization. In fact, Seidlhofer (2004: 229) has argued that 'The option of distinguishing ELF from ENL [i.e. English as National Language] is likely to be beneficial in that it leaves varieties of native English intact for all the functions that only a first language can perform and as a target for learning in circumstances where ENL is deemed appropriate, as well as providing the option of code-switching between ENL and ELF'. However, since ELF data has left out native speakers, we are unable to say if the research can address this question; observations of the interaction between different communities of speakers might be able to provide an answer.

As we will see in the next section, some ELF research, in particular that which focuses more on pragmatic strategies, as opposed to form, has moved towards including native speakers. Our study is more aligned with this school of research in that we will focus on pragmatic strategies as a way in which all global speakers of English may negotiate their differences in form (see Canagarajah, 2006).

Some Instances of Inclusion

While most empirically-based research seems to exclude native speakers from the ELF framework, some scholars have admitted them into the fold, at least on a theoretical basis.

Lesznyák (2004: 43–44), for example, suggests that 'communicative behavior' (pragmatic strategies?) is central to ELF and that, therefore, 'native speakers' could use ELF 'if empirical research proved that other situational factors, e.g. an international setting, have a stronger influence (...) than the presence or participation of a NS'.

Seidlhofer (2004: 211) also emphasizes situational factors when considering the inclusion of native speakers in ELF interactions which 'often also include interlocutors from the Inner and Outer Circles, and can indeed take place in these contexts, such as at academic conferences in Madras or meetings of the United Nations in New York'.

Meierkord's (2005) research has had a strong focus on pragmatic strategies and, in a recent paper, she too suggests that ELF2 needs to be studied in terms of the processes that take place when users of different Englishes interact. She includes speakers from Turkey, Jamaica and Guernsey in processes, her own title for which is IaE–Interactions across English.

House (2006: 89) goes about including all speakers into 'global ELF registers' by redefining Kachru's 'Expanding Circle', which now contains first, second and foreign language speakers. Importantly for our study, House also suggests that two of ELF's most important ingredients are negotiability and variability in terms of speaker proficiency.

Spoken ELF Data

The spoken data collected and analysed so far seems to suggest that ELF has its own characteristics separating it from other forms of English, most notably from ENL. According to researchers' different interests, these characteristics have to do either with language forms, or with communicative behavior.

As far as forms are concerned, Seidlhofer (2003: 18) has identified those which are 'commonly relied-upon', in particular where these appear to be different from forms used by 'native speakers', while Mauranen (2003: 515) notes a tendency 'towards some kind of structural simplification, or generally unmarked features' and James (2005: 140) indicates that ELF might be lexically simpler than what he terms EPL (English as a Primary Language).

Researchers focusing on communicative behavior find that ELF may be characterized by co-operative patterns of interaction: Meierkord (2000) cites six pieces of research, as well as her own, which all point in this direction and Lesznyák's (2004) work shows that sociolinguistic and pragmatic rules of interaction are negotiated by ELF users, while they seem to be fixed for native speakers.

A possible problem with the research findings mentioned above is that little has been done to contrast ELF with English used between 'native' and 'non-native' speakers. Work carried out in the 1980s (e.g. Thomas, 1983; Varonis & Gass, 1985) suggested pragmatic difficulties in this type of interaction, against which the cooperative nature of ELF conversation might be seen to stand out. But with increased interactions in the context of globalization, diaspora communities and transnational relations, added to the linguistic shift of power between 'native' and 'non-native' speakers, the research findings from the 1980s may not apply any more. We feel that there is at least a need for studies like the present one to observe the possible changes in patterns.

Lesznyák (2004) is among the few researchers providing comparative data: she finds that, in interactions with a majority of 'native speakers', 'non-native' users may no longer use their strategic flexibility to co-construct rules of topic management but have, instead, to accept those imposed on them by their native English interlocutors. It is worth noting, however, that Lesznyák's contrastive data has native speakers in a majority, rather than as individual participants in a multinational interaction.

In seeking to examine an ELF2 interaction, we therefore pay particular attention to the presence of a native speaker in an international group. In so doing, we are by no means seeking to influence debates concerning the possible cultural domination of native speakers, far less to challenge supporting or opposing opinions. Our purpose is simply to try to extend ELF research into ELF2.

Our Study

We set out to study English spoken by international users, in a group where a native speaker was present, but in a minority, and in a setting where he or she could not be thought of as having a major advantage.

Aims

We sought to find out:

- whether or not the characteristics of ELF still hold in ELF2;
- whether or not the presence of a native speaker changes the nature of the interaction.

The group

In order to achieve this, we brought together a group of five English users as follows (names have been changed):

(1) Hedda: a Norwegian female who started learning English at school at the age of eight. Like many Norwegians, she is able to understand Danish.

(2) Javier: a male from Equatorial Guinea who started learning English at school at the age of 11. He also speaks Spanish and Fang.

(3) Hao: a Chinese male who started learning English at school at the age of 11. He also speaks his home language (unidentified since he referred to it as 'only a dialect') and Standard Chinese.
(4) Sofia: a German female who started learning English at school at the age of nine.
(5) Milne: an American male who started learning Spanish at school at the age of 13.

None of the participants described her/himself as bilingual except Javier, who considered himself bilingual in Spanish/Fang. The group members were all students at the University of Hertfordshire, UK and aged between 19 and 23. They were all enrolled as 'international students' and had all been in the UK for three months at the time the data was gathered.

Collecting and analyzing the data

We asked the group members to participate in a simulation, requiring them to imagine the forthcoming visit to the University of an international dignitary and to make proposals for spending an imaginary visit budget.

We decided to use a simulation so that, in controlling the topics, any conversations we might later use for comparative purposes would have limited variables.

We asked Milne to enter the conversation only after 10 minutes so that we could assess any differences his participation might have made to the overall interaction.

We recorded the conversation, transcribed the recording and then analyzed the transcription, looking for the following items, corresponding to some of the characteristics of ELF mentioned above:

(1) Lexicogrammatical forms not normally used by native speakers, in particular those which appear to be simpler forms than those normally used by native speakers.
(2) Relative simplicity of lexis: we used Cobb's (2006) Lexical Tutor software to ascertain levels of lexical familiarity and rarity. We used the facility which calculates the number of 'tokens' and the number of 'types'. Each word is considered a 'token' while each different word is considered a 'type'. Thus a high type-token ratio suggests a more varied vocabulary than a low one. Words are also grouped according to their relative frequency in combined corpora. Cobb labels 'K1' all the words which belong to the thousand most frequent words and K2 those belonging to the next thousand. A further two categories are

'AWL' words, referring to those found in corpora of academic spoken and written texts, and 'off-list' words.

(3) Cooperation: we noted instances where speakers explicitly signal their cooperative approach by using hedging and downtoners, back-channeling signals, turns expressing explicit agreement, supportive laughter, inclusive use of 'we' and 'you', inclusive questions and collaborative turns (where speakers overlap with each other in a sup-portive way); we attempted to view these against instances where participants seemed to be explicitly uncooperative by using unhedged, unmuted or intensified transactional turns, turns expressing explicit disagreement or closure, challenging questions and turns marked with a 'high-fall' intonation pattern.

(4) Topic management: we sought to understand whether and how topics were managed through negotiation processes.

We looked at any changes in the conversation after Milne's entry, with specific attention to possible asymmetry, impinging on levels of coopera-tiveness and the negotiation of topic management.

We compared the conversation to a further set of international conver-sations (hereafter F-INT conversations), each involving a native speaker in a minority and each centered on the same simulation, and also to a set of nine conversations (F-NAT) where participants from F-INT conversations were in conversation with their co-nationals. The comparative observations are reported more fully in Roberts (2005).

Findings

Lexicogrammatical forms

Most lexicogrammatical forms in the conversation are those shared by native speakers and do not seem to be simplified. That said, there are instances of unmarked verbs in the third person singular present, one of the forms referred to by Seidlhofer as 'commonly relied-upon' (see above). These instances are confined to two out of the five participants, Javier and Sofia. Their use of third person singular present forms is unstable, how-ever, and the simplified form seems to compete with the unsimplified one. Javier has six relevant turns:

1 Yeah, that's what this University need its own security
2 own security in case there might be a student or somebody don't like
3 even if the person haves his own security and he come to visit
4 Depend how many people.

5   And security need to be too
6   the security don't need

and Sofia three:

1   Because maybe the important person have, has a security of
     his own.
2   Is it sure that he @he need one@?
3   You don't think that the VIP, important person uhm not has
     security of his own?

The 'native speaker', Milne, always uses 's' to mark third person singular
verbs, a characteristic he shares with both Hao and Hedda.

The F-INT conversations show a sprinkling of instances of unmarked
verbs in the third person singular present. On the other hand, corresponding marked forms are also found and, where they compete with unmarked
forms, are mostly more numerous. Whilst the native speakers never use
an unmarked form, other participants' turns mostly show that the use or
otherwise of 's' is unstable.

Apart from the use of unmarked third person singular present, there is
little evidence of simplified forms. Trace elements of grammatical simplicity do occur, however, in Milne's turns which, unlike those of other
participants, do not contain embedded clauses and make exclusive use of
the present tense.

Evidence of grammatical simplification processes is, however, absent:
in the one instance where Milne finds himself having to rephrase a turn,
he does so using the more complex passive form to replace the simpler
active one:

Mil: What is the bottom line. What, what's the-
Hao: bottom line, yes
Mil: least you can do it for? The least
       it can be done for?

At one time, Milne's slightly simpler grammar and vocabulary might
have been accounted for under the heading of 'Foreigner Talk' but in
reconsidering international interactions as ELF2 data, we will posit that he
is using language forms in a spirit of negotiation on equal terms with his
interlocutors rather than with an attitude of condescension. 'Foreigner
Talk' may then be abandoned along with other linguicist terms and Milne's
use of slightly simpler forms than those found in the F-NAT conversation
among Americans can be accounted for by his awareness that he is participating in an ELF2 conversation. The same could be said to be true of the
other, 'non-native-speaker' participants.

Lexical simplicity

The conversation seems at first to be characterized by rather simple vocabulary. When it is compared to the F-NAT conversations, however, judgement needs to be revised. Using Cobb's Compleat Lexical Tutor, the vocabulary statistics for the conversation are shown in Table 11.1.

The relatively low percentage of K2 and AWL words, and the low type-token ratio do not seem significantly different from equivalent figures in the F-NAT conversations. Table 11.2, based on the conversations among Germans, Americans, Norwegians and Chinese, serves to make the point.

Milne's contribution to the conversation does not make use of noticeably simpler or more complex vocabulary. His turns do show the highest frequency of the most common (the 'simplest'?) words (see Figure 11.1) and the second lowest frequency of K2 and academic words (see Figure 11.2), but these minimal differences are not great enough to be able to draw clear conclusions.

Table 11.1   Lexis statistics: international conversation

	Percent		
K1 words (1 to 1000)	88.86%	Words in text (tokens):	2070
K2 words (1001 to 2000)	2.69%	Different words (types):	345
AWL words (academic)	2.47%	Type-token ratio:	0.19
Off-list words	5.97%		

Table 11.2   Lexis statistics: F-NAT conversations

	Germans	*Americans*	*Norwegians*	*Chinese*
K1 words (1 to 1000)	89.09%	87.57%	88.44%	86.78%
K2 words (1001 to 2000)	3.56%	4.69%	3.33%	4.93%
AWL words (academic)	2.38%	2.06%	2.13%	2.46%
Off-list words	4.97%	5.68%	6.10%	5.83%
Words in text (tokens)	2558	3398	2004	1522
Different words (types)	492	546	360	284
Type-token ratio	0.24	0.23	0.21	0.20

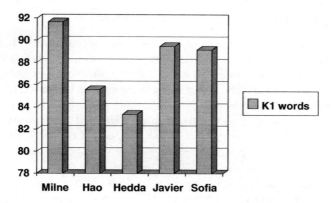

Figure 11.1   Lexis: individual participants' K1 words

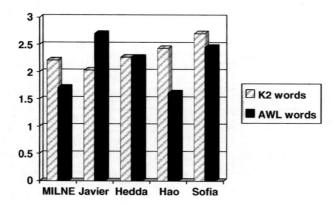

Figure 11.2   Lexis: individual participants K2 and AWL words

Turning to density and richness of vocabulary, a sample of around 140 words from each participant shows that the type-token ratio for Milne is slightly lower than ratios for other speakers but not sufficiently lower to warrant a special explanation (see Table 11.3).

The conclusion to be drawn here is that, if ELF conversation can be characterized as lexically simple, relative to conversation among mother-tongue users, then this is a characteristic shared by ELF2 conversations: the presence of a native speaker may even serve to make the conversation even simpler.

Table 11.3 Lexis: individual participants, type-token ratios

	Hao	*Milne*	*Hedda*	*Sofia*	*Javier*
Words in text (tokens)	141	142	144	143	144
Different words (types)	80	65	70	74	73
Type-token ratio	0.57	0.46	0.49	0.52	0.51

Cooperative interaction

The overall instances of explicit cooperative behavior in the conversation far outnumber instances of explicit lack of cooperation: there are altogether more than 100 manifestations of the former compared to fewer than 20 of the latter. Milne's entry into the conversation does not seem to make any difference. A total of 937 words have been uttered before Milne joins in, after which a further 1050 words complete matters. The two parts of the interaction (before and after Milne's entry) are therefore of roughly equal size. In the first part, we logged 67 manifestations of explicit cooperative behavior, 13 of its opposite; the corresponding figures in the second part were 62 and 15.

The two extracts below can be taken as typically illustrative. In the first one (Example 1), Milne has yet to enter the conversation and the four participants are discussing Hedda's proposal to spend money on making a film. It seems clear that neither Javier, Sofia nor Hao think that Hedda's suggestion and her budget requirement are reasonable but all three make an effort to show comity.

In the first instance, Hao explicitly supports Hedda with 'Good idea' (113) and, later, Javier concedes that 'film is important' (125). As participants begin to express their opposition to Hedda, they draw on a range of devices: Javier adds a question tag to 'That's quite a lot', thereby making an overt appeal for cooperation, which an untagged statement would not have achieved (119); the laughter attending his utterance may also be an attempt to soften this first open objection to Hedda's suggestion (120) in the same way that the later laughter may be in attempted mitigation of Hao's cold-water conclusion (134–135); Sofia also seems to use laughter in order to mitigate her own negative response to Hedda (126) and it is possible that Hao's use of 'By the way' is, similarly, an attempt at softening his negative point of view (131). Hedda herself also uses laughter in order, possibly, to make her counter-argument more acceptable (133) and she also prefaces utterances with 'yeah' which may, again, signal her desire to show comity while pushing forward an unpopular idea (117, 132). She joins with Sofia in a collaborative turn, again probably indicating a wish to show a willingness to cooperate (121–122).

Among all this explicitly cooperative behavior, there is almost no evidence of turns explicitly marked as uncooperative. One possible exception is Hedda's 'but that will look so unprofessional' (130) which is delivered with a rise-fall intonation pattern.

Example 1:

109	Hed:	And also we need to film the event so we can sell the movie
110		afterwards, maybe earn some money on the movie
111	All:	@@@
112	Hed:	But-
113	Hao:	Good idea.
114	Hed:	I don't know how much we are going to spend on the movie because
115		we need a crew.
116	Jav:	So how much is it going to cost?
117	Hed:	Yeah, it says about five thousand.
118	Hao:	Five thousand.
119	Jav:	That's quite a lot, isn't it?
120	All:	@@@
121	Sof:	Quite a lot-
122	Hed:	For a movie.
123	Jav:	That's going to stretch the budget-
124	All	@@@
125	Jav:	So...Yeah, film is important.
126	Sof:	You never will earn the five thousand @pounds@
127	Hed:	Maybe some of the money
128	Jav:	You can make a home movie just by Camcorder, (.you..) student, just
129		record it. Won't cost that much, isn't it?
130	Hed:	Yeah but that will look so unprofessional
131	Hao:	By the way I don't think this is very important
132	Hed:	That, yeah and
133		then the very important person will be @so disappointed@
134	Hao:	I don't think they want to see the movie after
135	ALL:	@@@

The second example (Example 2) comes from later in the conversation when Milne is participating. Sofia's idea of engaging journalists (308–309) and Hedda's objection to it (312) are the only notes of discord. Otherwise all participants continue to express comity, whether it is by making obvious concessions (292, 321) overlapping with each other in a collaborative way (297–299, 304–306), or laughing in order to maintain a patina of lightness (302). Milne's contribution does not stand out in any way: he participates in the collaborative overlapping (above) and softens his transactional turn, as other participants mostly do, by hedging, toning down and using a prosodically-marked (fall–rise) question (300–301).

Example 2:

290	Jav	My cost.....around, er..two grand and a half, or two thousand and a
291		half. Becau...So I, er..will be all right because the security don't
292		need...I can adjust the price for two thousand five hundred.
293	Hao	Two thousand five hundred.
294	Jav.	Yeah. So you can get security in...inside...inside the conference room
295		and in front of the door and control the people coming in and out.
296	Hao	So we are three thousand pounds better off
297	Jav	Yeah
298	Mil	Three thousand
299	Hed	And me...thousand....no.
300	Mil	Shall we switch from a movie and maybe just try and make a
301		booklet...with photos...and maybe writing about the story?
302	All	@@@
303	Jav	You mean just for newspaper?
304	Mil	Maybe do a newspaper story.
305	Jav	Yeah, newspaper story.
306	Hao	Yes whatever...
307	Jav	Can reduce the budget.
308	Sof	Journalists do it all....to write the article for the newspaper.
309		Journalists do it.

310	Hao	Journalists?
311	Mil	Yeah we...
312	Hed	Then we have to hire a journalist.
313	Hao	Yeah.
314	Jav	Yeah we can get a local journalist. It won't cost that much. (...) just
315		local.
316	Hao	I don't think you need..
317	Hed	But it all depends on....
318	Mil	If the person's very
319		important the journalist will want to write....
320	Hao	Yes
321	Hed	Yeah, that's true

The predominance of language marked as explicitly cooperative is also characteristic of the F-INT conversations where, again, the presence of a native speaker does not make any difference to the interaction in this respect. The F-NAT conversations, on the other hand, have an even balance of turns explicitly marked for cooperativeness and uncooperativeness.

It is important to point out here that we are not suggesting that turns marked as uncooperative were indicative of participants' antipathy towards each other or as signs of asymmetry in the conversation. The point about the conversation is that it contains far more turns which are explicitly marked for cooperativeness than it does turns explicitly marked as the opposite, even though participants have transactional goals, within the simulation, which put them in opposition to each other and even though, given that it is a simulation, they have no need to express cooperativeness, since any expression of its lack would presumably not be taken as a personal threat.

Rules of topic management

There is no evidence in the conversation that any rules of topic management are being followed. Unlike in the recordings made by Lesznyák (2004), no-one was designated to chair the proceedings: participants occasionally appear to take on the role of chairperson but relinquish it as swiftly as they adopt it. When Milne enters the conversation, he does so by establishing a new topic, his own budgetary requirements, but the other participants soon succeed in deviating him from this and return to insisting on their own ideas without allowing the conversation to take shape as a formal discussion. Towards the end of the conversation, there is still no evidence of adherence to fixed rules of topic management as this extract makes clear:

Example 3:

234	Mil	Because between all the media and computer and everything it's going
235		to need ...
236	Jav	And security need to be too, it's very important I think.
237	Hao	It's very (...) very important person. I don't think decorating too much
238		is very necessary.
239	Jav	No is necessary, yeah.
240	Hao	Yeah, just clean
241	Jav	We don't need to provide...
242	Sof	The clean is the same. we have to clean and to decorate the areas.
243	Hao	What kind of (br....)
244	Jav	cleaning
245	Sof	Where there are dirty. @@@
246	Hao	Let's hold it in a warehouse or something. To pay four thousand quid
247		to clean this up...
248	Jav	Yeah four hundred clean that is all right. Conference room.
249	Sof	Four...But it is not just the conference room. It's the area outside
250		and...
251	Jav	Yeah then make it, then make it eight hundred, yeah?, because
252	Sof, Hed	@@@
253	All:	@@@
254	Jav	@@@
255		thousand. For lights, I don't know something...
256	Mil	It's going to cost less to clean up than it does to decorate..
257	Jav	To decorate
258	Hed	Yeah. So it's
259	Mil	So how much to decorate and then less than that to clean up
260	Hed	Yeah
261		because it's so much more important that it's clean.

A few minutes later the interactants come to a conclusion, without ever having openly set any rules allowing them to do this.

Example 4:

326	Hao	So how much left?
327	Sof	How much we have? Two thousand five hundred
328	Jav	Two thousand five hundred
329	Hao	Three hundred both of us.
330	Sof	Three and five thousand
331	Jav	Three thousand make five thousand?
332	Mil	Yes. Five thousand five hundred between us...
333	Jav	Er...how many...?
334	Hed	Er...
335	Mil	I think we can do it for a thousand.
336	Jav	A thousand. Yeah.
337	Hed	Yeah a thousand.
338	Mil	Then let the media
339	Jav	So that makes six thousand five hundred
340	Sof	Then I have three thousand five hundred. OK.

The achievement of a conclusion is clearly the result of a negotiated process within which the native speaker appears to participate on an equal footing with the other interactants without seeking to impose any regularization of topic management along specific cultural lines.

Conclusion

Our findings show that ELF2 speakers have the capacity to negotiate English when the context demands it. Perhaps the negotiating capabilities have been ignored in the mainstream linguistic literature as scholars have been more concerned about homogeneous contexts of communication. Research from non-Western communities, where multilingual communication is the norm, shows that speakers develop intuitive competencies to negotiate differences. We also find from this body of research that multilingual communication is possible because participants do not focus on a uniform code or conventions. They negotiate the terms of communication in each intersubjective context, constructing the norms that would be operative in that context. The grammar for that communicative context is emergent – it arises out of the negotiation strategies which participants use in order to succeed in that communication (see Canagarajah, 2007 for further discussion).

The findings in our study encourage us to move further in the direction suggested by the work of those researchers who focus primarily on communicative behavior and to consider the negotiation strategies both 'native' and 'non-native' speakers may use to succeed in communicating in English as a global language. To answer the question posed in the introduction – that is, what would facilitate conversation in English as a global language (of the ELF2 variety)? – we arrive at a radical conclusion. Our data seem to show that grammatical forms are negotiated by individuals within ELF processes and are not necessarily shared by all interacting users. This would suggest that the center will not be 'World Standard Spoken English', 'Lingua Franca Core' or the traditional Anglo-American variety of English. It will not be lexicogrammar at all. Rather it will be the negotiation strategies which speakers of all communities bring to the interaction.

More work is required to focus on these strategies, leading perhaps to programs for the development of strategic skills among all speakers who wish to succeed in communicating in English as a lingua franca.

References

Canagarajah, S. (2006) In this issue. *TESOL Quarterly* 40 (1), 5–6.

Canagarajah, S. (2007) Lingua franca English, multilingual communicative practices, and second language acquisition. *Modern Language Journal* December

Cobb, T.M. (2006) The Compleat Lexical Tutor, version 3.5. On WWW at http://132.208.224.131/. Accessed 21.07.08.

Crystal, D. (1997) *English as a Global Language*. Cambridge: Cambridge University Press.

Crystal, D. (2004) *The Stories of English*. London: Allen Lane.

Davies, A., Hamp-Lyons, L. and Kemp, C. (2003) Whose norms? International proficiency tests in English. *World Englishes* 22 (4), 571–584.

Firth, A. (1996) The discursive accomplishment of normality: On 'Lingua Franca' English and conversation analysis. *Journal of Pragmatics* 26 (2), 237–260.

House, J. (1999) Misunderstanding in intercultural communication: Interactions in English as a Lingua Franca and the myth of mutual intelligibility. In K. Gnutzmann (ed.) *Teaching and Learning English as a Global Language* (pp. 73–89). Tübingen: Stauffenburg.

House, J. (2002) Developing pragmatic competence in English as a Lingua Franca. In K. Knapp and C. Meierkord (eds) *Lingua Franca Communication* (pp. 245–267). Frankfurt: Peter Lang.

House, J. (2006) Unity in diversity: English as a Lingua Franca for Europe. In C. Leung and J. Jenkins (eds) *Reconfiguring Europe* (pp. 87–104). London: BAAL/Equinox.

James, A. (2005) The challenges of the Lingua Franca: English in the world and types of variety. In C. Gnutzmann and F. Intemann (eds) *The Globalisation of English and the English Language Classroom* (pp. 133–144). Tübingen: Gunter Narr Verlag.

Jenkins, J. (2000) *The Phonology of English as an International Language*. Oxford: Oxford University Press.

Jenkins, J. (2006) Current perspectives on teaching World Englishes and English as a Lingua Franca. *TESOL Quarterly* 40 (3), 157–181.

Lesznyák, A. (2004) *Communication in English as an International Lingua Franca*. Norderstedt: Books On Demand.

Mauranen, A. (2003) Academic English as Lingua Franca – a corpus approach. *TESOL Quarterly* 37 (3), 513–527.

McArthur, T. (2004) Is it *world* or *international* or *global* English, and does it matter? *English Today* 20 (3), 3–15.

Meierkord, C. (2000) Interpreting successful lingua franca interaction. An analysis of non-native/native small talk conversations in English. In A. Fetzer and K. Pittner (eds) *Conversation Analysis: New Developments*. Linguistics Online, 5. Special Issue. On WWW at http://www.linguistik-online.com/1_00/MEIERKOR.htm. Accessed 21.07.08.

Meierkord, C. (2002) 'Language stripped bare' or 'linguistic masala'? Culture in lingua franca conversation. In K. Knapp and C. Meierkord (eds) *Lingua Franca Communication*. Frankfurt: Peter Lang.

Meierkord, C. (2005) Interactions across Englishes and their lexicon. In C. Gnutzmann and F. Intemann (eds) *The Globalisation of English and the English Language Classroom* (pp. 90–104). Tübingen: Gunter Narr Verlag.

Modiano, M. (1999) International English in the global village. *English Today* 15 (2), 22–28.

Roberts, P. (2005) English as a world language in international and intranational settings. PhD thesis, University of Nottingham.

Seidlhofer, B. (2000–2007) What is VOICE? On WWW at http://www.univie.ac.at/voice/voice.php?page=what_is_voice. Accessed 21.07.08.

Seidlhofer, B. (2003) *A Concept of International English and Related Issues: From 'Real English' to 'Realistic English'?* Strasbourg: Council of Europe, Language Policy Division, DGIV – Directorate of School, Out-of-School and Higher Education.

Seidlhofer, B. (2004) Research perspectives on teaching English as a lingua franca. *Annual Review of Applied Linguistics* 24, 209–239.

Thomas, J. (1983) Cross-cultural pragmatic failure. *Applied Linguistics* 4 (2), 91–112.

Varonis, E.M. and Gass, S. (1985) Miscommunication in native/non-native conversation. *Language in Society* 14, 327–343.

Widdowson, H.G. (1993) Proper words in proper places. *ELT Journal* 47 (4), 317–329.

Chapter 12
Pragmatics and EIL Pedagogy

SANDRA LEE McKAY

Introduction

Mauri: But don't you agree that all people of the world that they should speak English?

Joy: I would like to know erm what is English so important for the people in the globe.

(*Source*: House, 2003: 146)

The above exchange introduces three major themes of this chapter: first, today many people believe English is an important language to know; second, with the growing use of English, many interactions in English, as in this interaction, are taking place between L2 speakers of English; and third, the increasing use of English for cross-cultural communication makes the need for the teaching of pragmatics in language classrooms all the more important. As Boxer points out:

> Cross-cultural interactional competence is increasingly critical in societies where neighbors, coworkers, and colleagues are likely to come from distinct linguistic and cultural backgrounds. To ignore cross-cultural pragmatics entails running the risk of prejudice, stereo-typing, and ultimately alienation. Understanding these differences open doors, not only for those who are in less powerful status, but for all of us. (Boxer, 2002: 161–162)

The purpose of this chapter is to argue for the need to devote more attention to the teaching of pragmatics in English as an International Language (EIL) classrooms based on a context-sensitive view of pragmatics. In order to make this argument, the paper begins by reviewing several central tenets of pragmatics and relating these to the teaching of English as an international language. Then an argument is made for recognizing the hybridity of modern interactions in English, with a special focus on L2/L2 interactions. This is followed by a summary of existing research in the area of L2/L2 interactions. The paper ends by setting forth principles that should inform the teaching of pragmatics in EIL classrooms. In this chapter, EIL is being used as a comprehensive term to include L2/L2 English interactions as well as L2/L1 English interactions. In addition, the term international English is taken to include many legitimate varieties of English.

Central Tenets of Pragmatics

The field of pragmatics began largely as a reaction to Chomsky's (1957) view of language as a fixed universal property of the human mind that exists devoid of context. A major challenge to Chomsky's view of language was the work of Hymes (1974), a linguistic anthropologist, who argued that a description of language must take into account the social knowledge that individuals bring to linguistic interactions. Hymes argued that researchers interested in describing how language is used need to consider the context in which particular interactions take place and how this context affects the interaction. Specifically, Hymes (1972: 281) maintained that the following four questions must be raised in analyzing language use.

(1) Whether (and to what degree) something is formally *possible*.
(2) Whether (and to what degree) something is *feasible* in virtue of the means of implementation available.
(3) Whether (and to what degree) something is *appropriate* (adequate, happy, successful) in relation to a context in which it is used and evaluated.
(4) Whether (and to what degree) something is in fact done, actually *performed*, and what its doing entails. [emphasis in original]

It is item numbers three and four that are critical to the development of the field of pragmatics. For the first time linguists were being asked to consider whether or not a particular instance of language use was appropriate in relation to a specific context. In addition, linguists were asked to examine what was being accomplished by a particular use of language. Hymes's focus on appropriateness and context laid the foundation for several central tenets of pragmatics.

Pragmatics as appropriate language use

Hymes' third question resulted in an emphasis on determining appropriateness in language use. Traditionally in ELT pedagogy, appropriateness has been equated with native-speaker use. Cohen (1996), for example, refers to the Cross-Cultural Speech Act Research Project (Blum-Kulka *et al.*, 1989) that compared the speech act behavior of native speakers of several languages with the behavior of learners of those languages. For Cohen, the value of such studies is that they provide teachers and researchers with important information on how native speakers perform certain speech acts. In his view, this information should be used as a baseline to determine what should be done in the classroom. As Cohen puts it:

> Once descriptions of the speech acts are made available, the next task is to determine the degree of control that learners have over those speech acts . . .. Ideally, this information could then be used to prepare a course of instruction that would fill in the gaps in language knowledge and also give tips on strategies that might be useful for producing utterances. The role of the learners is to notice similarities and differences between the way native speakers perform such acts and the way they do. (Cohen, 1996: 412)

A similar stance is evident in Canale and Swain's (1980:16) discussion of communicative competence. In discussing the theoretical basis of communicative approaches to second language teaching, they state, 'knowledge of what a native speaker is likely to say in a given context is to us a crucial component of second language learners' competence to understand second language communication and to express themselves in a native-like way'. One of the major problems with this approach to ELT pedagogy is that it ignores another central tenet of pragmatics, namely that social norms regarding language use are open to negotiation.

Pragmatics as a negotiation of meaning

Whereas individuals in their social groups develop a historically derived set of understandings as to what is expected and appropriate to say and do in particular situations, what is said or done at any particular time is always open to negotiation. In other words:

> The linguistic resources we choose to use at particular communicative moments come to these moments with their conventionalized histories of meaning. It is their conventionality that binds us to some degree

to particular ways of realizing our collective history. However, while our resources come with histories of meaning, *how they come to mean* at a particular communicative moment is always open to negotiation. (Hall, 2002: 11)

Thomas (1995: 22) makes a similar point when she defines pragmatics as *meaning in interaction*. As she puts it, 'meaning is not something which is inherent in the words alone, nor is it produced by the speaker alone, nor by the listener alone. Making meaning is a dynamic process, involving the negotiation of meaning between speaker and hearer, the context of utterance (physical, social and linguistic) and the meaning potential of the utterance'. The fact that language use is open to negotiation suggests that what is appropriate will always be dependent on the dynamics of a particular interaction. This negotiation of meaning means that listeners must continually seek to understand a particular utterance in context, leading to a third central tenet of pragmatics.

Pragmatics as interpretation of meaning in context

Listeners are often called upon to make inferences about a speaker's intent. In arriving at a particular interpretation of a message, listeners frequently make use of contextual features. For example, the simple phrase, 'What are you doing?' can have a variety of meanings. It could express an actual request for information as to what an individual is doing at that moment. However, with a particular intonation pattern, the same phrase could also be a reprimand. In interpreting the intended force of the comment, a listener needs to consider the context of the utterance. Was the comment made over the phone in a conversation in which the speaker had an interest in knowing what the listener was doing, or was the comment made in a classroom where the teacher was surprised by the behavior of particular students? The context then provides the background information necessary to interpret the comment. As Yule (1996: 3) points out, pragmatics is 'the study of contextual meaning'. in the sense that a listener's interpretation of a message is dependent on the listener using contextual cues such as who is talking, where, when and under what circumstances to make inferences about the intended meaning of the speaker.

Challenging a Native-Speaker Model for Pragmatics

The fact that language use is open to negotiation and context-dependent calls into question a basic assumption of traditional ELT pragmatics, namely that native-speaker norms should be the pedagogical target. It is clearly naïve to assume that English native speakers today share the same sense of appropriateness. This is especially true given the fact that English is a widely spoken international language used by individuals of very diverse cultural backgrounds. The many speech communities within English-speaking countries make it impossible to describe what members of that society as a whole consider appropriate language use. There are, however, additional reasons for rejecting a native-speaker model in ELT pedagogy.

As Kasper (1997) notes, one problem that exists in applying a native speaker model to the development of pragmatic competence is that from the L2 learners' perspective there may be sociopragmatic aspects of the target culture that conflict with their beliefs and values. Sridhar (1996), for example, found that Indian speakers when making requests in English within India often used forms that would be considered overly polite by native speaker judges. If most Indian speakers believe that such formality is warranted, then it is unreasonable to require that these speakers use forms that so-called native speakers might use, given that Indian speakers themselves are legitimate users of EIL. Furthermore, a native speaker model is often not appropriate since the use of nativelike pragmatic competence by bilingual users of English may be viewed by some native speakers in the target culture negatively. In fact, some studies suggest that there may be benefits in not conforming to native speaker pragmatics.

Aston (1993), for example, suggests that not having nativelike competence may be a means of establishing comity between people of different cultures. He points out that there are a variety of grounds on which individuals can establish solidarity and support in cross-cultural contexts. In order to achieve solidarity and support, Aston contends that individuals have to focus on their identities as individuals rather than as representatives of members of their culture of origins. If this is done, then individuals in cross-cultural encounter might achieve comity by, for example, expressing a critical stance toward their own country. Individuals in such encounters can also establish comity by exploiting their own incompetence in either the language or specific areas of knowledge. For Aston, the potential to establish comity in cross-cultural encounters

> supports the argument that interlanguage pragmatics should operate with a difference hypothesis rather than a deficit hypothesis ... and not simply analyze NNS discourse in terms of failure to conform to NS conversational norms. Pedagogically, it implies that the learner's task in developing an ability for interactional speech using the L2 is

not simply one of acquiring nativelike sociolinguistic competence in the attempt to mimic the behavior of a native speaker, but requires the development of an ability to use specific comity strategies appropriate to the context of NNS discourse. (Aston, 1993: 245)

There are then many reasons for rejecting a native-speaker model in the teaching of EIL pragmatics, some of them related to the nature of pragmatics itself and others to the fact that English as a global language is used in a great variety of social contexts by many legitimate speakers of English. The question is what should be the basis for an alternate model? An answer to this question needs to be based on a recognition of the mobility and fluidity of modern life and an examination of what this means for language use. Canagarajah (2006) argues that since L2 users of English will frequently be confronting many varieties of English, the teaching of pragmatics should help L2 learners shuttle between language communities by promoting a view of language as process rather than product. This orientation would lead to the following shifts in pedagogy.

From:	To:
mastery of grammar rules	metalinguistic awareness
focus on rules/conventions	focus on strategies
correctness	negotiation
language/discourse as static	language/discourse as changing
language as homogeneous	language as hybrid
language as context-bound	language as context-transforming
language as transparent/instrumental	language a representational
L1 or C1 as problem	L1 or C1 as resources

(Canagarajah, 2006: 210)

What this suggests for the teaching of pragmatics is that L2 learners need to be encouraged to view each interaction as an opportunity to draw on their linguistic resources to accomplish a specific communicative purpose. As Canagarajah (2006: 211) points out, a shift from product to process is 'not radical or new in our field. We simply have to develop appropriate pedagogical practices motivated by these assumptions'.

One step toward developing such a pedagogy is to examine what is actually occurring pragmatically in L2/L2 interactions in various contexts. Doing so can provide insight into what resources L2 speakers use to achieve their communicative purposes. Furthermore, knowing more about what actually occurs in L2/L2 interactions may help eliminate negative social attitudes toward such interactions. As Seidlhofer (2004: 215) notes, 'if we are to think differently about English, we need to know more about what forms it takes in different contexts of use, including lingua franca sections'. As a way of thinking differently about English and providing a foundation for discussing a new approach to the teaching of pragmatics, we turn now to a summary of existing research on L2/L2 interactions. My focus will be exclusively on L2/L2 interactions since it is these interactions that form the majority of interactions in English today, with some arguing that over 80% of interactions in English are presently between L2 and L2 speakers. I realize, however, that many of the strategies enacted in such exchanges can also occur in L2/L1 interactions.

Research in English as a Lingua Franca

Recently more and more attention is being given to an analysis of interactions between L2 speakers of English, termed *English as a Lingua Franca (ELF)* talk. Firth (1996) provided one of the earliest definitions of ELF stating that ELF interactions are those in which English is used as 'a "contact language" between persons who share neither a common native tongue nor a common (national) culture, and for whom English is the chosen *foreign* language of communication' (Firth, 1996: 240). Such interactions occur frequently in Expanding Circle countries where English is used for business, political, academic and travel purposes. Perhaps it is for this reason that the majority of existing research has taken place in Expanding Circle countries, particularly in Europe. This type of interaction, however, can also occur in Inner and Outer Circle countries.

Firth's (1996) seminal article on ELF was one of the first to identify some typical pragmatic features of ELF interactions. Firth's data involved a collection of telephone calls from two Danish international trading companies involving Danish export managers and their international clients. As Firth (1996: 241) points out, one of the major advantages of analyzing such discourse from a conversation analysis perspective rather than as 'foreigner talk', 'interlanguage talk' or 'learner interaction' perspective is that the participant is viewed as 'a *language user* whose real-world interactions are deserving of unprejudiced *description* rather ... than as a person conceived *a priori* to be the possessor of incomplete or deficient communicative competence, putatively striving for the "target" competence of an idealized "native speaker."' The following excerpt between a Danish seller (H) and an Indian buyer (G) illustrates several common features of ELF interactions.

(1)
```
 1  H    fine than(k) you (.) you know now the summer time had- t-
          come to D'nmark
 2         as well (.) hh:uh ((laugh))=
 3  G    =((laughing)) huh hh:eh heh heh heh:.hh
 4  H    so for:: the:- us here in Denmark it's hot ((.) it's uh twenty
          five degree, (.) .hh
 5         but for y[ou it will be-
 6  G             [ya:h,
 7  H    it would be ↑cold (.) I think
 8  G    no, here in this pwu:h forty- forty two
 9  H    yes?
10         (1.0)
11  H    [[well
12  G    [[yes
13         (1.0)
14  H    well I prefer twendy five. (.) it's better to me
15         (0.9)
16  G    yeah
```
                (Firth, 1996: 242)

To begin, the interaction includes grammatical errors, unidiomatic clause constructions and pronunciation variants. But more significantly is the apparent misunderstanding that occurs in lines 4–9 when it appears that G has failed to understand that H is using *cold* in a comparative sense with the temperature in Denmark. What is remarkable is that the conversation continues in an orderly way with no recognition of the misunderstanding. Firth argues that one common phenomenon of ELF talk is the 'let it pass' principle in which participants appear to determine that during a particular interaction, a misunderstanding is 'non-fatal' so is allowed to pass. The problem, however, is that from the analyst's point of view, it is unclear whether or not the problem was missed by the participants or whether it was understood and allowed to pass.

Whereas the let-it-pass principle is evident in some ELF interactions, on other occasions, when mutual understanding is deemed essential, misunderstandings are not allowed to pass, as is evident in the following interaction.

(2)
```
 1  B    ... so I told him not to u::h send the:: cheese after the- (.) the
          blowing (.) in
 2         the ↑customs
```

```
3            (0.4)
4            we don't want the order after the cheese is u::h (.) blowing.
5H           I see, yes.
6  B         so I don't know what we can uh do with the order now. (.)
             What do you
7            think we should uh do with this is all ↑blo:wing Mister
             Hansen
8            (0.5)
9  H         I'm not uh (0.7) blowing uh what uh, what is this u::h too big
             or what?
10           (0.2)
11 B         no the cheese is ↑bad Mister Hansen
12           (0.4)
13           it is like (.) fermenting in the customs' cool rooms
14           H ah it's gone off↑.
15 B         yes it's gone off↓
16 H         we::ll you know you don't have to uh do uh anything
             because it's not ...
             ((turn continues))
             (Firth, 1996: 244)
```

When in line 9, H asks B a direct question regarding the blowing of the cheese, H is compelled to display his unfamiliarity with the term *blowing*. Because of a need for mutual understanding, the let-it-pass principle is not applied. Instances such as this demonstrate the danger of formulating principles that apply to all L2/L2 interactions, particularly since, as was noted earlier, pragmatics by nature involves a constant negotiation of meaning.

Firth's data also showed that on some occasions, participants formally recognize their lack of competence in the language, sometimes as a means of achieving comity, as is evident in the following excerpt.

```
(7)
1  L         ((Hungarian: name of company))
2            (0.4)
3  H         yes he↑llo: this is Hanne from ↑CellPhone
4            (0.2)
5  L         oh↓ ↑hello [how are you? ]
6  H                    [h e: ↓] [o::]
7            (0.2)
8  H         ↑fine↓ thank you an you::↓
9  L         .hh on fine thank ↓you
10 H         how are sales going in ↑Budapest
```

```
11          (0.3)
12    L     oh(.) ↑sorry↑
13          (0.2)
14    H     how are sales going in ↑Budapest=
15    L     =o:h I think now its- its a little bit ↑middle h(h)h. hh. middle
            power hu(h)
16          hu(h)h [h(h)u(h)
17    H            [(h)o:k(h)a(h)y::↓
18    L     it's not- it's not so ↑ni::ce
19          (0.2)
20    L     .hh=
21    H     =so [why's that
22    L         [but it's going hh. h(h)hu(h)
23    H     okay:
            (Firth, 1996: 254)
```

In line 15–16, L laughs at his own marked usage of *a little bit middle …*
power which displays his recognition of his own marked usage. This invites
H to do the same and creates a feeling of camaraderie. For Firth (1996:
256), one of the most significant insights provided by his analysis is that
although lingua franca interactions are linguistically marked, 'the parties
nevertheless *do interactional work* to imbue the talk with orderly and
"normal" characteristics'.

Subsequent research on ELF has yielded additional findings on the
pragmatic characteristics of ELF interactions. House's (2003), for example,
studied the interactions of international students at the University of
Hamburg in Germany. The students were asked to interact with one
another as they expressed their opinions on a reading text discussing the
role of English as a lingua franca. House noted several common features
of these exchanges. First, there was a lack of discourse markers like *well*
or *I think* when students started or completed a new turn or opportunity
to speak. The most common feature of turn-taking was what House terms
represents, that is, a repetition of the previous speaker's comments, as
shown in the exchange below.

Mauri: Yes but the grammar is quite differ[ent very different]
Wei: [it is very different]
Mauri: between Chinese and Japanese. (House, 2003: 145)

House points out that using these repetitions may be one strategy the students used to make the processing of English easier. In addition, it signals
acceptance and understanding of the previous speaker's statement.

A second feature in many of these exchanges was a high use of starting a turn with conjunctions like *and* and *but* rather than more common items like *yes, well,* or *I see.* Also, when speakers did disagree, they tended not to use any phrases to soften the disagreement such as 'I hate to disagree with you but ...'. Rather they used raw negation, rejection and disagreement, shunning the use of face-saving strategies. Fourth, the participants often took little account of their interlocutors' expectations, violating turn transition points. This is evident in the following interaction when Joy does not answer Mauri's question but proceeds to make her own comment on the use of English.

Mauri: But don't you agree that all people of the world that they should speak English?

Joy: I would like to know erm what is English so important for the people in the globe. (House, 2003: 146)

Meierkord's (2000) work highlighted additional pragmatic features of ELF interactions. Based on her analysis of conversations of overseas students in Great Britain, collected in a student hall of residence, Meierkord (2000) delineates the following characteristics of ELF conversations.

- Pauses often occur between conversational phrases, especially at the end of a conversation to make the transition from one phase of the conversation to the other.
- Participants prefer to discuss safe topics like talking about the meals and life in the hostel rather than more controversial and complex topics.
- Participants tend to keep the topics very short and not to deal with them at length.
- Participants display frequent and long pauses both within and in-between turns.
- The participants make considerable use of politeness phenomena such as routine formulae in openings and closings, back-channels, and other gambits. Most of their routines, however, were restricted to common phrases like 'How are you?' and 'Bye'.

Meirkord (2000) points out two possible explanations for these characteristics. The first is that they reflect the participants' own gaps in English proficiency. For example, the choice of topics could be interpreted as a reduction strategy employed because of a lack of vocabulary for dealing with more complex philosophical or political themes. On the other hand, it could be explained as being due to the participants' insecurity regarding the acceptability of the topics they introduce. Clearly both interpretations

are possible depending on the proficiency and intention of the participants, leading Meirkord to argue for a differentiated interpretation of
interactional data 'which takes into account both the intercultural situations as well as the fact that speakers need to be regarded as learners of the
language they use'.

Summarizing the findings of existing data on ELF interactions,
Seidlhofer (2004: 218) provides the following generalizations regarding
the pragmatics of ELF.

- Misunderstandings are not frequent in ELF interactions; when they
  do occur, they tend to be resolved either by topic change, or less often,
  by overt negotiation using communication strategies such as rephrasing and repetition.
- Interference from L1 interactional norms is very rare – a kind of sus-
  pension of expectations regarding norms seems to be in operation.
- As long as a certain threshold of understanding is obtained, interlocutors seem to adopt what Firth (1996) has termed the 'let-it-pass
  principle', which gives the impression of ELF talk being overtly
  consensus-oriented, cooperative and mutually supportive, and thus
  fairly robust.

In reaching generalizations regarding ELF interactions, it is essential to
fully define the contextual features of the exchanges on which such features
are based. This should include the demographics of the participants,
including the speakers' level of English language proficiency, as well the
social context and purpose of the interaction. This information is necessary for two reasons. First, an understanding of the language proficiency
of the speakers allows the researcher to determine if the features delin-
eated are typical of proficient bilingual users of English or if they are rather
a feature of learner discourse. Second, because social context is critical for
speakers in making choices as to what to say and how to say it, it is important that such background information be provided to correctly interpret
research findings, as was evident from the fact that the 'let-it-pass' principle seems to be put aside when speakers believe that a clarification of
terms is warranted.

Towards a New Pedagogical Model for EIL Pragmatics

The insight provided by current research in ELF pragmatics, as well as
the fact that English is an international language, has several implications
for the teaching of EIL pragmatics. First and foremost, a reliance on a
native-speaker model as the pedagogical target must be put aside. As

House (2003: 149) notes, since ELF research suggests that ELF participants belong to a rather vague but existing community of ELF speakers, in which negotiation of meaning is paramount, the L2 speaker should be measured against the 'bilingual or multilingual speaker under comparable goals for interaction in different discourse domains'. Hence, the curriculum should 'focus on the learners' need to be flexibly competent in international communication through the medium of the English language in as broad a spectrum of topics, themes, and purposes as possible'. If a curriculum is to achieve such a goal, several skills need to be developed. Among these are the following.

(1) Explicit attention should be given to introducing and practicing repair strategies, such as asking for clarification, repetition and rephrasing, and allowing for wait time. This focus is necessary since it is evident from many of the examples noted above that gaps in linguistic knowledge necessitate the development of mechanisms to solve communication breakdowns.

(2) A variety of conversational gambits should be introduced and practiced, including such items as managing turn-taking, back channeling, and initiating topics of conversation. The development of such strategies is necessary to avoid instances, noted in the research, of L2 speakers ignoring the topic at hand to follow their own agendas.

(3) Attention should be given to developing negotiation strategies that involve such features as suggesting alternatives, arguing for a particular approach, and seeking consensus. The reasons for such a focus are twofold. First, as was mentioned earlier, pragmatics by definition involves a negotiation of meaning, and second, as House (2000: 148) points out, ELF is typically not a language with which to identify but rather 'an instrumentally opportune medium of communication'.

One productive mechanism for promoting such skills is to use data from ELF interactions, as well as from L2/L1 interactions, as the basis for pragmatic materials. Students could be asked to identify discourse strategies and markers in the examples that help or hinder speakers' communicative intentions. When communication breakdowns are noted, mechanisms for avoiding such breakdowns can be introduced. L2/L2 and L2/L1 interactions could also be used to highlight cross-cultural misunderstandings and how these might be dealt with.

Last but not least, an EIL pragmatics pedagogy must recognize the hybridity of modern life and the manner in which English as a international language is often used to negotiate various identities. As Rampton (1997: 330) argues, the time has come for sociolinguists and educators to challenge the notion that societies are compact and systematic entities and instead to recognize the heterogeneity and fluidity of modern states in which 'being neither on the inside nor the outside, being affiliated but not fully belonging, is said to be a normal condition'. This is certainly true of many L2 speakers of English who often do not view themselves as insiders or outsiders. Rather they use English to negotiate 'a sense of self within and across different sites at different points of time' (Norton, 1995: 13). Because of this, EIL pragmatics cannot afford to offer a simplistic view of pragmatics based on native-speaker norms. Rather it must seek to foster the idea that each interaction is unique and a site for negotiating meaning and identity in a growing international language.

References

Aston, G. (1993) Notes on the interlanguage of comity. In G. Kasper and S. Blum-Kulka (eds) *Interlanguage Pragmatics* (pp. 224–250). New York: Oxford University Press.

Boxer, D. (2002) Discourse issues in cross-cultural pragmatics. *Annual Review of Applied Linguistics* 22, 150–167.

Blum-Kulka, S., House, J. and Kasper, G. (1989) Investigating cross-cultural pragmatics: An introductory overview. In S. Blum-Kulka, J. House and G. Kasper (eds) *Cross-Cultural Pragmatics: Requests and Apologies* (pp. 1–34). Norwood, NJ: Ablex.

Canagarajah, S. (2006) An interview with Suresh Canagarajah. In R. Rubdy and M. Saraceni (eds) *English in the World: Global Rules, Global Roles* (pp. 200–212). London: Continuum.

Canale, M. and Swain, M. (1980) Theoretical bases of communicative approaches to second language teaching and testing. *Applied Linguistics* 1 (1), 1–47.

Chomsky, N. (1957) *Syntactic Structure*. The Hague: Mouton.

Cohen, A.D. (1996) Speech acts. In S.L. McKay and N.H. Hornberger (eds) *Sociolinguistics and Language Teaching* (pp. 383–420). Cambridge: Cambridge University Press.

Firth, A. (1996) The discursive accomplishment of normality. On 'lingua franca' English and conversation analysis. *Journal of Pragmatics* 26, 237–259.

Hall, J. (2002) *Teaching and Researching Language and Culture*. New York: Longman.

House, J. (2003) Teaching and learning pragmatic fluency in a foreign language: The case of English as a *lingua franca*. In A. Martinez Flor, E. Usó Juan and A. Fernández Guerra (eds) *Pragmatic Competence and Foreign Language Teaching* (pp. 133–159). Castello de la Plana, Spain: Publicacions de la Universitat Jaume I.

Hymes, D. (1972) On communicative competence. In J. Pride and J. Holmes (eds) *Sociolinguistics* (pp. 269–293). Harmondsworth: Penguin.

Hymes, D. (1974) *Foundations of Sociolinguistics*. Philadelphia: The University of Pennsylvania Press.

Kasper, G. (1997) The role of pragmatics in language teacher education. In K. Bardovi-Harlig and B. Hartford (eds) *Beyond Methods* (pp. 113–141). New York: McGraw-Hill Company.

Norton, B. (1995) Social identity, investment and language learning. *TESOL Quarterly* 29 (1), 9–32.

Meierkord, C. (2000) *Interpreting Successful Lingua Franca Interaction: An Analysis of Non-Native/Non-Native Small Talk Conversations in English.* On WWW at http://www.linguistik-online.de/1_00/MEIERKOR.htm. Accessed 21.4.05.

Rampton, B. (1997) Second language research in late modernity. *The Modern Language Journal* 15 (3), 329–333.

Seidlhofer, B. (2004) Research perspectives on teaching English as a lingua franca. *Annual Review of Applied Linguistics* 24, 209–239.

Sridhar, K. (1996) Societal multilingualism. In S.L. McKay and N.H. Hornberger (eds) *Sociolinguistics and Language Teaching* (pp. 47–70). Cambridge: Cambridge University Press.

Thomas, J. (1995) *Meaning in Interaction.* London: Longman.

Yule, G. (1996) *Pragmatics.* Oxford: Oxford University Press.

Chapter 13

Cultural Conceptualizations in English as an International Language

FARZAD SHARIFIAN

Introduction

In this chapter I make an attempt to explore the concept of 'English as an International language' using the framework of *cultural conceptualizations* (Sharifian, 2003, 2008b).

Beginning with a discussion of the notion of *cultural conceptualizations*, this chapter then explores how EIL may be viewed from a cultural-conceptual perspective when speakers draw on various systems of conceptualizations in EIL speech situations. This is followed by a discussion of the need for a revised model of communication in EIL contexts. Some preliminary principles and strategies are discussed in this section. Notions such as 'language proficiency' and 'variety' are then revisited in the light of this discussion.

The Notion of Cultural Conceptualizations

I use the term *cultural conceptualizations* to refer to units of conceptual knowledge such as *schemas* (e.g. Bartlett, 1932; D'Andrade, 1995; Malcolm & Sharifian, 2002; Rumelhart, 1980; Sharifian, 2001; 2003; Strauss & Quinn, 1997), *categories* (e.g. Lakoff, 1987; Rosch, 1978), and *conceptual metaphors* (e.g. Lakoff & Johnson, 1980) that emerge from the interactions between the members of a cultural group. A schema largely reflects a thematic relationship between its composing concepts, while categories are developed on the basis of class membership. However, schemas and categories are related to each other in so far as the concepts that are part of a schema may themselves be a category. For example, the 'restaurant' schema contains the concept of 'food', itself a category, which includes 'sandwich', 'pasta', and so on, as its instances. Conceptual metaphors are basically formed by mapping from a category, schema or image schema onto another schema (Lakoff & Turner, 1989). For example, in American English marriage can be conceptualized as a 'journey', reflected in expressions such as *We have reached a crossroads in our relationship* (Quinn, 1996). In African English, 'political leadership' is often conceptualized in terms of 'eating' (e.g. *They have given him plenty to eat*, which is used in Cameroon when a new government official is appointed) (Polzenhagen & Wolf, 2007).

Cultural conceptualizations are 'negotiated' and 'renegotiated' across time and space by generations of speakers so that the members of a group are able to think, so to speak, in one mind. From this perspective, conceptual structures such as 'schemas' are not just the properties of an individual's mind but also emerge at the cultural level of cognition (Sharifian, 2008b).

Apart from being 'emergent', cultural conceptualizations are *heterogeneously distributed* across the minds of a cultural group. In other words, they are not imprinted equally in the minds of every individual in the group. Members of a cultural group may share conceptualizations *more or less* with one another, but they often operate on the assumption that conceptualizations in their communication are completely shared.

Groups develop complex systems of conceptualization that serve to form or inform their worldviews over time. Worldviews are not the result of one person's imagination, but rather, the result of systems of conceptualizations that have emerged from years of interaction between people across various groups and the 'negotiation' of how to conceptualise experiences. Cultural conceptualizations are also often used as a basis or frame of reference for reasoning and, as such, serve as the 'logic' underlying our thoughts and actions in our daily routines. New cultural conceptualizations may also be triggered by influences from, or contact with, other communities.

Language has an intrinsic and significant link with our system of conceptualizations. Human beings communicate their various systems of conceptualizations using language and, in fact, many aspects of language are largely embedded in the conceptualizations that are used to interpret and organize our cultural experience. Scholars in anthropological linguistics have long shown how lexical items in various languages may encode the way speakers have conceptualized their experiences in the past, shaping the frames of understanding available for interpreting new experiences.

Numerous studies have revealed how certain features of a language may reflect the way their speakers categorize or schematize experiences (e.g. Palmer, 1996). In addition, recent studies within the framework of cognitive linguistics and cognitive anthropology have shown how our use of language reflects metaphors, which are largely culturally constructed (e.g. Kövecses, 2005; Quinn, 2005; Yu, 2003). These metaphors often provide a basis for how we conceptualize and structure our experiences (e.g. Lakoff & Johnson, 1980). Even our basic understanding of notions such as 'time' is based on conceptual mappings, which do not appear to be universal (e.g. Núñez & Sweetser, 2006).

Within the area of pragmatics, what has come to be known as 'implied meaning', or 'implicatures', are in fact understandings that we associate with linguistic expressions due to the schemas that we more or less share with other members of our speech community (Sharifian, 2004, 2005b, 2008a). It is now well-known that even the organization of our discourse is largely the result of our 'negotiated conceptualizations' in the form of *formal schemas* (Carrell, 1987; Sharifian *et al.*, 2004) that are culturally constructed. Against this background, I now turn to a discussion of how EIL may be described in terms of the notion of *cultural conceptualizations*.

EIL as a Language of Various Cultural Conceptualizations

I make sense of English as an International language in terms of a language which can be used to communicate various systems of cultural conceptualizations. Consider the following examples from Aboriginal English and from Australian English.

> Aboriginal English: This land is me.
> Australian English: This land is mine.

The two English sentences above encode two different systems of conceptualizations with regard to the relationship between an individual and the land. The Aboriginal English sentence draws on a schema according to which people and the land are linked in various ways, such as by totemic connection. One system of conceptualization may appear patently ridiculous from the point of view of another. An Aboriginal person made the remark that the land was there before he was born, so how could *he* own the land? Often in response to 'this land is mine', Aboriginal people respond, 'but the land owns us'. From the perspective of Aboriginal cultural conceptualizations, people and the land have reciprocal responsibilities towards each other. For example, the land provides food for people and people are supposed to 'look after' the land. The

Australian English sentence, on the other hand, encodes the Anglo conceptualizations of the relationship between the individual and the land, in which an individual's possession of a piece of land involves being able to transfer that possession to other individuals, usually for money. From a different perspective, the Australian sentence may also suggest political possession, that is, 'This land is mine because I am Australian' (Ian Malcolm, personal communication). This example clearly shows how different cultural conceptualizations are encoded in two varieties of English.

Aboriginal English speakers often use English words to communicate their own cultural conceptualizations that have evolved throughout the history of their existence (see further in Sharifian, 2006). Even everyday words such as 'family', 'home' and 'shame' often evoke conceptualizations in Aboriginal English speakers that are different from those of Anglo-Australians (Sharifian, 2005a). For example, in some varieties of Aboriginal English the word 'mum' is associated with a category that encompasses aunts, grandmother, and so forth. The word 'home' for many Aboriginal people may mainly be associated with the company of their extended family rather than being confined to a building (Sharifian, 2008c). It should also be noted here that as a result of contact, certain new and overlapping systems of conceptualizations have also developed (Malcolm & Sharifian, 2005).

Similarly, bilingual learners and speakers of English may draw on their first language systems of cultural conceptualizations when using English. For example, a Persian speaker of English may draw on the Persian cultural schema of *Shekasteh-nafsi* 'modesty' in responding to compliments (Sharifian, 2005b, 2008a). Consider the following example.

Lecturer: I heard you've won a prestigious award. Congratulations! This is fantastic.
Student: Thanks so much. I haven't done anything. It's the result of your effort and your knowledge. I owe it all to you.
Lecturer: Oh, no!!! Don't be ridiculous. It's all your work. (Personal data)

In the above conversation between an Iranian student and an Australian lecturer, the student's reply to the lecturer's congratulations appears to have discomforted the lecturer, leaving him with the feeling that his contribution to the student's success has been overestimated. The lecturer commented that the student 'has stretched the truth too far'. The student on the other hand maintained that she did not find anything wrong with her remarks.

Here, the Iranian speaker appears to have responded to the compliment in a way that is appropriate to the Persian cultural schema of *shekasteh-nafsi* while the Australian lecturer's response seems to be in consonance with the Anglo-Australian schema of 'individual merit'.

The point is already obvious. Unfamiliarity with the systems of conceptualizations on which the international speakers of English are relying may lead to various forms and degrees of discomfort and even miscommunication.

Different solutions have been presented to this situation, among which is a proposal for a 'nuclear' English (e.g. Quirk, 1981). If, however, we take the idea of systems of cultural conceptualisations emerging from the inter-actions between people seriously, then it is obvious that even if we could come up with a 'nuclear' English, this itself would in time develop its own new systems of conceptualizations. I am not sure what the nuclear English developed out of interactions between Japanese and Malays would have in common with one which would develop out of the interactions between Chinese and Anglo-Australian speakers.

The alternative I am offering here in response to the observations made so far in this chapter is to accept and appreciate the idea that English can be associated with an array of cultural conceptualizations from various cultural groups, but to also explore the implications of this for a revised model of communication.

The Need for a Revised Model of Communication

As mentioned above, instead of trying to explore how English as an International Language could be turned into a 'nuclear' language or trying to turn the whole world into a 'homogenous' speech community, it might be more helpful to offer a revised model of communication. The one that I have in mind would have at its core the following principle: the need to recognize that in international contexts two interlocutors may not share the same system of cultural conceptualizations even though they both use English to engage in communication with each other. In routine inter-actions, speakers rely on the tacit assumption that their cultural conceptu-alizations are shared by their interlocutors. This may achieve for them a certain degree of communicative efficiency. Speakers of different languages and varieties may of course do this in different degrees. Aboriginal English speakers often rely to a relatively large extent on the assumption of shared conceptualizations (Sharifian, 2001). Consider the following example:

No big boy A ... reckon
he help K ...
was drivin back from Wiluna or whatever some place
an light behind,

look in revision mirror
no he's gone,
drivin along
saw i',
look in the 'vision mirror again,
look in the back seat,
an ole ole blackfella sittin in the back seat, lookin at im
(from Aboriginal English Database)

Here the speaker makes a reference to a 'light behind'. This 'light' is known as the *minmin light* and is variously associated with spiritual presence for different Aboriginal cultural groups (Sharifian, 2001). One version is that the 'light' is a spiritual presence that can mislead people and therefore people should flip down their rear vision mirror (which in Aboriginal English may be referred to as 'revision mirror'). The 'ole blackfalla' is another spiritual reference which is associated with the presence of *minmin light* (Glenys Collard, personal communication). It should be obvious that interpreting this text, the way in which it is interpreted by the speakers would require knowledge of particular Aboriginal cultural conceptualizations.

In contexts such as the production of the above text, often speakers build on the assumption that their cultural conceptualizations are shared by their hearers. In the revised model of communication for English as an International Language, interlocutors would first need to minimize the assumption of shared cultural conceptualizations. That is, participants in EIL communicative events would need to constantly remind themselves that 'other interlocutors may not share the same schema, category or metaphor that I am drawing on as a frame of reference in my production and comprehension'. This may result in adopting several strategies such as the one highlighted below.

Consider the following conversation between two people from different cultural backgrounds:

A: You stupid!
B: Can I ask in what contexts you usually use this expression in your culture?
A: hmm, we can use it as a term of endearment between husband and wife, like the wife saying this to husband to say, 'you're not kind to yourself'.
B: (Surprise and smile) Ah, right! So I should take it as a compliment.

As it can be seen, here the hearer has asked for clarification of how the concept of 'stupid' may be used in the speaker's culture. To the extent that this strategy can be used without interrupting the flow of conversation too much, it may prove to be effective for avoiding misunderstandings caused by the interference of different systems of cultural conceptualizations.

Another example of the use of this strategy follows:

A: As a friend I expected more from you!

B: Can I ask you to tell more about the way you perceive friendship in your culture?

A: (explains the concept of 'friendship' in her culture for about 15 minutes)

B: It is quite clear that in my culture, we have a different understanding of 'friendship' ...

The above two excerpts clearly show that even a notion such as 'friendship', which may be thought to be universal, can be associated with widely different cultural conceptualizations and hence expectations depending on the culture in question. The notion of 'friendship' appears to be a category with specific culturally defined boundaries about who we consider as our 'friend'. This is, of course, in addition to the conceptualizations that each individual may associate with such words based on their own life experiences and expectations.

It is acknowledged here that asking for clarification may not always work for a variety of reasons. For example, with some cultures, direct interrogation may prove to be inappropriate. The Aboriginal cultural conceptualizations of 'communication' do not allow for much direct interrogation (Eades, 1996; Walsh, 1994). In such contexts, cultural conceptualizations may unfold themselves gradually as the conversation continues for a while.

Moreover, we need to revise our understanding of some traditional models of communication in order to operate effectively in EIL communicative events. Even the notions of 'sender' and 'receiver' prove to be less clear-cut in EIL contexts. As the above examples suggest, both parties in a communicative event may need to actively and equally collaborate with each other in order to clarify the cultural conceptualizations that serve as starting points for them. As has been mentioned above, when encoding our 'messages', it is easy to overestimate what we share with others particularly if they come from different cultural or sub-cultural backgrounds. Within the revised model of communication laid out in this chapter, I argue that there is a need for the interlocutors participating in a communicative setting to constantly monitor the assumptions they are making about the systems of conceptualisations on which the other interlocutors are drawing.

Similarly, using the famous credo 'think globally, act locally', interlocutors in an EIL communicative event may benefit from thinking 'globally', so to speak, by keeping in mind that English is now used globally to express various systems of cultural conceptualizations, and at the same time acting and collaborating 'locally' with their conversants to explicate conceptualizations that more directly inform and contextualize the here-and-now communicative event. I now turn to a discussion of the implications of the notion of EIL for some fundamental concepts in ELT.

EIL and the notions of 'Language Proficiency', 'Native Speaker' and 'Teaching Model'

One of the basic notions discussed in the context of EIL is the 'native speaker'. Here I have nothing to add but to refer the reader to the relevant discussions in the literature (e.g. Arva & Medgyes, 2000; Braine, 1999; McKay, 2000, 2002; Medgyes, 1992, 1994). It would be obvious from the discussions that are presented here and also those by McKay and others on the notion of EIL that 'native' speaker competence may not necessarily enable individuals to be effective speakers in EIL contexts, particularly if their competence has been exclusively developed in monocultural contexts.

The notion of 'language proficiency', however, may need further discussion, as the notion of 'being proficient' in EIL appears to require more than just the mastery of grammar and lexicon in EIL contexts. In the light of the revised model of communication in EIL presented above, we may need to consider the notion of EIL proficiency, at least partly, in terms of exploring various systems of cultural conceptualizations and practice in adopting effective communicative strategies when communicating in EIL contexts. That is, 'more proficient' speakers are those who have been exposed to, and show familiarity with, various systems of cultural conceptualizations, participating with flexibility in EIL communication and effectively articulating their cultural conceptualizations when their interlocutors need this to be done. The kind of competence that underpins the skills that are described here may best be termed *meta-cultural competence*.

In answer to the question of which variety to choose as the EIL teaching model, I believe no matter what variety the teacher speaks, students need to be exposed to several varieties, to get the real sense of EIL speech situations, in which people who communicate with each other speak different varieties of English. It should be noted that the variety that each student develops in their language learning is unlikely to replicate in every detail the one(s) to which they have been exposed. Some students may develop a phonological system close to varieties such as American English while drawing on cultural conceptualizations from their 'native' cultures or the culture that is associated with the taught variety, or even blend aspects of the two. Here it should be repeated that the notion of 'cultural conceptualizations' used here does not refer to any static set of conceptual structures, but includes conceptualizations that emerge out of the interactions between people from differing cultural backgrounds.

This is one of the most significant implications of the notion of cultural conceptualizations for EIL: as speakers from diverse cultural backgrounds come to interact with each other in English, new systems of cultural conceptualizations may develop, both at the individual level and at the level of communities. As an example, we have observed Aboriginal children may bring their *Hunting* schema and map it onto the schema that they have learned in English about football and thus they talk about football using vocabularies and discourse patterns that reflect the Aboriginal Hunting schema (Malcolm & Sharifian, 2002: 176).

With regard to the notion of 'variety', it should be noted that varieties that may be associated with EIL do include but also move beyond those that have been identified as New Englishes. As mentioned above, communities of EIL learners and users may develop varieties of EIL based on their L1 phonological and grammatical characteristics as well as on the conceptual systems with which they are informed.

One of the characteristics of these varieties may be a prominent use of particular English words to express certain culturally important 'key words' (Wierzbicka, 1997), or what Roslyn Frank (personal communication) calls 'signatures of identity'. Speakers of Persian may use words such as 'honor', 'reputation' or 'face' in their use of English much more frequently than speakers of American English, for example. As I have discussed elsewhere (Sharifan, 2007), in many cases these words are used by Persian speakers to instantiate their Persian cultural schema of *aaberu* 'face'. I believe this to be the most significant schema for many Persian speakers (Sharifian, 2007), one which constructs their identity in profound and emotionally motivated ways. It is also associated with a schema that embodies the image of a person, a family or a group, particularly as it is viewed by others in the society. O'Shea (2000: 101) maintains that for Iranians '*Aberu* or honor, is a powerful social force. All Iranians measure themselves to a great extent by the honor they accumulate through their actions and social interrelations'. This Persian cultural schema surfaces very frequently in conversations among Persian speakers and often motivates much of the content of their communication. Thus it would not be surprising to see its translated versions surface very frequently in Persian speakers' English, although some simply use the Persian word instead. Consider the following examples from some internet postings:

> ... I think the problem is more giving too much value to your social picture. We have even an important word for it in Farsi, Aberoo, that I don't know of a good English equivalent for it.[1]

> ... However, in any case, denying the existence of the problem never helps solving it. It is much easier to face the issue here without feeling that 'aaberoo' is lost ...[2]

Concluding Remarks

In this chapter, I have explored the cultural conceptual dimension of EIL observing specifically that in EIL communicative events, speakers are likely to draw on their L1 systems of cultural conceptualizations, perhaps not always realizing they are doing so. Since in such contexts English, a common language, is being used for communication, speakers may too easily assume that they mean the same thing when they use the same or similar words. In situations where this assumption is unwarranted, there is a need for interlocutors to consciously adopt communicative strategies, explicating and clarifying underlying conceptualizations. This chapter provides a sketch of strategies, although further and more systematic research is necessary.

Acknowledgements

I would like to thank Roslyn Frank, Ian G. Malcolm, Hans-Georg Wolf, Eric A. Anchimbe and Susan Stanford for their helpful suggestions and comments on the earlier drafts of this chapter.

Notes

1. http://freethoughts.org/archives/000594.php.
2. http://parents.berkeley.edu/madar-pedar/transex.html.

References

Arva, V. and Medgyes, P. (2000) Native and non-native teachers in the classroom. *System* 28 (3), 355–372.
Bartlett, F.C. (1932) *Remembering*. Cambridge: Cambridge University Press.
Braine, G. (ed.) (1999) *Non-Native Educators in English Language Teaching*. Mahwah, NJ: Lawrence Erlbaum Associates.

Carrell, P.L. (1987) Content and formal schemata in ESL reading. *TESOL Quarterly* 21 (3), 461–481.

D'Andrade, R. (1995) *The Development of Cognitive Anthropology.* Cambridge: Cambridge University Press.

Eades, D. (1996) Legal recognition of cultural differences in communication: The case of Robyn Kina. *Language and Communication* 16, 215–227.

Kövecses, Z. (2005) *Metaphor in Culture: Universality and Variation.* Cambridge: Cambridge University Press.

Lakoff, G. (1987) *Women, Fire, and Dangerous Things: What Categories Reveal about the Mind.* Chicago: University of Chicago Press.

Lakoff, G. and Johnson, M. (1980) *Metaphors We Live By.* Chicago: University of Chicago Press.

Lakoff, G. and Turner, M. (1989) *More than Cool Reason: A Field Guide to Poetic Metaphor.* Chicago: University of Chicago Press.

Malcolm, I.G. and Sharifian, F. (2002) Aspects of Aboriginal English oral discourse: An application of cultural schema theory. *Discourse Studies* 4 (2), 169–181.

Malcolm, G.I. and Sharifian, F. (2005) Something old, something new, something borrowed, something blue: Australian Aboriginal students' schematic repertoire. *Journal of Multilingual and Multicultural Development* 26 (6), 512–532.

McKay, S. (2000) Teaching English as an international language: Implications for cultural materials in the classroom. *TESOL Journal* 9 (4), 7–11.

McKay, S.L. (2002) *Teaching English as an International Language: Rethinking Goals and Approaches.* Oxford: Oxford University Press.

Medgyes, P. (1992) Native or non-native: Who's worth more? *ELT Journal* 46 (4), 340–349.

Medgyes, P. (1994) *The Non-Native Teacher.* London: Macmillan.

Núñez, R.E. and Sweetser, E. (2006) Aymara, where the future is behind you: Convergent evidence from language and gesture in the crosslinguistic comparison of spatial construals of time. *Cognitive Science* 30, 1–49.

O'Shea, M. (2000) *Cultural Shock: Iran.* Portland, Oregon: Graphic Arts Publishing Company.

Palmer, G. B. (1996) *Toward a Theory of Cultural Linguistics.* Austin: University of Texas Press.

Polzenhagen, F. and Wolf, H. (2007) Culture-specific conceptualizations of corruption in African English: Linguistic analyses and pragmatic applications. In F. Sharifian and G.B. Palmer (eds) *Applied Cultural Linguistics: Second Language Learning/Teaching and Intercultural Communication* (pp. 125–168). Amsterdam/Philadelphia: John Benjamins.

Quinn, N. (1996) Culture and contradiction: The case of Americans reasoning about marriage. *Ethos* 24 (3), 391–425.

Quinn, N. (ed.) (2005) *Finding Culture in Talk: A Collection of Methods.* New York: Palgrave MacMillan.

Quirk, R. (1981) International communication and the concept of nuclear English. In L.E. Smith (ed.) *English for Cross-Cultural Communication* (pp. 151–165). New York: St Martin's Press.

Rosch, E. (1978) Principles of categorization. In E. Rosch and B. Lloyd (eds) *Cognition and Categorization* (pp. 27–48). Hillsdale, NJ: Lawrence Erlbaum.

Rumelhart, D.E. (1980) Schemata: The building blocks of cognition. In R.J. Spiro, B. Bruce and W.F. Brewer (eds) *Theoretical Issues in Reading Comprehension.* Hillsdale, NJ: Erlbaum.

Sharifian, F. (2001) Schema-based processing in Australian speakers of Aboriginal English. *Language and Intercultural Communication* 1 (2), 120–134.

Sharifian, F. (2003) On cultural conceptualisations. *Journal of Cognition and Culture* (3) 3, 187–207.

Sharifian, F. (2004) Cultural schemas and intercultural communication: A study of Persian. In J. Leigh and E. Loo (eds) *Outer Limits: A Reader in Communication Across Cultures* (pp. 119–130). Melbourne: Language Australia.

Sharifian, F. (2005a) Cultural conceptualisations in English words: A study of Aboriginal children in Perth. *Language and Education* 19 (1), 74–88.

Sharifian, F. (2005b) The Persian cultural schema of *shekasteh-nafsi*: A study of complement responses in Persian and Anglo-Australian speakers. *Pragmatics & Cognition* 13 (2), 337–361.

Sharifian, F. (2006) A cultural-conceptual approach and world Englishes: The case of Aboriginal English. *World Englishes* 25 (1), 11–22.

Sharifian, F. (2007) L1 cultural conceptualisations in L2 learning. In F. Sharifian and G.B. Palmer (eds) *Applied Cultural Linguistics: Implications for Second Language Learning and Intercultural Communication* (pp. 33–52). Amsterdam/Philadelphia: John Benjamins.

Sharifian, F. (2008a) Cultural schemas in L1 and L2 compliment responses: A study of Persian-speaking learners of English. *Journal of Politeness Research* 4 (1), 55–80.

Sharifian, F. (2008b) Distributed, emergent cognition, conceptualisation, and language. In R.M. Frank, R. Dirven, J. Zlatev and T. Ziemke (eds) *Body, Language, and Mind (Vol. 2): Sociocultural Situatedness* (pp. 241–268). Berlin/New York: Mouton de Gruyter.

Sharifian, F. (2008c) Cultural model of Home in Aboriginal children's English. In G. Kristiansen and R. Dirven (eds) *Cognitive Sociolinguistics: Language Variation, Cultural Models, Social Systems* (pp. 333–352). Berlin/New York: Mouton de Gruyter.

Sharifian, F., Rochecouste, J, and Malcolm, I.G. (2004) "It was all a bit confusing …": Comprehending Aboriginal English texts. *Language, Culture and Curriculum* 17 (3), 203–228.

Strauss, C. and Quinn, N. (1997) *A Cognitive Theory of Cultural Meaning*. Cambridge: Cambridge University Press.

Walsh, M. (1994) Interactional styles and the courtroom: An example from Northern Australia. In J. Gibbons (ed.) *Language and the Law* (pp. 217–233). London: Longman.

Wierzbicka, A. (1997) *Understanding Cultures Through Their Key Words: English, Russian, Polish, German, Japanese*. New York: Oxford University Press.

Yu, N. (2003) Metaphor, body, and culture: The Chinese understanding of *gallbladder* and *courage*. *Metaphor and Symbol* 18 (1), 13–31.

Chapter 14

English as the International Language of Scholarship: Implications for the Dissemination of 'Local' Knowledge

ANDY KIRKPATRICK

Introduction

The emergence of English as the international language for the dissemination of knowledge is well-attested. It is 'by far the most important language of scientific and scholarly conferences' (Ammon, 1996: 260). The European Science Foundation's working language is English and its journal *Communication* is exclusively in English (Ammon, 1996). Over 90% of the information contained in influential databases such as the Science Citation Index (SCI) 'is extracted from articles in English taken mostly from English language journals' (Truchot, 2002: 10).

This phenomenon has a number of potential consequences. First, the role of other languages is becoming diminished. For example, European languages are not developing appropriate scientific terms (Hoffmann, 2000: 10). And the move from German into English has raised concerns that a once powerful European lingua franca is being reduced to a sub-variety, used only in restricted local domains (Görlach, 2002: 16). Second, writers for whom English is not a first language may naturally feel a resentment and injustice in being obliged to use English (Ammon, 2000). The need to work with an empirical-scientific knowledge paradigm and 'Anglo' rhetorical styles can greatly disadvantage those unfamiliar with both (Kandiah, 2001). Third, the status of 'traditional wisdom' and 'indigenous knowledge' has become devalued, not least by local people themselves (Canagarajah, 2005; Fernando, 1996), or has been reframed by being disseminated in English.

In this chapter, drawing on examples from the context of Chinese medicine, I want to consider the implications of the rise of English as the international language of scholarship for the dissemination of indigenous knowledge.

Background

The increasing growth of English as an international language is considered inevitable, at least in the foreseeable future (Graddol, 2006). One major role it plays in this context is as the language of international education and scholarship. Along with the growth of English as an international language, however, nativized and indigenous new varieties of English continue to develop. A major role that these new Englishes play is as a conduit for reflecting local cultures. For example, many 'new' literatures in English have flourished over recent decades, although the extent to which these new literatures in English can indeed adequately reflect or represent local cultures remains the subject of much debate. In this chapter, I shall first briefly review this debate. My aim in doing this is to see whether the development of new literatures in English offers any insight into the parallel development of new 'academic Englishes'. In other words, if English can be adapted and indigenized to reflect local cultures, can it also be adapted to represent and disseminate indigenous knowledge? In addressing this question I shall consider the case of Chinese medicine. This will require exploring whether Chinese medicine is a unified and utterly indigenous form of knowledge, or whether it is diverse and dynamic and subject to outside influence. It will also require a brief investigation into translation and the processes through which knowledge is disseminated.

The Rise of New Englishes

There is evidence that new varieties of English in Africa and the Indian subcontinent have developed creatively to produce new African and Indian literatures in English (Kirkpatrick, 2007). In both Africa and the Indian subcontinent, however, voices promoting the use of English as the language of local experience are challenged by voices decrying this and calling for the use of local languages. Famous African novelists who have decided that English can carry African cultures include the Nigerian writers, Chinua Achebe, Wole Soyinka and Ken Saro-Wiwa. According to Achebe (2003: 171), 'the writer should aim at fashioning out an English which is at once universal and able to carry his personal experience'. Soyinka agrees, 'When we borrow an alien language, we must stretch it, impact and compact it, fragment and reassemble it' (cited in Schmied, 1991: 126). There are, however, those who oppose the use of English, arguing that it is elitist and the cause of 'psychological amputation'. The best known voice of this camp belongs to the Kenyan writer Ngugi wa Thiong'o (2003: 176) who accuses Achebe and others like him of kowtowing to their former colonial masters. 'It is the final triumph of a system of domination when the dominated start singing its virtues.'

Similar arguments for both sides can be heard on the Indian subcontinent. In a quote that echoes the sentiments expressed by Soyinka above, the Pakistani novelist Sidhwa (1996: 231) writes, 'English ... is no longer the monopoly of the British. We, the excolonised, have subjugated the language, beaten it on its head and made it ours'. These views are nicely captured by the authors of a recent survey of Indian literature in English. In a style illustrating distinctive Indian rhetorical tropes, including an extended use of metaphor (Kachru, 1983: 41), they write:

> Years ago, a slender sapling from a foreign field was grafted by 'pale hands' on the mighty and many-branched Indian banyan tree. It has kept growing vigorously and now an organic part of its parent tree, it has spread its own probing roots into the brown soil below. Its young leaves rustle energetically in the strong winds that blow from the western horizon, but the sunshine that warms it and the rain that cools it are from Indian skies; and it continues to draw its vital sap from 'this earth, this realm, this India'. (Naik & Narayan, 2004: 253)

As with the case of Ngugi mentioned above, however, not all agree. The Sri Lankan poets, Yasmine Gooneratne and Lakdasa Wikkramasinha, represent strongly dissenting voices. Gooneratne argues that 'there is still deep-seated resentment' against English, especially 'in countries such as India, Pakistan and Sri Lanka, perhaps Africa too, but certainly in regions that possess an ancient and written literature, and a creative literary tradition of their own' (cited in Bailey, 1996: 40). Wikkramasinha is explicit in his contempt for English and writing in it. 'I have come to realise that I am writing the language of the most despicable and loathsome people on earth ... to write in English is a form of cultural treason' (cited in Canagarajah, 1994: 375).

The question is whether we can expect the development of new academic Englishes which reflect local rhetorical styles to parallel the development of new Englishes which reflect the cultural values and conventions of their speakers and writers.

The Dissemination of Knowledge: Some Key Issues

While there is obvious disagreement here about the value, even the morality, of writing in English, literatures in African and Indian Englishes have developed, if not flourished, in Africa and on the Indian subcontinent. Indeed, Naik and Narayan's book cited above lists 54 successful Indian-based authors writing in English. This gives rise to the following question: if local writers can write novels and poetry in nativized forms of English can local scholars write academic articles and disseminate local knowledge in nativised forms of English? At first glance this may appear a naïve question. One might say that this is not so much about the ability of English to adapt, but about the power of journal editors to insist on academic articles conforming to Anglo-rhetorical and disciplinary styles. As Truchot (2002) has pointed out, over 90% of information contained in influential databases is 'extracted from articles in English taken mostly from English language journals', and Burrough-Boenisch's (2003: 238) research suggests that non-native speakers preparing articles for those journals are required to acquire 'an American accent'. This not only causes linguistic problems for the authors concerned, but also gives rise to questions of identity. In a study of Chinese scholars who were trained in the West and who have returned to China, Shi (2003: 376) reports they felt a division between 'us' bilingual and Western trained scholars and 'they' monolingual scholars, and that they also now preferred to write in English rather than Chinese. Belcher (2007) has raised the possibility of editors accepting new standards of text conventions and different varieties of English. Swales (1997: 380) has called for a sober reflection on 'Anglophone gate-keeping practices' and Ammon (2000: 114) for a 'new culture of communication'. Yet Ammon himself remains pessimistic that this is imminent. On the other hand, Flowerdew (2001) found some evidence of a tolerance for non-Anglo styles, as a percentage of the journal editors he interviewed were sympathetic to the problems facing non-native speaker (NNS) writers and were also keen to include their work. However, the fact that these were editors of applied linguistics journals – including *World Englishes* – may explain their positive attitudes towards NNS writers.

There are two related concerns here. On the one hand, there is the clear disadvantage facing non-native speaker writers of English in having to submit journal articles in English that conform to Anglo rhetorical and disciplinary styles. Phillipson (2006: 68–69) reiterates Bourdieu's challenge: 'How can one go along with the use of English without exposing oneself to the risk of being anglicised in one's mental structures, without being brainwashed by the linguistic routines?' This leads to the second concern which touches upon the very nature of the knowledge itself. Is indigenous knowledge fundamentally altered if it has to be reframed to fit Anglo rhetorical patterns on the one hand and empirical-scientific knowledge paradigms on the other? For example, Fernando (1996) argues that Sri Lankans traditionally valued metaphysical and religious knowledge, but these values have been undermined by the current insistence on a 'western' scientific-technological paradigm. And does the dominant position of the empirical/scientific paradigm not lead to a devaluing of other types of knowledge? Canagarajah points to an underlying unfairness here. Although empirical science and empirical methods are now required internationally and dominate other paradigms and methods of enquiry, they themselves were once only forms of local knowledge. In his view, there is something unethical about one tradition of local knowledge 'lording it over' others (Canagarajah, 2005: 7). These two concerns lead to a third, which is that the flow of knowledge is essentially one way. Knowledge is processed and then disseminated by Anglo-journals. But is it not time, as Kandiah has eloquently argued, 'to effect a significant reversal in the directionality of the flow of ideas' and to fight for 'a truly equal and participatory academic community made up of scholars from across the world?' (Kandiah, 2001: 107–108).

These are extremely complex questions, not given to easy answers. They can be expressed in this way:

(1) Does the insistence on dissemination through English restrict the spread of local knowledge or does it allow for the greater spread of local knowledge?
(2) Can local knowledge be transmitted through processes other than those associated with conventional academic practices?
(3) Does the dissemination of local knowledge through English fundamentally alter the essence of the local knowledge?'

In an attempt to provide preliminary responses to these questions, I consider the case of Chinese medicine with a particular focus on the manner of its dissemination to the 'West'.

Chinese Medicine as Diverse Practice

Chinese medicine has a history as long as China's. Canonical medical texts that are still in use include the Confucian Classic, *The Book of Changes* (the *Yi Jing*), and the earliest Classical text on Chinese medicine, the *Yellow Emperor's Inner Canon* (*Huang Di Nei Jing*) (Hsu, 1999). The precise dates of the '*Inner Canon*' are unknown but it is at least 2300 years old

(Unschuld, 2003). It is important to point out, however, that, despite this continued reliance on such canonical texts, Chinese medicine has been subject to external influences for centuries. Alter draws attention to the striking similarities between various Asian medical systems and also points out that forms of 'Western' medicine have been adapted or integrated by Asian systems over many centuries (Alter, 2005a: 2–3). 'One can imagine an ancient chain of links in medical knowledge connecting what is now China to what is now Greece or India ...' (Alter, 2005a: 14).

Chinese medicine has therefore to be seen as a constantly changing phenomenon. 'There are no fixed borders between medical traditions or between different regions of a cultural space' (Scheid, 2002: 263). Aspects of Chinese medical knowledge have been known in Europe at least since Matteo Ricci's (1552–1610) translations (Ma & Grant, 1999: 214). The notion, then, that Chinese medicine is a purely indigenous form of knowledge cannot be supported. On the contrary, it has been and remains a developing and dynamic body of knowledge which has shaped and been shaped by other medical systems.

Here, some issues surrounding translation need to be briefly considered. There is always the danger that what has been called 'ideological manipulation' (Chang, 2005: 44) may subvert the message in fundamental ways. Ideological manipulation can be defined as the ways in which bodies of knowledge have been manipulated during the process of borrowing ideas from one place or a combination of places (Alter, 2005b). Chang (2005: 45) gives the following example from Xuan Zang's (600–664) translation of Buddhist texts into Chinese, where the translator was forced to respect Confucian prejudices. The original text reads, in English translation, 'We, my daughter are prostitutes, we give pleasure to all people, we do not make our living by serving one man only.' This explanation that her status as a prostitute made it impossible for her daughter to marry a prince is coyly rendered for the Chinese reader as 'We of a humble position are not fit to marry princes.'

In addition to the dangers of the message being essentially altered through ideological manipulation, there are those who argue that the very relationship between language and thought makes it impossible to accurately translate thought from one language into another. As it happens, Chinese represents an excellent research site for the followers of this version of the Sapir-Whorf hypothesis. For example, Chinese, especially Classical Chinese, is characterized by ambiguity. Wardy quotes Matteo Ricci as saying, 'there is so much ambiguity (in the Chinese language) that there are many words that can signify more than a thousand things ...' (Wardy, 2000: 6). This is one reason why Classical Chinese poetry has proved so difficult to translate as the ideas expressed within the poems are open to so many different, but plausible, interpretations. Yet, as Wardy (2000: 7) reminds us, ambiguity is itself simply a 'technical term which derives its meaning from this or that linguistic theory' (but *cf.* Empson, 1930). In a rebuttal of the Sapir-Whorf hypothesis, he illustrates how successfully Aristotle's *Categories* was translated into Chinese in the 17th century. But, this is not to say that translation of this sort is easy. Ambiguity is not restricted to Chinese poetry, as the examples of the translations of *qi* given below will illustrate.

To return to the nature of Chinese medicine itself, Hsu (1999) describes the diverse practices of Chinese medicine and the diversity of Chinese medical knowledge. In research that saw her studying Chinese medicine in different settings, she identified three social settings for the knowledge and practice of Chinese medicine: secret, personal and standardized. To investigate the differences in the medical practices used in these three settings, Hsu learned (1) *qigong*, which is described as a Daoist-based 'meditative practice with life-maintaining therapeutic effects' (Hsu, 1999: 21) from a *qigong* master, (2) 'real' Chinese medicine from an elderly doctor, Doctor Zhang, whose few remaining patients were mostly old friends, and (3) the 'new' version of Chinese medicine, TCM, at the Yunnan Province TCM College. The different ways in which knowledge was transmitted in these three settings serves to underline the diversity of knowledge and practice associated with Chinese medicine. The *qigong* knowledge was veiled in secrecy (Hsu, 1999: 225). Students did not need to understand the *qigong* spells but solely needed to be able to pronounce them correctly. This meant, of course, that the spells could only be transmitted orally and that the *qigong* master therefore had control over the transmission of this knowledge.

Doctor Zhang, on the other hand, expected his students to learn in a specific way. 'The promise was that one day we would just know' (Hsu, 1999: 227). 'Knowing Chinese medicine meant acquiring profound knowledge by memorising the "experience" (*jingyan*) of the ancients in the text and combining it with one's own experience in medical practice' (Hsu, 1999: 227). The students' task was to learn passages from canonical texts and assist in therapy. Doctor Zhang did not translate these literally, but used them to convey his own conviction and experience.

At the Yunnan TCM College, students rote-learned excerpts from textbooks with little attention to meaning. As Hsu points out, rote-learning was common to all three traditions, with *qigong* students learning short spells, Zhang's students texts from medical canons and TCM students shorter texts from TCM textbooks. However, the TCM students were also taught by the 'didactic method of post-Enlightenment education' (Hsu, 1999: 228) through a combination of explanation and method. It is this third setting, standardized, that has seen the development of a legitimized Chinese medicine which has come to be called, despite its relatively recent origins, Traditional Chinese Medicine (TCM). It could, more appropriately, be called Modern Chinese Medicine.

While some key terms were common in all three traditions, they were not interpreted in the same way. For example, the concept of *qi* is central to all three traditions, yet it is differently interpreted. A glimpse of the complexity of the concepts represented by *qi* can be seen from this excerpt taken from Scheid (2002: 48):

> In early Chinese writings about nature *qi* simultaneously refers to that which 'makes things happen in stuff' and 'stuff in which things happen'. According to Pockert, *qi* is both an 'energetic configuration' and a 'configuration of energy', while Unschuld translates the terms as '(finest matter) influences', 'emanations' or 'vapours'.

As Hsu (1999: 81) explains:

> The all-pervasive *qi* that permeated macrocosm and microcosm(s) had, in Chinese medical doctrine, innumerable facets. Although unifying, the concept of *qi* lent itself to the expression of great diversity.

Given this, her comment that, 'Use of the same terminology need not be taken as a sign that the same therapeutic practice is being performed' (Hsu, 1999: 240) would seem something of an understatement. A key difference that Hsu identifies between Chinese and Western science is that terms in Western science are constructed in such a way as to be unambiguous, while Chinese terms are 'therapeutically useful precisely because of their vagueness and polysemy' (Hsu, 1999: 233). This obviously means that any attempt to translate such vague and polysemous terms into English will necessarily turn them into qualitatively different concepts. A goal of TCM is to disambiguate these terms so that they can be transmitted.

TCM as Modern Chinese Medicine

This need for Chinese medicine to become modern and scientific is behind the development of this 'new' branch of Traditional Chinese Medicine. The Chinese Government is the key driver in the move to disambiguate Chinese medicine and to make Chinese medicine conform to Western 'scientific' principles. Mao's 1940 article, 'On New Democracy', calls for a new scientific democratic culture which is opposed to super-stition and feudal ideas. Things had to be 'new scientific, unified' (Taylor, 2001: 357). A critical and empirically tested evaluation of Chinese medi-cine is now seen by many Chinese scholars as crucial for its international legitimacy (Qu, 2004).

This has led to a tension between the supporters of the older version of Chinese medicine and the new TCM; between 'plasticity, diversity, adaptability and stochastic reasoning' on the one hand and the need for a unified and homogeneous knowledge as required by TCM on the other (Scheid, 2001: 270). The debate within China is between those who see Chinese medicine as essentially different from Western biomedicine and those who feel Chinese medicine must modernize in order to survive. This tension was nicely captured in a recent report in Hong Kong's South China Morning Post newspaper (SCMP, 2006), a summary of which is provided here. The President of China's University of Science and Technology, Professor Zhu Qingshi argued that what he called TCM must have an empirical basis. Professor Zhang Gongyao of Central South University in Hunan agreed, 'TCM is an ineffective and sometimes dangerous approach to treating the sick'. Others, including the Minister of Health, disagreed, saying that discarding TCM would be a 'betrayal of our ancestors.' They unswervingly take the view that Western medicine and TCM cannot be compared as they are different approaches to different systems.

As we have seen, however, the argument that Chinese and Western medicine are two different and unrelated systems is impossible to sustain. Rather, these and other systems of medicine have influenced each other over centuries. This plurality has led Scheid to argue for plurality across health systems as a whole. 'The plurality of agents that impinge on human health may best be engaged by means of a similar plurality in the domain of medicine' (Scheid, 2002: 273). This position is probably adopted by many patients all over the world, who, if they feel that one system is not working, are more than happy to try another. But as Qu (2004) points out it cannot just be a question of seeing a Western doctor and taking Chinese herbs; there must be dialogue. The importance of traditional medicines and the financial value attached to them is being increasingly recognised. For example the 'Traditional Knowledge Digital Library' (TKDL) is being developed in India to patent traditional cures and medicines and to pre-vent them from being 'discovered' by Western drug companies (2007).

The brief account above has demonstrated the complexity of the issue. Chinese medicine is not a unified 'single' form of knowledge and practice, which has been disseminated in a uniform way. On the contrary, it comprises a diversity of knowledge and practices which have been disseminated in equally diverse ways. Nor has it developed in isolation. Rather, medical traditions have been influencing each other for thousands of years. The current 'official' form of Chinese medicine, TCM, owes its scientific approach as much to the Chinese Communist Party as to anyone else. The debate surrounding the fundamental alteration of Chinese medical knowledge and practice is already in full swing in China itself, even though the knowledge is being transmitted in Chinese. A major problem lies in the translation of deliberately vague and ambiguous Chinese medical terms into the modern form of TCM, and this is as much of a problem for translation from Classical Chinese into Modern Standard Chinese as it is for translation from Chinese into English.

Despite these linguistic difficulties, Chinese medical knowledge and practices have been transmitted beyond China for centuries. In the remaining part of this chapter, I shall look briefly at the transmission of Chinese medicine in selected countries outside China and consider the extent to which this transmission is aided or hindered by a need for Chinese medicine to be transmitted through English (and other languages).

The International Transmission of Chinese Medicine: Some Examples

The plurality that exists within Chinese medicine itself is reflected even in a country of a relatively small population such as Denmark. Here, five different types of Chinese medicine are practised (Hog, 1999). TCM is the least popular, as it is considered the most abstract and intellectually challenging. Those practising 'traditional' acupuncture and herbal medicine – and these include a Sri Lankan school – are more popular as they emphasize 'short training and practicability against common illnesses' (Hog, 1999: 237). In general, however, Chinese medicine's chances of official recognition by the Danish Ministry of Health are slim, and the case of chiropractice helps explain why. The Danish Ministry now recognizes the study of chiropractice, but only because it has been able to fulfil the following two fundamental conditions: providing a common curriculum; and conforming to scientific biomedical reasoning. It has now been renamed 'clinical biomechanics' (Hog, 1999: 242–243). In addition to being unable to satisfy scientific criteria, Hog lists two further problems that Chinese medicine will have to overcome before it can become officially recognized in Denmark. The first concerns the tendency of schools of Chinese medicine to run in competition with each other with the major aim of achieving a profit. The second, which is of particular relevance to this chapter, concerns the difficulty of conveying certain Chinese medical concepts into Danish, especially if they come through German or English first. This is perhaps not surprising given the deliberately vague nature of many Chinese terms noted above. However, it has led translators to simply leave out difficult passages, thus inevitably seriously compromising the knowledge itself (Hog, 1999: 244).

In the United Kingdom, Chinese medicine is better established than in Denmark because of the large number of Chinese migrants, especially in the 19th century. This gave Chinese medicine a viable patient pool from early on. The success of Chinese acupuncture in Britain, for example, was established when Chinese migrants went to acupuncture clinics when they felt that 'local' medical practices were not working (Ma & Grant, 1999). Acupuncture has a long tradition in England. In the 1820s many papers were published in *The Lancet* and other medical journals describing acupuncture treatments, and Leeds Infirmary was a famous acupuncture centre (Ma & Grant, 1999: 217). Among the reasons that Ma and Grant offer for the current popularity of Chinese medicine, in particular acupuncture, are a British tradition for alternative treatments (shared by the current Prince of Wales) and the presence of so many different cultures living in Britain.

This plurality of cultures allows for a plurality of medical practices. This is also a reason that Chinese medicine has become popular in the United States (Hui & Lee, 2002). When this plurality is coupled with an increasing suspicion of scientific 'experts', places like Britain and the United States may provide more promise for the ability of Chinese medicine to survive in a wider variety of forms than in China itself. A brief survey of the current situation in Hong Kong may help justify this claim. When Hong Kong was a British colony, Chinese medical practitioners were able to operate without a licence. This made it difficult to maintain standards and weed out charlatans (Hong Kong Museum of Medical Sciences Society [HKMMSS], 2006: 248). The first law regulating the practice of Chinese medicine in Hong Kong, 'The Chinese Medicine Ordinance' was passed only in 1999, two years after Hong Kong's handover back to China (Hokari, 1999) and this gave TCM official status for the first time (HKMMSS, 2006: 250). The Hong Kong government is now keen to establish Hong Kong as an international centre for Chinese medicine, but by this they mean TCM. They have therefore imported several hundred TCM practitioners from China. In 1998 the Hong Kong Baptist University (HKBU) offered the first full-time degree course in the subject, soon to be followed by the University of Hong Kong and the Chinese University of Hong Kong. These courses require internship in China, with the HKBU course including an internship at the Beijing University of Chinese

Medicine and Pharmacology. The texts are all imported from Mainland China so that, interestingly, the TCM being transmitted in Hong Kong is certified by the Beijing government as one adopting 'Western scientific methods' (Hokari, 1999: 233–234). From a pre-handover environment, therefore, in which a wide variety of schools of Chinese medicine were allowed to practise, now all practitioners must be licensed and the official school is represented by 'scientific' and 'modern' TCM as promulgated by Beijing.

The influence of Beijing-approved TCM extends beyond Hong Kong. The Hong Kong Baptist University degree is now offered as a joint degree with the Royal Melbourne Institute of Technology (RMIT) in Australia. In fact, several Australian universities now offer degrees in TCM and, as far as I can determine, these are all based on Mainland Chinese 'official' TCM.

The potential tension between the standardization required by TCM and the diversity of other Chinese medical practices is captured in the editorial notes of the *Australian Journal of Acupuncture and Chinese Medicine* (AJACM). This claims, and then appears to discount, the acceptance of plurality under its Aims and Scope section:

> The AJACM acknowledges the diversity of Chinese medicine theories and practice, and encourages the integration of research, practice and education. It promotes the use of rigorous and appropriate research methodologies in the field of Chinese medicine ...

It also endorses the 'Uniform Requirements for Manuscripts Submitted to Biomedical Journals' and requires prospective authors to follow the Standards of Reporting Interventions in Controlled Trials of Acupuncture (STRICTA) which were drawn up by Hugh Macpherson in his role as the Research Director of the Foundation for TCM. While these requirements may be perfectly understandable, the journal's insistence on them may be incompatible with the claim that it acknowledges the diversity of Chinese medicine.

What would seem to be happening is that the TCM officially promoted by the Chinese government is being adopted in Hong Kong and in universities overseas. This has been made possible by the Chinese Government's drive to make TCM a 'modern' and 'scientific' subject of study. As Hsu has pointed out, it is within the institutions of the Chinese state that Chinese medicine 'has been modernised, westernised, standardised and made scientific' (Hsu, 1999: 7). It is not, as might have been expected, its transmission through English that has caused this. The reformulation occurred within the original society, not as a result of its transmission through

English into other societies. Doubtless this reformulation into a 'modernized, Westernized, standardized' and 'scientific' subject has made its transmission through English easier. However, as indicated earlier, the picture is not as clear cut as that. As we saw in the case of Denmark, several different schools of Chinese medicine are operating. Paradoxically perhaps, it is the plurality that exists in countries such as Britain and the United States – those English speaking countries whose rhetorical and scientific paradigms dominate the dissemination of knowledge – that has allowed older varieties of Chinese medicine to gain a foothold, and it is in these countries that scholars are confident that these practices can flourish. This may be because there have been enough Chinese speakers over a long enough period of time in these countries to allow Chinese medicine to be disseminated via popular, informal and non-academic processes, even through the 'secret' oral transmission described by Hsu above. A second explanation may be that these diverse practices are able to flourish 'precisely because the legitimisation of Asian medicine through discourses of science has made it possible to transform discourses of health into commodified regimens of medicalised self-help' (Alter, 2005a: 17).

Conclusion

At the beginning of this chapter I raised three questions. By way of conclusion, I shall attempt here to answer them in relation to Chinese medicine.

(1) Does the insistence on dissemination through English restrict the spread of local knowledge or does it allow for the greater spread of local knowledge?

It would seem safe to argue that knowledge about TCM has increased significantly via its transmission through English. It is now available as a subject of study through English in a number of international universities and the number of TCM practitioners outside China is increasing dramatically.

(2) Can local knowledge be transmitted through processes other than those associated with conventional academic practices?

The increasing popularity of what Hsu classified as 'personal' and 'secret' Chinese medicine in pluralistic societies is evidence that the knowledge and practices associated with these versions of Chinese medicine are indeed being successfully transmitted. This knowledge is not being transmitted through conventional academic means, however, but through a variety of informal, personal and popular channels. Perhaps ironically these 'other' Chinese medicine practices are flourishing in countries such as the United States, Australia and the UK – where English is the main language – because these countries are so multicultural and pluralistic. A second reason for the increasing popularity of these unscientific forms of Chinese medicine is an increasing distrust of 'scientific' methods and the resultant need for people to seek out alternative methods. The popular transmission of these older versions of Chinese medicine through more informal and non-academic processes has taken place precisely because they do not conform to standardised scientific paradigms.

(3) Does the dissemination of local knowledge through English funda-mentally alter the essence of the local knowledge?

This is an issue that deserves a field of study on its own. The focus of this chapter has been more on the dissemination of the knowledge than the effect of the dissemination upon the knowledge. Nevertheless a number of points can be made in the context of Chinese medicine. First, the essence of the local knowledge has been shaped and altered through contact with other knowledge systems over centuries. Second, the 'local' knowledge in fact comprises several different knowledge systems. It is not a unified body of knowledge but a highly diverse one. Third, in the case of TCM, the essence of the knowledge was re-shaped by demands of the Chinese Communist Party and *before* its international dissemination through English. This reshaping of Chinese medicine into a modern scientific body of knowledge referred to as TCM has made it easier to transmit through English via conventional academic avenues such as university courses and academic journals.

Chinese medicine has been subject to constant change through many outside influences over many centuries. Far from being represented by a unified body of knowledge it is characterised by diversity of knowledge and practice. The development and transmission of the more 'scientific' and 'modern' TCM has been driven more by the Chinese government than the demands of editors of Anglo academic journals. Just as the devel-opment of African and Indian literatures in English has required the adaptation of English to reflect and represent local cultural traditions, it is the Chinese government-promoted adaptation of Chinese medicine into the 'scientific' and 'modern' version of Traditional Chinese Medicine which is being transmitted through journals and being taught in 'Anglo' universities. Thus the *World Englishes* paradigm discussed at the beginning of the chapter is not being mirrored in international scholarship in English about TCM. At the same time, however, older and other types of Chinese medical knowledge and practice have been transmitted through Chinese and other languages for several centuries and continue to be transmitted. It would appear this knowledge is being successfully transmitted though language and resources other than those assumed necessary for academic dissemination (*cf.* Pachler, 2007). Interestingly, official support for these other kinds of Chinese knowledge and practices is greater in pluralistic societies outside China than within China itself. It is also worth noting that these countries include Britain and the United States, countries which are home to the journals and scientific paradigms that are considered to provide major obstacles to the transmission of local knowledge. The transmission of knowledge is thus not solely dependent upon its transmission through English via traditional academic avenues or means.

References

Achebe, C. (2003) The African writer and the English language. In J. Jenkins (ed.) *World Englishes* (pp. 169–172). London: Routledge.

Alter, J. (2005a) The politics of culture and medicine. In J. Alter (ed.) *Asian Medicine and Globalisation* (pp. 1–20). Philadelphia: University of Pennsylvania Press.

Alter, J. (2005b) *Asian Medicine and Globalisation.* Philadelphia: University of Pennsylvania Press.

Ammon, U. (1996) The European Union. Status change during the last 50 years. In J. Fishman, A. Conrad and A. Rubal-Lopez (eds) *Post-Imperial English* (pp. 241–267). Berlin: Mouton de Gruyter.

Ammon, U. (2000) Towards more fairness in international English: Linguistic rights of non-native speakers? In R. Phillipson (ed.) *Rights to Language: Equity, Power and Education* (pp. 111–116). Mahwah, NJ: Lawrence Erlbaum Associates.

Bailey, R.W. (1996) Attitudes towards English: The future of English in South Asia. In R.J. Baumgardner (ed.) *South Asian English: Structure, Use and Users* (pp. 40–52). Illinois: University of Illinois Press.

Belcher, D. (2007) Seeking acceptance in an English-only research world. *Journal of Second Language Writing* 16 (1), 1–22.

Burrough-Boenisch, J. (2003) Shapers of published NNS research articles. *Journal of Second Language Writing* 12 (3), 223–244.

Canagarajah, S.C. (1994) Competing discourses in Sri Lankan English poetry. *World Englishes* 13 (3), 361–376.

Canagarajah, S.C. (2005) Reconstructing local knowledge, reconfiguring language studies. In S. Canagarajah (ed.) *Reclaiming the Local in Language Policy and Practice* (pp. 3–24). Mahwah, NJ: Lawrence Erlbaum Associates.

Chang, N.F. (2005) *Yes Prime Manipulator: How a Chinese Translation of British Political Humour Came into Being*. Hong Kong: Chinese University Press.

Empson, W. (1930) *Seven Types of Ambiguity*. London: Chatto and Windus.

Fernando, C. (1996) The ideational function of English in Sri Lanka. In R.J. Baumgardner (ed.) *South Asian English: Structure, Use and Users* (pp. 206–217). Illinois: University of Illinois Press.

Flowerdew, J. (2001) Attitudes of journal editors to nonnative speaker contributors. *TESOL Quarterly* 35 (4), 121–150.

Görlach, M. (2002) *Still More Englishes*. Amsterdam: John Benjamins.

Graddol, D. (2006) *English Next*. London: The British Council.

Guardian Weekly (2007) From palm leaf to database. 176 (7), 2–8 Feb.

Hoffmann, C. (2000) The spread of English and the growth of multilingualism in Europe. In J. Cenoz and U. Jessner (eds) *English in Europe: The Acquisition of a Third Language* (pp. 1–21). Clevedon: Multilingual Matters.

Hog, E. (1999) Traditional Chinese Medicine (TCM) in Denmark: Conditions in a new host culture. In A.K.L. Chan, G.K. Clancey and H-C. Loy (eds) *Historical Perspectives on East Asian Science Technology and Medicine* (pp. 236–250). Singapore: Singapore University Press.

Hokari, H. (1999) The presentation of traditional Chinese medicine (TCM) knowledge in Hong Kong. In A.K.L. Chan, G.K. Clancey and H-C. Loy (eds) *Historical Perspectives on East Asian Science Technology and Medicine* (pp. 236–250). Singapore: Singapore University Press.

Hong Kong Museum of Medical Sciences Society (HKMMSS) (2006) *Plague, SARS and the Story of Medicine in Hong Kong*. Hong Kong: Hong Kong University Press.

Hsu, E. (1999) *The Transmission of Chinese Medicine*. Cambridge: Cambridge University Press.

Hui, K.K. and Lee, G.K. (2002) Meiguo Zhongyiyao-de xiangzhuang jiqi fazhan (Current status and future outlook of Chinese Medicine in the USA). In Y.C. Kong (ed.) *Xiandai Zhongyiyao-zhi Jiaoyu, Yanjiu yu Fazhan (Modern Chinese Medicine: Education, Research and Development)* (pp. 25–30). Hong Kong: Chinese University of Hong Kong.

Kachru, B.B. (1983) *The Indianization of English*. New Delhi: Oxford University Press.

Kandiah, T. (2001) Whose meanings: Probing the dialectics of English as a global language. In R. Goh (ed.) *Ariels – Departures and Returns: A Festschrift for Edwin Thumboo* (pp. 102–121). Singapore: Oxford University Press.

Kirkpatrick, A. (2007) *World Englishes: Implications for International Communication and English Language Teaching*. Cambridge: Cambridge University Press.

Ma, B-Y. and Grant, A. (1999) The transmission of TCM to England. In A.K.L. Chan, G.K. Clancey and H-C. Loy (eds) *Historical Perspectives on East Asian Science Technology and Medicine* (pp. 214–221). Singapore: Singapore University Press.

Mao Zedong (1952) *Mao Zedong Xuanji Di Er Zhuan (The Selected Works of Mao Zedong Vol 2)* (pp. 633–682). Beijing: Renmin Chubanshe.

Naik, M.K. and Narayan, S.A. (2004) *Indian English Literature 1980–2000: A Critical Survey*. New Delhi: Pencraft International.

Ngugi wa Thiong'o (2003) The language of African literature. In J. Jenkins (ed.) *World Englishes* (pp. 172–177). London: Routledge.

Pachler, N. (2007) Choices in language education: Principles and policies. *Cambridge Journal of Education* 37 (1), 1–15.

Phillipson, R. (2006) Figuring out the Englishisation of Europe. In C. Leung and J. Jenkins (eds) *Reconfiguring Europe* (pp. 65–86). London: Equinox.

Qu, J. (2004) *Dang Zhongyi Yudaoshang Xiyi (When Chinese Medicine Meets Western Medicine)*. Hong Kong: Sanlian Chubanshe.

Scheid, V. (2001) Shaping Chinese Medicine: Two case studies from contemporary China. In E. Hsu (ed.) *Innovation in Chinese Medicine* (pp. 370–404). Cambridge: Cambridge University Press.

Scheid, V. (2002) *Chinese Medicine in Contemporary China*. Durham: Duke University Press.

Schmied, J. (1991) *English in Africa*. London: Longman.

Shi, L. (2003) Writing in two languages: Chinese professors return from the West. *Canadian Modern Language Review* 59 (3), 369–391.

Sidhwa, B. (1996) Creative processes in Pakistani English fiction. In R.J. Baumgardner (ed.) *South Asian English: Structure, Use and Users* (pp. 231–240). Illinois: University of Illinois Press.

South China Morning Post (SCMP) (2006) Status of Chinese medicine comes under attack. 21 October.

Swales, J. (1997) English as Tyrannosaurus rex. *World Englishes* 16 (3), 373–382.

Taylor, K. (2001) A new, scientific, and unified medicine: civil war in China and the new acumoxa, 1945–49. In E. Hsu (ed.) *Innovation in Chinese Medicine* (pp. 343–369). Cambridge: Cambridge University Press.

Truchot, C. (2002) *Key Aspects of the Use of English in Europe*. Strasbourg: Council of Europe.

Unschuld, P. (2003) *Huang Di Nei Jing Shu Wen. Nature, Knowledge, Imagery in an Ancient Chinese Medical Text*. Berkeley: University of California Press.

Wardy, R. (2000) *Aristotle in China*. Cambridge: Cambridge University Press.

Chapter 15

Local or International Standards: Indigenized Varieties of English at the Crossroads

ERIC A. ANCHIMBE

Introduction

This chapter examines the dilemma facing Indigenized Varieties of English (IVEs) – also commonly called New Englishes, non-native Englishes, postcolonial Englishes, vernacular Englishes and nativized Englishes – with regard to the issue of standard or norm; and seeks to situate them within the broader framework of English as an international language. The norms of these varieties are often rejected internationally (and nationally) and are regarded as *degenerate* and *unintelligible*. The spread of English to (post)colonial areas preceded the generally acknowledged status of English as a world or international language. The desire to maintain an 'international monochrome standard' for the language was not part of the agenda to spread it. This is because colonialism or colonizing groups had mixed feelings about spreading English to colonized people. In some areas, colonized people had no access to the language and had to appropriate it – resulting in Pidgins and Creoles. In other areas, the language was reserved for the settled colonial population and was a weapon of class demarcation – resulting in the development of transplanted (native) varieties of the language in such areas. In yet other areas, the colonized population was allowed limited access to the language through colonial schools – this led to the emergence of the educated varieties of English, which are the focus of this chapter. I therefore contend that, since the transmission, mix of populations, languages and exposure to English during colonialism were all different and determined by political factors, and since (in the later years) English was not taught by a homogeneous group of native speakers, there were bound to be as many standards as there were complete sociohistorical communities of speakers. In spite of pressure from prescriptivists, each community tends to use English from its own ecological and sociocultural standpoint. It inscribes, by necessity, its regional ecology onto the language so that this new version of English comes to reflect and transmit this ecology.

English as International Language (EIL) and Indigenized Varieties of English (IVEs)

Before going any further, it is important to show the relationship between EIL and IVE. When Quirk (1985: 6) declared that for English to be an effective world language it needed to have 'an international mono-chrome standard that sounds as good in speech as it looks on paper', his intention was to make one of the widespread old (native) varieties (British or American English) the worldwide standard. Such a move would have transformed the variety chosen into some sort of an international English. This was however impossible because, Standard English, difficult as it is to define, 'does not have an associated accent' (Trudgill, 1998: 38). In other words, the so-called native countries' versions of English span dialects and accents that are just as divergent as the indigenous languages in most of the other (especially postcolonial) areas to which English spread and is used as a second language. What then is EIL, from the point of view of this chapter?

Smith's (1983: vi) notion of English as an International Language, refers to the international 'functions of English, not to any given form of the language [... and of course to], the use of English by people of different nations and different cultures in order to communicate with one another'. He insists, '[i]t is not a new form of BASIC English'. More than a decade later, Widdowson (1997, 1998) revisits EIL and, ignoring the broad scope proposed by Smith, narrowly limits it to a written language used for inter-national, professional and academic purposes. EIL, he says, should be looked upon in terms of register, since most users need it for professional reasons rather than for communication within their community. To make this distinction clearer, Widdowson (1998: 400) defines EIL as a 'composite lingua franca which is free of any specific allegiance to any primary variety of the language'. Although it is unclear what 'primary varieties' are, the expression implies there are peripheral or secondary varieties. In one way Widdowson's position, though milder, reflects Quirk's (1990) reliance on older varieties. It nevertheless, opens the door to the non-primary varieties as Quirk's position does not.

Modiano (2001: 170) views EIL from a different perspective. He suggests it is a more accurate alternative to 'Standard English'. His notion provides an avenue for speakers to be culturally, politically and socially neutral in a way that earlier notions of Standard English did not. EIL, he continues, should consist of internationally intelligible features contributed by both L1 and L2 speakers. In his model of EIL (Modiano, 1999: 10), he characterizes EIL as the common core of English where 'the major varieties, the foreign language varieties and the other varieties' overlap. He excludes extreme regional accents, Pidgins and Creoles, marked RP usage, and terms that have different meanings in British and American English from this common core. Although Modiano (1999) agrees that EIL is difficult to define, he does not propose solutions to the definition debacle, which revolves around the varying functions, users and uses of English in L1 and IVE areas. He mentions 'competent speakers' but does not explain who qualifies as one. For more on the EIL debate, see Jenkins (2000), Holland (2002) and Seidlhofer (2001).

It is clear from the above discussion that the IVEs or New Englishes have been overlooked in the conception and definition of EIL. All criteria either for or against EIL have been drawn with the older, native varieties in mind – see 'primary varieties', 'major varieties', 'other varieties' above. The hidden motivation behind this is the colonial tendency to consider colonial peoples and everything they produce second class. Thus these varieties are treated, according to Mufwene (2001), as illegitimate offspring of the mother language. This insidious bias limits them to descriptions like 'deficient', 'degenerate', 'maturing' or less used varieties that are still growing and have yet to attain the perfection found in the older varieties. As a result, these varieties are overlooked when international and even national standards of the language are considered. Rather, the older varieties are put in an authoritative position above them. This defeats any attempt to characterize English as an international language. First, that construct implies a particular variety would be imposed upon others. Second, those who constitute the higher number of speakers (i.e. the L2 speakers) would not have been included in the classification.

The above concerns notwithstanding, EIL, as it is considered here (and perhaps as it is considered throughout this volume), is more important in terms of its status from a functional point of view (its sociolinguistics and its communicability) than in terms of its relationship to older or new varieties of the language. Thus EIL is that variety of English (consistent or not – does not matter much) that speakers around the world use for interpersonal and professional communication. While it might have certain features of some known varieties; it is not an extended version of them and should therefore not be understood thus. Since communicability is of primary importance, EIL could be realized in any accent provided those involved understand each other. Speakers coming from regional backgrounds should not expect to be immediately understood by inter-locutors from other regions, whether they are native and non-native, national and international. They must, as in any situation of idiolectal contact, involve themselves in a give-and-take process of acquiring new speech habits, until they can communicate more easily.

The unbalanced relationship between native and indigenized Englishes is clearly visible in the names given to the IVEs. In some way, the issue of 'standard' is controlled by these names. Names grade varieties on scales of acceptability, which also means setting up their standards on similar scales of acceptability and correctness.

And Now it is Called . . .? Naming *Disease* in IVE Research

The field of New (World) Englishes has been ridden with terminologies of all kinds: conflicting and compromising, complementary and exclu-sionary, upgrading and downgrading, and so on. What I refer to here (harshly though not unfairly) as the 'naming disease' simply follows on the heels of the debates about the status, acceptability, standards and the relevance of these Englishes. The encompassing term, English as an inter-national language puts a lid over a field that has seen researchers on the one hand, trying to reestablish the authenticity of the variety of the language they speak, or on the other hand, trying to project it over the millions of other tongues that speak it differently. The outcome has been a cline of similar perspectives on the same subject under divergent names. Over 20 years ago Kachru (1982) found out that the first enemy of Indigenized Varieties of English were their nations – speakers of these national varieties. He found himself, with many others, fighting the battle for the 'linguistic human rights' of these varieties on two fronts: against home-grown enemies and against the foreign conservative native speaker who nursed the 'fear of seeing *his* language disintegrate in the hands of (or shall we say, on the lips of) non-native users' (Kachru, 1985: 34). The exchange of creatively coined 'missiles' like 'liberation linguistics', 'deficit linguistics', 'Quirk concerns', 'Kachru catch', 'half-baked quackery' (see Abbott, 1991; Bamgbose, 1998; Kachru, 1991, 1996; Quirk, 1990) in the 1990s by the different combatants indicates that the field of postcolonial Englishes was (as it still is) a controversial one. Attention has been drawn to the naming habit by Afendras (1995), Singh *et al.* (1995), Mufwene (1994, 2001), Erling (2005) and Anchimbe (2006). After reviewing the inconsistencies in the naming of English-derived languages, Mufwene (2001) concludes that those varieties of non-European descent are named as if they were illegitimate offspring of the language. To him, the structural evolutionary patterns of all languages are similar and, that being so, there is no reason why Nigerian English should be described as a localized or domesticated variety. A brief overview of the names used for IVEs follows.

Non-native Englishes

Coined in the 1960s and 1970s (i.e. during and shortly after colonialism), this term divides the world of English speakers into two: the native and the non-native, and treats the native as the norm-setter and the non-native as the norm-receiver. The non-native speaker was considered as a perpetual learner striving to reach perfection in the native speaker's variety. The term '*non-native* is one for disenfranchising the relevant varieties as not really legitimate offspring of English, because their norms are set by non-native speakers' (Mufwene, 2001: 108). Although this terminology was descriptive during colonialism, it is no longer accurate as the so-called non-native varieties now have native speakers of their own.

New Englishes

Although this term does not indicate either a 'genetic relationship or a history/chronology, it was suggested to counteract the negative connotation of 'non-native' and to reflect the fact that these varieties have only recently become salient in terms of research efforts and status recognition' (Kachru, 1995: 305). Several decades after this coinage, these languages are not 'new' anymore. Again, some of the New Englishes are chronologically older than some of the native or by implication 'older' Englishes – Indian English, for instance, is older than New Zealand English.

Indigenized Englishes

Still in line with finding a befitting terminology, 'the term *indigenized*' Mufwene (2001: 108) explains 'reflects the struggle for legitimizing them, a stand that is consistent with the position that every dialect has its own set of distinctive features and norms by which a speaker is identified as a typical or non-typical member of the community'. This term reflects a process-nominalization of the impact of the local ecology on the language and, although the term itself does not imply this, it could be interpreted somehow, as Schmid (2007: 136) does as, 'this is what proper native English has been turned into in the mouths and minds of African [or IVE] speakers'. Although used predominantly to describe IVEs, indigenization affects *all* languages in new environments.

Localized, regionalized and domesticated Englishes

Wild though English may have been in its spread, it needed to be 'localized' or 'domesticated' to become the language of communities on which it had been imposed (as the language of education, administration, diplomacy, etc), but within which it had to live, for better or for worse, forever. Like the term *indigenized Englishes* above, these process-nominalizations place the IVEs in categories that imply (incorrectly) that the evolution or restructuring of the language in these contexts are different from what happens in other contexts.

Nativized Englishes

Nativization is thought to be structurally motivated just like indigenization. It sees English as having been submerged in the local fabric into which it moved. Kachru (1986: 22) insists 'nativisation must be seen as a result of those productive linguistic innovations which are determined by the localised functions, [...] "the culture of conversation" [...] and "the transfer" from local languages'. It is hard to accept that the IVEs are still in the process of being nativized, given that they emerged several decades or centuries ago.

Second language Englishes

Based on the premise that postcolonial contexts are multilingual and that English is foreign to the speakers there, so it must normally be a second language. Even though this is true from a classificational point of view, this premise occasioned the use of ready-made European models of bilingualism and multilingualism in these regions. All native speakers of English are first of all native speakers of non-standard dialects (Trudgill, 1998). They, technically speaking, are also L2 users of the standard variety of the language, and hence are just as far away from it as L2 speakers in postcolonial regions.

Although the terminology I adopt in this chapter (i.e. IVEs) adds yet another to the existing list, it is also not bias-free. It simply suits the structural evolutionary path of the varieties under study. Some of the other terms have outlived their usefulness due to the enormous changes that have taken place ever since they were first employed: there are native speakers of these varieties already, making them no longer exclusively non-native Englishes; they are no longer new as such given the long history of their existence; nativization took place and they have now been completely indigenized; and they are second language varieties only in the *normal* sense that most people in these areas speak an indigenous language learnt before English. This notwithstanding the question remains, why is it that postcolonial Englishes are referred to by process-based terminology suggestive of their origins? For this we must all be held accountable. But I wonder if it has anything to do with a desire to maintain 'standards' of the language?

Keeping the *Standard* Standard

Does the status of a language depend on its ability to maintain a universal standard? Prescriptivists and conservatives insist on keeping the standard of languages standard, ignoring differences across speech communities and their ecological and historical peculiarities. The *disease* referred to above is also responsible for the refusal to accept alternative standards of the English language in *other*, so-called 'non-native' or 'IVE' contexts. If we agree with Trudgill (1998: 39) that 'the further down the social scale one goes, the more nonstandard forms one finds', then it is obvious that the criteria of what is standard in a language depend strongly on societal prejudices – in other words, it was from the onset based on social stratification.

If we liken the social class system of the imperial British society to the social classification system put in place by colonialism – construing colonial subjects as second class subjects – it would also become clear that the rejection of the standards of IVEs is prejudicial on the same or similar lines. The native varieties are taken as the determiners or keepers of the standard as the educated, upper social classes of old used their standards on the poor. This puts the IVEs in a dilemma. Which standard should be adopted for formal, educated and official duties in countries where English is the sole official language (or where perhaps it shares that function with another European language)? This is because the home-grown 'standard' forms are generally treated as non-standard varieties that are likely to cause unintelligibility and trigger deterioration of the language. However, as this chapter asserts, languages evolve according to the dictates of their hosts who form communities within complete sociohistorical contexts. If such communities are complete and speakers are able to use the language in ways they define as correct and acceptable, then a standard *has* taken root and should be allowed to flourish. More attention, Wilkinson (1995: 21–23) argues, should be paid to the variability of the language, because 'for English to retain its vitality and creativity, it has to be seen in the context of its continuing adaptability to use in a wide variety of differing situations'. The common refusal to acknowledge the standards of IVEs is based on three reflexes: intelligibility, prestige and the fear of deterioration or degeneration.

The intelligibility argument

To allow English *degenerate* into regional, second language standards – referred to by Prator (1968) as *heresy* – meant for some jeopardizing world-wide intelligibility in the language. The regional varieties, which proponents of this crusade feared would be heavily influenced by indigenous languages, were regarded as a major source of forms and speech patterns that would cause unintelligibility across borders. Intelligibility was therefore advanced as a solid reason for a native-speaker-like standard to be imposed on peoples who had never had, or were not likely to have, any contact with it. The call for an international standard modelled on one of the native varieties (see Abbott, 1991; Prator, 1968; Quirk, 1985, 1990) defeats the very essence of English as an international language. Today the worlds of education, commerce, law and science are all linked by English. Although the actors in these domains are from different parts of the world and use different regional standards of the language, intelligibility is still maintained. Take the following examples from various varieties of English:

(1) Whether had you rather lead mine eyes, or eye your master's heels? (Shakespeare: *Merry Wives of Windsor.* III.ii.3)
(2) Tomorrow Sunday, lor. [Tomorrow is Sunday] (Gupta, 1994: 72 – Singapore English)
(3) It was all thatched houses was here one time, you know. (Filppula, 1991 – Hiberno-English)
(4) Dr Bobga informs relatives and friends that his wife has just put to birth a male baby named George Babilla Bobga. (Simo Bobda, 2002: 2 – Cameroon English)
(5) That hat was not belonging to you. (Schmied, 1991: 67 – East African English)
(6) I jumped highly. (Sey, 1973: 38 – Ghanaian English)

Most speakers of English reading the above statements will definitely understand them although they have been produced by people from different areas and historical periods. Mutual (un)intelligibility therefore should not be used as an excuse for rejecting regional standards. Two reasons can be given for the mutual intelligibility illustrated here: (1) the core vocabulary of English remains similar across all speech communities of the language; and (2) English language teaching methods and pedagogic materials are predominantly the same making any substantial changes to the grammar difficult to come by. To claim regional embellishments could lead to unintelligibility is therefore not sustainable. The excerpt from Shakespeare (1) above is at least as far removed from the standard as the Hiberno-English excerpt (3); and even further away from it than the Ghanaian English example (6).

With globalization and the free movement and settlement of people in the 21st century, intelligibility is more likely than ever before. This is because the ELT industry has grown so big that teachers are no longer drawn from the so-called native-speaking countries. More and more of them come from countries where English is spoken as a second language, that is, they are speakers of indigenised varieties of English.

The prestige argument

Since it spread to Africa, the Caribbean and South Asia through colonialism, the status of English in these areas has often been judged from the standpoint of its prestige and social stratification. Attempts to redress the colonial impression that postcolonial Englishes are 'linguistic flights [...], which jar upon the ear of the native Englishman' (Whitworth, 1907: 6) started decades ago. While it is generally accepted that these are varieties in their own accord, the issue of them having autonomous standards seems to linger on. This stratification of standards could be likened to *colorism* or *shadism* in the linguistic landscape of Jamaica. Farquharson (2007) uses the following expressions to show the racial strata of the Jamaican society, which clearly have linguistic undertones. The acrolect could be likened to the native standard and the basilect to the IVE standard, which are generally required to 'stay back' on the international platform:

If yuh white, alright.	Acrolect
If yuh brown, stick around.	Mesolect
If yuh black, stay back.	Basilect

Chevillet (1992), for instance, is blunt on the prestige issue when she wonders: 'would it be reasonable for an EFL teacher to recommend to his students to acquire a Nigerian or Indian accent? Certainly not [...]'. Even though standard English, whatever we may (dis)agree it is, does not have an accent attached to it, it is, however, realized in given communities using accents that suit those communities and express their position in a number of different social hierarchies. And since accents are inseparable from speech communities, it makes no real sense to insist certain varieties of the language are substandard and so do not have the right to exist simply because they lack prestige. This is because a variable such as prestige is a social construct validated by other realities that have no linguistic substance. Was it not an expression of the old colonial status quo when Trudgill (1995: 316) declared Irish English 'still has some way to go, however, before it achieves full autonomy and respect as a variety of English in its own right'? If it were judged on the linguistic basis alone, then Irish English would deserve all the respect linguists attach any autonomous variety, given that all Irish people speak the language daily and use it for all national purposes. What these perspectives ignore is the ecological relevance of foreign standards on local users. How effective would the American standard and accent, with the prestige they supposedly command, be in the Singaporean context?

The prestige factor is also expressed from within IVE contexts. Certain IVE speakers, generally educated conservative elites, remnants of the 'been-tos' of the 1970s, and social esteem seekers, continue to call for, and insist they speak, British or some other foreign *native* English. Along the very lines of the colonial discourse hinted on above, they call for the adoption of foreign English language standards in education in the IVE areas. This conforms to the phenomenon of postcolonial 'mimicry', in other words, of the colonial linguistic and cultural practices and 'hybridity' elaborated on by Bhabha (1994).

The *degeneration* argument

At the beginning of the last century, speaking in disapproval of the way British settlers in South Africa were using English, Pettman (1913: 34) said: 'It gives an Englishman, who loves the sentence that is lucid and logical, a shock to hear his native tongue maltreated by those who are just as English in blood as himself.' Advocates of the degeneration argument feared that if the language was entrusted to the hands of non-natives or colonial subjects, it would not only be *maltreated* but indeed *destroyed* or *dismembered*. This non-linguistic argument continued for several decades after Pettman's comment, with Prator (1968) branding the recognition of regional standards in ELT as a *heresy* to which he would like to take exception. In the early 1990s, Quirk (1990: 6) called Kachru's and other pro-IVE standards linguists' demand for the introduction of IVEs in educational curricular, 'half-baked quackery'. The question that arises is: did these people imagine that English would be spoken in foreign contexts the same way it is spoken in Britain? Even if native British teachers had been deployed in all parts of the world, would the standard of the language learnt have remained homogenous? The writing on the wall should have been obvious given that, even Englishmen by birth spoke the language differently once they had settled elsewhere. On these lines, Smith (1983: 11) asserts:

> Native speakers must realise that there are many valid varieties of English and that non-native speakers need not sound or act like Americans, the British, or any other group of native speakers in order to be effective English users. [...] Native speakers need as much help as non-native speakers when using English to interact internationally. There is no room for linguistic chauvinism.

Thus, regional varieties should not be treated as *degenerate*. Rather they should be understood as peculiar to the evolutionary patterns of the societies where they have developed. From a more critical angle, the non-standard dialects of Britain could as well be compared to the indigenous languages of Africa and Asia which also exist side-by-side English.

English Language Teaching: A World of Dilemmas

> No latitude is given to learners to be themselves with their own identity or to strive for intelligibility rather than the perfect English accent. (Berns, 2005: 86)

None of the three arguments presented above approaches the issue of standards from a realistic linguistic point of view. None of them is directly concerned with how autonomous communities actually use a language, which may be of foreign origin, in ways determined by the evolution of the people and their society. The impact of these arguments is heavy on the transmission of the language from one generation to the other, as seen in ELT.

ELT has grown over the last half decade into one of the most flourishing international industries stretching far beyond the British colonial empire to regions that do not have any historical links with either Britain or America. In EFL regions the appeal of English has been irresistible due to the economic advantages the language can bring. The choice of which standard to adopt has been only between the two major varieties, British English and American English (including the accents associated with them). The curriculum comes with experiences of 'living the foreign experience of English at home' in the way described by Berns. For the EFL learner:

> English means British English, literature means Shakespeare, the cultural monuments are those of London, Big Ben and the Beefeater guards, and the daily life of native speakers consists of tea-time and its components – tea cosies, scones, and lemon curd. In fewer cases it has been acceptable to read Edgar Allen Poe, take an imaginary trip to New York to see Central Park and its homeless denizens, appreciate the national costume of T-shirt and jeans, and catch glimpses of an everyday routine of shopping at malls and eating fast food. (Berns, 2005: 86)

This imaginary trip forces learners and the home-trained teachers 'to relocate themselves in some fantasy world when they are asked to hear, see, and imitate English dialogues' (Piepho, 1988: 19). So like the IVE speakers described below they live constantly on standards borrowed from abroad. However, their discomfort is less complex than that of IVE speakers because they have another language (their L1) that serves them as an official language.

In the ESL or postcolonial or IVE regions the dilemma or discomfort has been greater. English is an official language (in some cases the only one), in these regions. This implies that the speakers are bound to acquire and use it in whatever ways dictated by the competing proponents of the different native-speaker-like standards. Since these varieties have been generally treated as clines of errors, their speakers seek for higher social esteem through foreign standards and accents. Teachers are, therefore, in a dilemma: which standard should they recommend and teach? The local standard which is what both the teacher and the students grew up learning? The foreign British or American standards which the teacher does not use? Which accent does the pedagogic material prescribe? Can the students and teacher realistically use such an accent? These and similar dilemmas have resulted in hybridized ELT programs that do not have any real focus. Teachers find themselves teaching the British Standard English found in textbooks while using a local variety (accent and standard), which is what they know. Then writing is taught using a mixture of the American English and British

English spelling systems. The potential negative impacts of such mixed policies are many:

- The risk of variety restructuration triggered by foreign norms, that is, obliging a stable local variety of the language to adopt features from foreign varieties that do not reflect the context in which it is used.
- Temptations for speakers of the local variety to falsely claim and sometimes insist they speak the foreign variety promoted in education and the mixed policies. For instance, Anchimbe (2006) reports the case of Cameroon in which over 75% of a total of 300 respondents agreed that Cameroon English existed. In a follow-up question, 60% of the same respondents vehemently claimed they spoke British English.
- The risk of false and unrealistic standard of evaluation being asserted, so that institutions evaluate speakers' competence not according to the (local) standard broadly accepted at home but according to some imaginary foreign standard which everyone is forced to try, very often unsuccessfully, to approximate.
- The danger of stifling the further nativization or indigenization of the language in line with the local ecology. This could occur through banning certain widespread local forms, editing textbooks and other pedagogical material according to foreign standards or in extreme cases hiring only foreign teachers for the local market.
- The risk of inculcating in learners or speakers an inferiority complex since, as the case may be, they have to constantly look up to foreign standards even though they have used the locally appropriate English all their lives. This is particularly pernicious for those who have no prospects of travelling abroad to use the foreign standard.

All these issues put together make the choice of standards complex and pressing too, not so much in its linguistic interpretation and application but in terms of the social and extra-linguistic pressures that are brought to bear on it. Speakers may not be aware that the language they speak is called 'Creole'. So, if English in its new home was left to those who speak it among themselves, there would be no anxiety about the kind of prestigious embellishments or foreign norms that would make it more acceptable to linguists (like Quirk, 1990; Trudgill, 1995).

Conclusion: Which Way Forward for Regions and their Standards

This chapter has raised pertinent arguments about certain (mis)conceptions about local varieties versus international standards of English.

It has also demonstrated the extent to which international standards of English are both products of asymmetrical power relations as well as social constructs sustained through colonially-inherited discourses. The 'naming disease' discussed in the first part of the chapter is evidence of this asymmetrical power relationship. If names alone were able to resolve the issue of the acceptance of the standards of these IVE varieties, then there would have been more consensus on which name to use by now.

From the above discussion, we could be confident in asserting that the acceptance of regional or national standards of English does not in any way undermine the authority of English itself. These regional or national standards, it must be emphasized here, are acquired through education and are sustained by educated speakers, that is, they have international currency beyond local borders, and are 'normally used in writing, especially printing [... are] associated with the educational system [... and are] spoken by 'educated people' (Trudgill, 1998: 35). For English as an international language to maintain its currency and vitality, it will have to be spoken by different voices yet understood by different ears. The differences, community-based as they are, are inevitable since, due to the specificity of ecology, no two communities can be found to use a language in exactly the same way. As a result, therefore, 'it is generally accepted that communities [...] should be granted the rights of ownership and allowed to fashion the language of their needs' (Widdowson, 1994: 377). This should not be otherwise because as Mufwene (2001: 106) adds 'it is those who speak a language on a regular basis – and in a manner normal to themselves – who develop the norms for their communities'. Any attempts to homogenize standards across communities or to force communities to endorse the standards of other communities are bound to result in one or more of the negative impacts listed above. A standard should always be allowed to develop according the needs of its users. Difference is not deficiency and the two should not be confused in the case of IVE standards and norms.

References

Abbott, G. (1991) English across cultures: The Kachru catch. *English Today* 7 (4), 55–57.

Afendras, E.A. (1995) On 'new/non-native' Englishes: A gamelan. *Journal of Pragmatics* 24 (3), 295–321.

Anchimbe, E.A. (2006) *Cameroon English: Authenticity, Ecology and Evolution.* Frankfurt am Main: Peter Lang.

Bhabha, H.K. (1994) *The Location of Culture.* London: Routledge.

Bamgbose, A. (1998) Torn between the norms: Innovations in World Englishes. *World Englishes* 17 (1), 1–14.

Berns, M. (2005) Expanding on the expanding circle: Where do WE go from here? *World Englishes* 24 (1), 85–93.

Chevillet, F. (1992) English or Englishes? *English Today* 9 (4), 29–33.

Erling, E.J. (2005) The many names of English. *English Today* 21 (1), 40–44.

Farquharson, J.T. (2007) Folk linguistics and post-colonial language *politricks* in Jamaica. In E.A. Anchimbe (ed.) *Linguistic Identity in Postcolonial Multilingual Spaces* (pp. 227–242). Newcastle: Cambridge Scholars Publishing.

Filppula, M. (1991) Urban and rural varieties of Hiberno-English. In J. Cheshire (ed.) *English Around the World: Sociolinguistic Perspectives* (pp. 51–60). Cambridge: Cambridge University Press.

Gupta, A.F. (1994) Almost a Creole: Singapore colloquial English. *California Linguistic Notes* 23, 9–21.

Holland, R. (2002) Globospeak? Questioning text on the role of English as a global language. *Language and Intercultural Communication* 2 (1), 5–24.

Jenkins, J. (2000) *The Phonology of English as an International Language*. Oxford: Oxford University Press.

Kachru, B.B. (ed.) (1982) *The other Tongue: English Across Cultures*. Illinois: University of Illinois Press.

Kachru, B.B. (1985) The pragmatics of non-native Englishes. In L.E. Smith (ed.) *English for Cross-Cultural Communication* (pp. 15–39). Wiltshire: Macmillan.

Kachru, B.B. (1986) *The Alchemy of English: The Spread, Functions and Models of Non-Native Englishes*. Oxford: Pergamon.

Kachru, B.B. (1991) Liberation linguistics and the Quirk concerns. *English Today* 7 (1), 3–13.

Kachru, B.B. (1996) The paradigms of marginality. *World Englishes* 15 (3), 241–255.

Kachru, Y. (1995) World Englishes and linguistic research. *Journal of Pragmatics* 24, 305–308.

Modiano, M. (1999) International English in the global village. *English Today* 15 (2), 22–28.

Modiano, M. (2001) Ideology and the ELT practitioner. *International Journal of Applied Linguistics* 11 (2), 159–173.

Mufwene, S.S. (1994) New Englishes and the criteria for naming them. *World Englishes* 13, 21–31.

Mufwene, S.S. (2001) *The Ecology of Language Evolution*. Cambridge: Cambridge University Press.

Pettman, C. (1913) *Afrikanderisms: A Glossary of South African Colloquial Words and Phrases and Place and other Names*. London: Longman.

Piepho, H.-E. (1988) English as lingua franca in Europe: An appeal for didactic moderation in the field of English and its representatives. In E. Kleinschmidt (ed.) *Foreign Language Teaching Between Language Policy and Practice* (pp. 41–49). Tübingen: Gunter Narr. [Title translated by Berns (2005)].

Prator, C. (1968) The British heresy in TESL. In J. Fishman, C.A. Ferguson and J.D. Gupta (eds) *Language Problems of Developing Nations* (pp. 459–476). New York: John Wiley & Sons.

Quirk, R. (1985) The English language in a global context. In R. Quirk and H.G. Widdowson (eds) *English in the World.* (pp. 1–6). Cambridge: Cambridge University Press.

Quirk, R. (1990) Language varieties and standard language. *English Today* 21, 3–10.

Schmid, H-J. (2007) *Light* English, *local* English and *fictitious* English. Conceptual structures in North-Eastern Nigerian English and the question of an English-language identity. In E.A. Anchimbe (ed.) *Linguistic Identity in Postcolonial Multilingual Spaces* (pp. 119–147). Newcastle: Cambridge Scholars Publishing.

Schmied, J. (1991) *English in Africa: An Introduction.* London: Longman.

Seidlhofer, B. (2001) Closing a conceptual gap: The case for a description of English as a lingua franca. *International Journal of Applied Linguistics* 11 (2), 133–158.

Sey, K. (1973) *Ghanaian English.* London: Macmillan.

Simo Bobda, A. (2002) *Watch Your English: A Collection of Remedial Lessons on English Usage* (2nd edn). Yaounde: B&k Language Institute.

Singh, R., D'souza, J., Mohan, K.P. and Prabhu, N.S. (1995) On 'new/non-native' Englishes: A quartet. *Journal of Pragmatics* 24 (3), 283–294.

Smith, L.E. (ed.) (1983) *Readings in English as an International Language.* Oxford: Pergamon.

Trudgill, P. (1995) Linguistic oppression and the non-native speaker. Comment in the discussion: On 'new/non-native' Englishes: A gamelan. *Journal of Pragmatics* 24 (3), 315–316.

Trudgill, P. (1998) Standard English: What it isn't. *The European English Messenger* VII (1), 35–39.

Whitworth, G.C. (1907) (reprinted 1932) *Indian English: An Examination of the Errors of Idioms Made by Indians in Writing English.* Lahore: Letchworth.

Widdowson, H.G. (1994) The ownership of English. *TESOL Quarterly* 28 (2), 377–388.

Widdowson, H.G. (1997) The forum: EIL, ESL and EFL: Global issues and local interests. *World Englishes* 16 (1), 135–146.

Widdowson, H.G. (1998) EIL: Squaring the circles. A reply. *World Englishes* 17 (3), 397–404.

Wilkinson, J. (1995) *Introducing Standard English.* London: Penguin.

Index